BRIAN FRIEL: BEGINNINGS

Brian Friel: Beginnings

KELLY MATTHEWS

FOUR COURTS PRESS

Set in 10.5pt on 13.5pt CaslonPro by
Carrigboy Typesetting Services for
FOUR COURTS PRESS LTD
7 Malpas Street, Dublin 8, Ireland
www.fourcourtspress.ie
and in North America for
FOUR COURTS PRESS
c/o IPG, 814 N Franklin St, Chicago, IL 60610.

© Kelly Matthews and Four Courts Press 2024

ISBN 978-1-80151-140-7

A catalogue record for this title is available
from the British Library.

All rights reserved.
No part of this publication may be reproduced, stored in or introduced
into a retrieval system, or transmitted, in any form or by any means
(electronic, mechanical, photocopying, recording or otherwise),
without the prior written permission of both the copyright
owner and publisher of this book.

Printed in England
by CPI Antony Rowe, Chippenham, Wilts.

*To Rory and Andrew,
with love and gratitude*

Contents

LIST OF ILLUSTRATIONS		8
ACKNOWLEDGMENTS		9
PROLOGUE	Border crossings, February 1965	13
1	Rehearsals, 1952–9	17
2	Understudy, 1959–60	37
3	Off book, 1960–1	57
4	Stage directions, 1961–2	75
5	The giant of Minneapolis, 1962–3	94
6	Waiting in the wings, 1963–4	112
7	Broadway, here I come!, 1964–6	128
EPILOGUE	Curtain call	155
NOTES		161
BIBLIOGRAPHY		203
INDEX		209

Illustrations

Cover: Author photo of Brian Friel for *The saucer of larks*, 1962.

1.1 Brian and Anne Friel wedding photo, 28 December 1954. Courtesy of the National Library of Ireland.   21

1.2 Ronald Mason directing Tom Fleming as Columba in *The enemy within* for BBC television, March 1965. Courtesy of BBC Northern Ireland.   25

2.1 Roger Angell in his *New Yorker* office, photograph by Janet Malcolm. Courtesy of the estate of Roger Angell.   38

4.1 Abbey director Ernest Blythe, Fr Edward Daly, and Brian Friel in Derry, October 1962. Courtesy of the National Library of Ireland.   85

4.2 Brian Friel with cast of *The enemy within*, October 1962. Courtesy of the National Library of Ireland.   87

5.1 Sir Tyrone Guthrie amid Guthrie Theater multicoloured seats, 21 April 1963, photograph by Earl Seubert, Minneapolis *Tribune*. Copyright © Star Tribune Media Company LLC. Used with permission. All rights reserved.   101

7.1 Brian Friel, Hilton Edwards, and cast of *Philadelphia, here I come!* boarding plane to New York, December 1965. Courtesy of the National Library of Ireland.   151

7.2 Brian Friel, Hilton Edwards, and *Philadelphia, here I come!* cast with Mayor James Tate in Philadelphia, January 1966. Courtesy of the National Library of Ireland.   152

Acknowledgments

My work on this book began with the discovery of seventy-five previously uncatalogued letters from Brian Friel to his radio producer Ronald Mason in the BBC Written Archives Centre, unearthed during research into Northern Irish radio plays, and it continued with the excavation of an additional seventy-five letters from Friel to his editor Roger Angell, dispersed across a dozen different folders in the *New Yorker* archives at the New York Public Library. I am grateful to all the librarians who lit the path toward these and other subsequent discoveries, beginning with BBC archivists Samantha Blake and Kate O'Brien, who have been knowledgeable and responsive guides from beginning to end. I thank Peter Stewart and Gillian McIntosh of BBC Broadcasting House Belfast, Abbey Theatre archivist Mairéad Delaney, and all in the Manuscripts department of the National Library of Ireland, the Brooke Russell Astor Reading Room for Rare Books and Manuscripts at the New York Public Library, the Performing Arts Archives at the University of Minnesota, and the Wisconsin Center for Film and Theater Research – with special thanks to Jason Nargis at Northwestern University, who patiently leafed through Gate Theatre archival folders with me via Zoom during the COVID–19 pandemic.

As a work of literary biography, *Brian Friel: beginnings* aims to complement prior critical analyses of the playwright's early work. There are numerous excellent studies of Friel's early drama, fiction and journalism which have been instrumental to my understanding of his development as a writer. While this book's bibliography lists those works for readers who would like to delve further, I specifically acknowledge my debt to prior scholars who have traced Friel's influences and his early writing for a variety of audiences, as well as those who have comprehensively explored his recursive focus on fathers and sons, memory and truth, and spoken and unspoken desires.

Richard Pine, for example, interviewed Ronald Mason for his study *Brian Friel and Ireland's drama* (London, 1990), and Graham Morison's interview with Friel for *Acorn*, reprinted in Paul Delaney's compilation *Brian Friel in conversation* (Ann Arbor, 2000), pointed me toward Roger Angell as editor of Friel's short stories. I would not have known about Friel's *Irish Times* and *Irish Press* columns were it not for extensive archival research by scholars Scott

Boltwood and George O'Brien to recover the playwright's early journalism. As Boltwood noted in the *Irish University Review* in 2014, Friel's newspaper columns 'occupy a shifting, often overlapping space between journalism and fiction'; I have generally cited those columns whose facts are verifiable by other sources, and categorized the others as less reliably biographical.

I am particularly indebted to Anne Friel and the Brian Friel Estate for their generosity in allowing the reproduction of quotations from Brian Friel's papers as well as photographic reproductions in this text. I also thank Queen's University Belfast, who commissioned my work within their *Friel Reimagined* exhibit; the *Irish University Review* and *American Journal of Irish Studies*, who published my first essays on Friel's early work; and Martin Fanning and Anthony Tierney of Four Courts Press, who have embraced this book with enthusiasm.

As first readers of this manuscript, Talaya Delaney, Clare Dwyer Hogg and Claudia Springer offered keen insights and key suggestions for improvement, as did the peer reviewers for Four Courts Press, to whom I am very thankful. My longtime writing group friends Laura E. Miller and Emily Rubin provided encouragement and continual moral support. My colleagues at Framingham State University are a valued source of intellectual fellowship, and I am especially grateful to the university's Center for Excellence in Learning, Teaching, Scholarship and Service (CELTSS) for generous funding of my research-related travel and publication costs, as well as for opportunities to share my findings with fellow researchers and receive feedback on my work in progress. I am also grateful to the American Conference for Irish Studies, whose annual regional and national conferences have gifted me with a true community of high-minded scholars who welcome debate, discussion and laughter.

Finally, I am deeply grateful to everyone who has stood by me with love and fortitude, first and foremost my sons Rory and Andrew Millar; my siblings Mike Matthews, Katie Allen, Meghan Martin and Molly Banas and their spouses; my aunts, uncles and cousins in Wisconsin, Minnesota, Nebraska, Maine, Idaho and farther afield; and lifelong family and friends in Northern Ireland, Belgium, Wisconsin, Massachusetts and elsewhere.

Quotations and photographic reproductions have been allowed with the kind permission of the Estate of Brian Friel and courtesy of the National Library of Ireland.

Quotations from Roger Angell's letters and interview are allowed with the kind permission of the Estate of Roger Angell.

BBC copyright content is reproduced courtesy of the British Broadcasting Corporation. All rights reserved.

Quotations from the Gate Theatre Archive are allowed with the acknowledgment of the Estate of Hilton Edwards and Micheál macLiammóir and courtesy of the Charles Deering McCormick Library of Special Collections and University Archives, Northwestern University Libraries.

Quotations from the Tyrone Guthrie papers, folders D3585/F/5/2/25, D3585/F/5/1/10 and D3585/F/7/7/5 are allowed with the acknowledgment of the Deputy Keeper of the Records, the Public Record Office of Northern Ireland (PRONI) and courtesy of the Trustees of the Tyrone Guthrie Centre.

Quotations from the Guthrie Theater records in the Performing Arts Archive of the University of Minnesota are allowed with the permission of the Guthrie Theater.

PROLOGUE

Border crossings, February 1965

CROSSING THE ATLANTIC in the early days of jet travel was never routine. For Brian Friel, a young father of three trying to earn a living as a full-time writer, it must have been slightly surreal. From his modest terraced house at the end of its whitewashed row, he drove out of Derry, crossed the border into the Republic and travelled 140 miles to Dublin airport, an outpost of gleaming new technology rising amid pastures outside the capital city. There he walked the concrete apron and climbed the stairs onto a shamrock-tailed Boeing, one of a handful newly purchased by Aer Lingus for its inaugural flights to New York's Idlewild airport, ferrying American tourists lured by John Hinde postcards, Clancy Brothers recordings and John Ford's film *The quiet man*. After settling into his seat and lighting a cigarette to calm his nerves, Brian could contemplate the scenery below as the plane soared over patchwork fields and the stormy sea beyond.

What did he think when he looked out the window? Perhaps of his protagonist, Gar O'Donnell, in whose voice Brian had written an imagined journey of emigration as Gar fled the sleepy countryside of Donegal, 'Up in that big bugger of a jet, with its snout pointing straight for the States, and its tail belching smoke over Ireland'. Unlike Gar, whose journey was a humble one, bound for an entry-level job in a Philadelphia hotel, Brian was flying to New York to meet Gower Champion, a celebrated director who, it was hoped, would sign on to his play *Philadelphia, here I come!* and give it a future on Broadway. Champion's newest hit *Hello, Dolly!*, produced by the impresario David Merrick, was beginning year two of its eventual seven-year run after sweeping the Tony awards. His previous winner, *Bye bye Birdie*, had been released as a film starring Ann-Margret and Dick Van Dyke. The trip could have been overwhelming for Brian, who just a few years before had been teaching maths in the Christian Brothers school at Brow o' the Hill – but he held fast to his aspirations and ambitions. He had joked that on a previous flight to London the air hostess had to fasten his seatbelt when he was 'seized by a quiet panic'; now he struggled to suppress his excitement because he was 'superstitious' about his play's success in America.

Brian had cause to be concerned. For over a year, he had been trying to stage *Philadelphia* in London, and its prospects were growing dim. The play had been the toast of the Dublin Theatre Festival in October 1964, where its one-week run was extended to two, but plans to launch it on a larger scale had stalled. With no London production on the horizon, Brian had adapted the play for radio broadcast, leaning on the advice and support of his earliest friend in the theatre business, BBC drama producer Ronald Mason. After meeting with Champion in Manhattan, he would seek advice from his *New Yorker* editor Roger Angell, who agreed that 'This theatrical world is frightening to all writers'. Angell and his wife Carol hosted Brian for dinner in their apartment, and later commiserated by mail after the playwright's pitch to Champion came to nothing. (Angell wrote, 'I don't know anyone who has written for the stage who hasn't had to suffer through these disappointments and insults'.) It would be months before the American theatre agent Audrey Wood, best known for discovering Tennessee Williams, would rescue *Philadelphia* from rejection and sign David Merrick to produce it on Broadway.

Meeting with Champion was Brian's second trip to America. The first had been in 1963, when he went to Minneapolis, along with his wife Anne and their young daughters, to observe and learn from Tyrone Guthrie as he directed his new theatre company. But Brian's work had crossed the Atlantic even before he did. Since 1959, he had published short fiction in the *New Yorker*, beginning with his story 'The Skelper', about two Donegal salmon poachers and their skinny-dipping attempt to win a bet. Over months and years of correspondence, Brian developed a deep connection to Angell, his editor, and learned how to balance humour and pathos, how to convey Irish speech and ideas to an American audience, and how to bring each story to a satisfying close. Before that, Brian's writing had crossed the Irish Sea, borne invisibly by the airwaves of BBC Belfast and the Home Service's Third Programme. He revised and refined his theatrical technique by writing radio plays under the guidance of Ronald Mason, who helped Brian get his first scripts accepted for broadcast in 1957 and 1958: two plays about embittered, middle-aged Belfast men, a far cry from the youth and exuberance of *Philadelphia, here I come!* And before that, Brian's work had crossed the border between Northern Ireland and the Republic, with his first publication in Dublin literary magazine *The Bell* in 1952, and weekly humour columns for Dublin newspapers the *Irish Times* and *Irish Press*.

Each of these crossings demanded patience and diplomacy, and each one taught the young writer new ways to connect to new audiences. Brian Friel's first decade as a writer was shaped by his persistence and perseverance; by experimentation, as he tried out different modes for different listeners, readers and theatregoers; by occasional successes and, more commonly, rejections. Throughout these lean years Brian never tired of producing new work. In his irrepressible energy and creativity, he resembled his own most vibrant protagonists – Gar O'Donnell, the Francophile, St Columba. Along the way he was guided by directors and editors who have until now been unseen helpers in his trajectory, but whose contributions have come to light in the archives of the BBC's Northern Ireland bureau and the *New Yorker* magazine. The young Brian Friel that emerges from his letters to these early mentors is different from the reclusive, tight-lipped, even stubborn writer the world would come to know, or to think we knew. He is funny, self-deprecating, open to endless revisions, eager to please, hungry for honest criticism and encouragement.

Above all, he is a working writer. Not bound to any particular genre, moving fluidly from drama to fiction to humour and back again, letting his typewriter lead him to any new market that might offer publication and success. While much has been made of Brian's shift from short fiction to drama, the truth is that in his early career, he was working in multiple genres at once. His newspaper columns were often refashioned into short stories, and he later transposed stories into theatre: his play *Lovers* incorporates his story 'The highwayman and the saint', first written in 1964; *Aristocrats* includes a key scene from 'Foundry House', written in 1961; and *Dancing at Lughnasa* can be traced to the story 'A man's world', which Brian wrote thirty years earlier, in 1960. Although he moved on quickly each time he finished a new piece, ever fascinated with 'whatever work I have on hands' rather than past projects, his early work shows that he kept ideas on simmer for years, sometimes for decades.

When Brian boldly abandoned his teaching career to focus on writing full time, his New York agent and Roger Angell were 'equally horrified' at the leap of faith he was taking. Financial stability eluded Brian for several years afterward, as he channelled his boundless energies into stories, scripts and journalism to provide for his growing family. Stepping away from 'cosy security' meant risking rejection and failure; each disappointment could derail the writer's dream of success. To achieve it, he would have to get noticed. And he would have to make his way along the troubled borders between bitterness and laughter.

CHAPTER 1

Rehearsals, 1952–9

A BOY GROWING UP IN IRELAND in the 1930s and 40s could find reasons to be bitter. As a modern nation, it was a fledgling country, striving to fly on its own after gaining independence from Britain. Its partitioned northeast corner, where Brian Friel was born on 9 January 1929, was known by many names, none of them neutral: Northern Ireland, the North, the Six Counties, Ulster – a province, a region, a statelet, depending on one's political point of view. Economically, the entire island lagged behind its imperial neighbour, with pockets of rural poverty that rivalled the slums of its largest cities, Dublin, Cork and Belfast.

But there were signs of hope, too, and a boy could find reasons to laugh. Throughout the 1940s, rural electrification schemes brought light and time-saving water pumps, cookers, kettles and farm machinery to much of the country. Civil War enemies managed a peaceful transition of power when Éamon de Valera's anti-treaty Fianna Fáil party won election over pro-treaty Cumann na nGaedheal. The Free State claimed its place among the nations of the world by declaring itself a Republic in 1948. In the North, the Education Act of 1947 made post-primary schooling free and compulsory for all children to age 15. Brian's father, Patrick Friel, was head teacher of Culmore Primary School on the Tamlaght Road in Omagh (a three-classroom building now used as a practice hall by St Eugene's Brass & Reed Band) until 1939, when he was appointed principal of St Columba's, Long Tower, the school for Derry's oldest Catholic parish.

Master Friel, as he was known – or as 'Scobie', among his students – was described as 'a soft-spoken, courteous man and very well-liked by all his pupils' when he later won the prestigious Carlisle and Blake Premium, a national prize. Brian was his father's pupil at Culmore and recalled him differently. 'I can see him now, standing behind his desk, his hands deep in the pockets of his plus-fours ... I remember his first lesson on letter writing: "Begin without a beginning, end without a conclusion, and I'll beat the scrap out of any lurcher who fills his page with padding!"' In similar scenes at home, Master

Friel tasked his son with evening school work in the family dining room, a room that conjured 'vivid memories of complete despair' in later life. On weekends, Brian and his two sisters, Mary and Nanette, strained to stifle giggles while their father subjected them to 'Sunday singing episodes' that were 'a torture'. They always 'ended in the same way: Father in a fury, mother trying to placate him, and us … us huddled together at the back of the house and licking our wounds and snivelling miserably and accusing one another, "It was your fault! You laughed first! It was all your fault!"' Brian would later write of a fictional schoolmaster father 'troubled by an ambition I never understood until years later', one of many stern, unapproachable fathers who appeared in his stories and plays over the decades. Like their father, Brian and his two sisters all became teachers. Brian's sister Nanette taught at Loreto Convent, Omagh, before marrying an RAF officer and moving to Yorkshire, where she taught primary school. His sister Mary taught at St Columba's, Long Tower, where their father stayed on as headmaster for twenty-one years.

The family's move to Derry brought Master Friel back to his home town and brought young Brian, age 10, to a city on the brink of becoming a staging area for US and Allied troops during the Second World War. The war supplied work for Northern Ireland's shipbuilders, textile mills and farmers, as the payrolls of Belfast's Harland and Wolff shipyards tripled to over 35,000 men, and the linen and cloth industries produced 200,000,000 yards of material for the UK armed services. The total acreage of land under tillage was doubled to keep up with demand, and 25,000 gallons of milk were exported to Britain every day. Up to 149 ships were based in Lough Foyle, representing the United States, Canadian, French, Dutch, Norwegian, Polish and Russian marines, crewed by 20,000 sailors. At the peak of the war, the number of troops billeted in Derry between air raids on Germany and practice manoeuvres for the D-Day invasion reached 40,000, a number equal to the city's entire pre-war population. American soldiers, though segregated into Black and white regiments by the US Army, mixed eagerly into Derry's social life, spending their dollars in dance halls and pubs, playing poker and dice, chewing gum and flirting with local girls.

Brian's family moved into a brick terraced house at 5 St Joseph's Avenue, in view of the Ebrington barracks across the river Foyle, and it was likely in these years that his fascination with Americans began. Throughout his early career, he would mimic the American accent, from cowboy movies to dime store novels to academic prose, in his humour columns for the *Irish Times* and *Irish Press*, in Gar O'Donnell's monologues for *Philadelphia, here I come!* and biting social commentary within the play *The freedom of the city*. As a child, Brian watched from his window 'the whole drama of military life – of marching soldiers, and tanks, and artillery, and bayonet practise – a splendid and continuous tattoo, and all put on just for my entertainment'. He gathered with other boys at the gangways of naval ships and bought duty-free cigarettes from sailors, he roller skated down Abercorn Road between concrete blocks placed as barricades to German tanks, and he hoarded red glass reflectors prised from air raid shelters around the city. His father, meanwhile, tutored Brian in the evenings for the grammar school entrance exam. 'I don't remember the details of those private lessons', Brian later recalled, 'but I do know that they always ended with my father in a towering rage and me in tears, and I have a vivid recollection of crawling up to bed night after night, weighed down by the very terrible and imminent prospect of turning into a "Yahoo".' Fortunately, Brian passed the exam and won acceptance to St Columb's College, then a school of fewer than 300.

In his childhood summers, Brian returned with his family to his mother's home place, Donegal, where his aunt Kathleen, a teacher, still lived near the town of Glenties in the family home, a house imprinted in Brian's 'special and sacred' memories forever after. 'I remember in detail the shape of cups hanging in the scullery, the pattern of flags on the kitchen floor, every knot of wood on the wooden stairway, every door-handle, every smell, the shape and texture of every tree around the place.' It was to this house, The Laurels, that Brian's uncle, missionary priest Bernard Joseph MacLoone, returned in 1946, suffering from malaria after thirty-five years in Uganda and a decade in charge of the leper colony at Nyenga. He had served as a chaplain in West Africa during the war, and when he died in 1950, a requiem high Mass for the 'Wee Donegal Priest' was celebrated in St Connell's Church by four priests, joined by the lord bishop of Raphoe and fourteen more members of the Catholic clergy. Twenty-one-year-old Brian, along with his parents, sisters and Father MacLoone's six other surviving siblings, was listed among the mourners, but readers of tributes in the *Ulster Herald* could not have guessed how the young writer, then newly appointed to teach at Omagh Technical School after earning his credentials at St Joseph's College, Belfast, would mould and transform the story of the ailing missionary in his future work. Brian himself had considered the priesthood – after St Columb's, he spent two years in seminary at Maynooth – and he remained captivated by his uncle's life history, using it to frame two short stories that were rejected by the *New Yorker*, as well as an early play, *The blind mice*, before reshaping it into a subplot for his Tony-winning script *Dancing at Lughnasa*.

Brian's first published short story 'The Child' appeared in *The Bell* in July 1952, alongside writing by Kate O'Brien, James Plunkett, Val Mulkerns, Anthony Cronin and *The Bell*'s founding editor Seán O'Faoláin. The magazine was approaching the end of its fourteen-year run, having launched in Dublin in 1940 as a liberal voice for writers in the Emergency era. It took an inclusive approach to writers from the North, which they valued because, as John Hewitt wrote (in the same issue that featured Brian's story), 'there is no publishing house in Ulster as yet able to accept and distribute their volumes. Nor is there here a literary journal, not even a journal with cultural pretensions enough, to offer hospitality to and payment for the short story or the poem'. Landing a story in *The Bell* was a coup for any writer. Brian's two-page vignette marked his début with Joycean imagery, as its fearful child protagonist crouches at the top of his stairs in darkness, the tail of his torn nightshirt tucked between his feet and the cold linoleum floor, praying for his parents' nightly row to end. '"Dear God. Don't let me Ma and me Da fight ... I'll say a rosary – I'll say two if you'll stop it and ... Help me. Mary. Make him stop them."' Earlier the boy had lain in bed as 'Pleasant memories of the day floated through his mind', but when his father came home for the night, pleasant memories were displaced by raised voices and the image of his mother, still in her boots as she 'moved about the kitchen, doing trivial things with over-anxiety. The wellingtons made her untidy-looking'. As his parents roar at each other in the kitchen below, the boy returns 'blinded with tears' to a room 'thick and black because the night had entered'. Brian would choose similarly dark themes for his earliest radio plays as he moved among teaching posts in Derry primary schools and continued writing stories after hours.

On 28 December 1954, Brian married Anne Morrison, who grew up in a large house overlooking the Foyle and graduated with her BSc from University College Dublin at a time when women made up a slim percentage of each year's class. Smiling in cap and gown, Anne's photo brightened the front page of the Dublin *Evening Herald* the day she received her degree. She and Brian met as teenagers in Derry because their parents were friends – Brian's father had been best man at Anne's parents' wedding. With her sharp mind and 'sharp Waterside tongue' (as Brian once joked), Anne became Brian's first reader, his confidante and champion in career decisions, and his fearless travelling companion, journeying to Minneapolis and Dublin alongside him even when their children were babies. As newlyweds, the couple moved into 13 Marlborough Street, steps from St Eugene's Cathedral and the green expanse of Brooke Park, where Brian, wearing a 'checked cap' and 'brown shoes', would daily walk their Lakeland terrier, projecting himself to his middle-class neighbours as 'pleasant, honest, easygoing, good-natured, prepared to take a risk, kind, fond of a good yarn, happy-go-lucky, quick-witted, generous to a fault, considerate, popular with children, breezy, content, the idol of his wife and family, a real sport, the heart of corn.'

1.1 Brian and Anne Friel wedding photo, 28 December 1954.

The Bell published its final issue in the same month as Brian and Anne's wedding, leaving a void for Irish writers seeking a literary audience. But radio offered a lucrative alternative: the BBC had a regional station in Belfast, established three decades earlier by a young Tyrone Guthrie, and it paid by broadcast time. The starting rate was one guinea per minute, far beyond *The Bell*'s rate of one guinea per thousand words, which might add up to five guineas at most for a full-length story. Thanks to BBC Belfast producer John Boyd, Brian received twelve guineas (£12 12s.) for a twelve-minute story 'The good old days', broadcast on the BBC Northern Ireland Home Service in 1956, the year his daughter Patricia was born. But he was eager to try a longer format and appeal to a larger audience. He sent his first dramatic script, *A cottage in Devon*, directly to Broadcasting House, London, accompanied by a diffident query letter. 'Dear Editor, I am enclosing the script of a radio play which I hope you like … I think (perhaps in my innocence) that in style and treatment it is closer to the tradition of your Wednesday Evening Matinee.' A BBC editor pencilled an exclamation point and underlined the 'Evening Matinee' oxymoron, and unfortunately for 27-year-old Brian, the script was turned down by its London readers. It chronicled, in the words of Mollie Greenhalgh, script unit staff, 'The mental rehabilitation of an architect who thinks he has failed'. In her assessment, Brian's first attempt at radio drama was an 'Amateurish playlet, which wanders off the point and is badly characterised. Quite useless.' It was returned to Brian with a polite rejection slip.

He kept writing. Edith Sewell Haggard, based in the US office of the Curtis Brown literary agency, agreed to represent him, and in February 1957, she sent his short story 'The Nest' directly to *New Yorker* editor Katharine White, asking for consideration.

> I am not at all sure that this particular story is right for you, but Brian Friel is someone to watch. He is a young school teacher in Northern Ireland and I think he has real talent and a rare sensitivity. I hope you can encourage him.

Mrs White's response was swift but not dismissive. 'We can't use Brian Friel's "'The Nest'", but we'd like to see more of his work.' For an unknown writer, this was high praise from an esteemed source. Katharine White had joined the *New Yorker* six months after its founding in 1925, and was credited by editor William Shawn and others with shaping the magazine as it evolved into America's foremost literary and cultural journal of the twentieth century.

Divorced from her first husband, Ernest Angell, she had married essayist E.B. White, seven years her junior, after persuading *New Yorker* founder Harold Ross to hire him as a staff writer. When she received Brian's story, she was close to retirement as head of the fiction department, having brought writers such as Marianne Moore, Nadine Gordimer, John Cheever and John Updike to the magazine in her thirty-five years on staff. She promised Brian's agent that a new fiction editor, Roger Angell, would be in touch. She declined to mention that Roger was her son.

Brian's rejections by the BBC and *New Yorker* coincided with his essay 'For export only' in the American Catholic journal *The Commonweal*, published just days after Mrs White sent her rejection. The journal described him as 'an Irish writer', though he modestly pointed out that he was one of the 'small men' of Irish literature, 'journalists and writer-teachers and writer-barristers and writer-civil servants', each desperately vying for publication 'in a small community which cannot possibly support him'. Gone were the 'big men' – Shaw, Joyce, O'Casey – and gone were the 'little magazines', and gone with the war was British readers' appetite for writers from neutral Ireland. The only 'market' left, though Brian disdained the very word, was the American one, and, as he reported, Irish writers were justifiably doubtful. '"Write for Americans? I don't even speak their language!" or "Americans? Heavens, man, they are dedicated to Elvis Presley and the Dodgers! They're scarcely civilized!"' Even worse, acceptance was not guaranteed, as proven when Brian's 'writer-teacher friend' – or is it Brian himself? – 'produces a plausibly worded rejection slip from the United States'. In the end, Brian proposed a compromise. The Irish writer 'must keep in mind that you are writing for export only. This does not mean that you tell lies. It means that there are certain aspects of Irish life that you ignore' and instead focus on 'whitewashed, thatched cottages' and 'dances held at crossroads and lame fiddlers to play at them'.

He did not follow his own advice. Pitched closer to home, Brian's next effort at radio drama delved into social divides within Northern Ireland, and it would lead to the most instructive working relationship of his early writing career. In March 1957, Brian submitted a new radio play, *A sort of freedom*, directly to Ronald Mason, who had been appointed the BBC's Belfast-based drama producer two years earlier. Again he sent a hesitant, apologetic query. 'I am enclosing the opening pages of the script of a radio play which I hope you will like. You will find too a précis of the plot which, I am sorry to say, is not nearly as coherent as I would like.' He shied from sending the entire script, instead offering a three-page synopsis – and a confession.

I have no experience of radio drama. Mr John Boyd knows my stories; he has in fact one on hands at the moment which is to be broadcast some time soon. But I am a complete amateur at plays. If you give me the green light, I shall be delighted to go ahead, now that the theme is fresh but if you do not like it, I would be grateful for criticisms. I will be eager to hear your reply.

Ronald Mason was only three years older than Brian, but he had wider access to the world beyond Ireland and more direct experience of the theatre. Born in Ballymena in 1926, he was a schoolmate of Ian Paisley and spoke with a similarly stentorian Ulster accent. At Queen's University Belfast, Mason performed in student theatrical productions, but decided not to pursue acting professionally after receiving his degree. Instead he taught grammar school English and French in Coleraine, a post he held for six years before joining the BBC staff. As drama producer for Northern Ireland, he carried numerous responsibilities: cultivating new talent, commissioning plays, writing lead-in text and *Radio Times* blurbs, revising scripts and directing productions in the studio. According to his colleague John Tydeman, Mason excelled as 'both poet and politician, creator and administrator', and, when he later ascended to head of BBC radio drama, London, in 1976, 'The public servant, Ronald, came together with the slightly Bohemian drama director, Ronnie.'

Brian was to know and benefit from both sides of Mason's personality. Mason was gregarious, funny and 'larger-than-life'. He maintained contacts with theatre directors and playwrights as well as with administrators in BBC Broadcasting House, London – Tydeman in particular, who worked in the radio script unit in the early 1960s and thus would receive Brian's later submission, *The blind mice*, as well as *Philadelphia, here I come!* before its onstage success. In his role as regional drama producer, Mason travelled frequently to London and established networks beyond Brian's reach, anchored as the young father was by his teaching job and family in Derry. Internal memos hint that Mason was much loved on both sides of the Irish Sea: in one exchange, Tydeman signs off, 'Trust you are not missing London too much, though London is missing you'. Though many who knew Mason suspected he was homosexual, the mores of mid-century Belfast would never have allowed him to live openly as gay.

Mason's response to Brian's proposed script was careful and encouraging, and he soon became a trusted mentor. After conferring with H.W. McMullan, head of Northern Ireland programmes, who agreed that 'The dialogue is really v. good & he characterises well', Mason wrote to Brian, telling him the material 'looks very promising indeed, and is certainly worth the "green light"

1.2 Ronald Mason directing Tom Fleming in *The enemy within*, 1965, courtesy of BBC NI.

asked for'. While he cautioned that he could pay no commission nor promise an acceptance, he offered Brian his ongoing assistance. 'If at any stage in the writing of it you should like advice, or should like to discuss it with me, I would be only too happy to see you here in Belfast ... Don't hesitate to let me hear from you about its progress.' Mason's hands-on approach to nurturing talent epitomized the BBC's policies throughout the United Kingdom in the 1950s. No other country offered as much support to radio playwrights – efforts warranted because a typical afternoon play on the Home Service was heard by 750,000 listeners. Unlike magazine editors, who turned away more stories and poems than they could fit into their budgeted pages per month, BBC producers had weekly time slots to fill, so it behoved them to coach writers on adapting their talents to the medium of radio. Brian was not the only one to benefit. The BBC's national and regional stations aired 600 new plays per year, including early work by Harold Pinter and Tom Stoppard, launching their careers and making theatre available to far flung audiences who would never journey to London's West End.

By tapping into the BBC, Brian capitalized on his liminal position as a Northern Irish writer, traversing the cultural, political and economic borders between the UK and the Republic. Resources for radio drama were much more limited in Dublin, where government funding was leaner and television broadcasting did not yet exist. In May 1957, Brian submitted his full script for *A sort of freedom* to BBC Belfast and asked Mason, 'Could you let me know when you might reach a verdict on it? As this is really my first serious attempt at radio drama, you will appreciate my anxiety.' The play follows an ambitious dual storyline. Jack Frazer, owner of a road haulage firm outside Belfast, faces a planned strike by his thirty-three lorry drivers unless long-term employee Joe Reddin submits to joining their union. Meanwhile Frazer's newly adopted baby must be immunized against tuberculosis, an inoculation Frazer opposes on the grounds of individual parental rights. Frazer's tenderness toward his eight-month-old son barely offsets his bitterness as a boss and husband. When the baby succumbs to cot death, his wife mocks his despair. 'Grief for what? For an infant that wasn't ours and that was lucky to be spared the ordeal of growing up in this emotional desert? ... Twenty years earlier it might have been different, before your soul withered in you and mine withered because yours had. But it came too late.' Reading the script, Mason may have been reminded of the vicious marital arguments in John Osborne's *Look back in anger*, which had premiered with the English Stage Company the previous year and aired on BBC television in October 1956. Frazer's loyal employee, Joe Reddin, fares little better with his own wife, who chides him when he is unable to find work after standing up for his principles.

> REDDIN: I can't fill my belly on your pride.
> MARY: Will you look who's talking! The man that was too proud to sign his name to the union. Surely you've got your fill now, me boy.

Brian explained, 'If the play has any moral purpose it is this, that in our age, personal liberties have been forfeited to what we hope is a greater common democracy ... Was Frazer right in not defending his friend Reddin? Was Reddin right in accepting a cash settlement? Was it necessary for the baby to be inoculated?'

Mason reported to the head of programmes that 'Apart from a few obvious constructional flaws, Friel has made a promising start. The ending is peculiar, and at first reading the last scene seems to leave the whole thing hanging in the air'. McMullan agreed, 'He has something here. I suggest we get an opinion ... on its Trade Union side – which is dangerous. It's a promising script which doesn't quite ring true.' They conferred with John Boyd, who eventually engaged David Bleakley, then a member of the Northern Ireland Labour Party and later a member of parliament, to 'vet the Trade Unionism' within the story. In the politically charged environment of Northern Ireland, such topics had to be handled with care. Brian assured the BBC that 'I have been very careful not to mention Frazer's business in the play in case any Trade Union could identify itself with the mythical Union in the story.' Any misstep could be explosive: Sam Thompson's radio drama *Tommy Baxter, shop steward* had already aired on the BBC without incident, but his stage play *Over the bridge* would soon cause an uproar with its portrait of sectarianism in the shipyards.

While Brian's script was under review, Mason conveyed his measured appreciation and offered more help. 'Dear Brian Friel ... I am sure you have a play here, but it still needs a considerable amount of work done on it.' Mason applauded Brian's 'clear, precise, and clean-cut' dialogue and the distinct characterization of each voice to be heard on the air, but the trade union and domestic plots did not parallel one another as closely as they might. 'I am not sure that the play says quite what you intended. On reading it I ask myself, "how do the two conflicts tie up together?"' He invited Brian to Broadcasting House, and Brian travelled from Derry to Belfast on 21 June 1957 for their first meeting – the BBC reimbursed his train fare. Over lunch, the two men's personalities clicked, despite the polarities of their differing backgrounds and experiences. Brian and Anne were now the parents of two daughters, Patricia (nicknamed Paddy) and Mary, while Brian continued as a Catholic primary school teacher; Mason never married, and he shuttled between Belfast and London after having grown up in Ulster's Protestant heartland. But they were both well read, and witty, and ambitious. Brian wrote the following week: 'Dear Ronald Mason ... I enjoyed our talk immensely, possibly all the more because I come from a Philistine city. And thank you too for being young (do have your hair cut often) and for remembering Fowler'. From then on, Brian's trust in Mason deepened as he shared his struggles in the creative process with his newfound advocate and friend.

In his letters to Mason, Brian was always more eager to discuss his work's shortcomings than its strengths. When he sent the revised script for *A sort of freedom*, which had not yet been accepted by the BBC, he admitted his misgivings about the play.

> To be quite honest, I have battled with it for so long and throughout seven almost sleepless nights, I'm damned if I now know whether I've made a complete mess of the whole thing or whether the old copy, with

all its imperfections on its head, was not better. After all we said and planned, the only thing I'm sure of is that the fades out and in are not quite so bald as they were. Beyond that, I just <u>don't know</u>.

Brian listed the changes he made to the script, all suggested by Mason. He strengthened the subplot and shored up parallelism between his two themes. He rewrote dialogue in which Frazer tries to bribe the baby's doctor, fact-checked rules about adoption and inoculation, and revised the final domestic scene so that Mrs Frazer 'gets her platform and states her case.' But he ended his comments by stating, 'the more I think of it, the less I like it' – hardly a persuasive pitch by an aspiring author. He hungered for Mason's feedback, whether it be positive or negative. 'I will be very anxious to hear what your verdict will be. Do let me have it as soon as you can.' And he thanked Mason again for his 'kindness and helpfulness' as well as for three radio scripts Mason gave Brian at their lunch meeting, the first of Mason's many concrete acts of guidance in the art of playwriting.

Mason was equally struck by feelings of comradeship with Brian. Although he wrote that 'you have cleared up a good many of the points which we made here in my office', he cautioned that the parallels were now 'rather consciously plugged, I fear'. Some of Brian's revision went 'a little beyond what is necessary, and sacrifices economy ... to elaborate statement'. Still, he reassured the novice playwright that 'Most is within the remedy of a blue pencil', and promised that after his summer holidays they would plan for 'a few hours working over it together, and discussing each detail in turn. I think it is well written, and deserves the extra polish which a little time and careful thinking can so easily give it.'

In his next letter Mason dropped formalities and addressed his new friend by first name only, declaring: 'Dear Brian, Enough of this "Brian Friel" nonsense!' Brian replied from Kincasslagh in the Donegal Gaeltacht, where he and Anne had rented a cottage for the summer (he apologized for delay because 'the post office is playing hell with our letters'). Rather than travelling to Belfast, Brian invited Mason to his Marlborough Street home in Derry, where the two devoted a Saturday afternoon to a second round of rewrites. Brian returned the marked-up script to Mason a scant five days later, confessing, 'The MS is in a horrible state and I can only hope that [her holiday in] Spain will have built up your secretary's strength sufficiently to tackle it'. John Boyd had rejected his latest story submission, but he graciously accepted the verdict. 'All his criticisms were valid and quite coherent.' Brian again thanked Mason for his 'help and patient attention' to *A sort of freedom*, acknowledging that 'Whatever its merits now, it was a lumpy, ungroomed thing when you first saw it.' Before mailing, he typed a postscript that affirmed his commitment to his new genre. 'I am at present devouring all plays within arm's reach.'

Mason congratulated Brian on the revisions, confirmed that the play had been accepted for broadcast, and advised Brian that he would soon receive payment for it. 'What remains to be done is of minor importance; a little trimming here and there, and the addition of a few microphone perspectives to complete it as a radio script.' There were also a few changes needed for accuracy in the trade union plot. Most importantly, Mason encouraged the first-time playwright not to rest on his laurels, but to turn his energies quickly toward the next project. 'I hope you won't sit back and wait until this goes out before dreaming up something new. I am always available in the office here should you like to call on me.'

Brian's acceptance by the BBC came just days before his first humour column, a satire on Derry's new television transmitter, appeared in the *Irish Times*. Although he had spent the summer corresponding and meeting with Mason, he now told readers that he refused to watch BBC television, despite the new transmission mast being built on Sheriff's Mountain outside Derry. His imperfect eyesight was one factor; another was the cost of a TV licence. The only time he watched the new medium, he wrote, was if invited to a friend's house, where he and Anne 'discover all sorts of unlikely facial resemblances between our neighbours and the actors on the screen ... we get wonderful fun out of it all.' The warmth and humour of Brian's newspaper writing struck a far friendlier tone than his dark-edged radio drama, so that when he closed his anti-television complaint by stating, 'My only hope ... is that the I.R.A. will blow up the new transmitter', it was impossible to take him seriously. But he may have hoped that Mason wouldn't read it.

In fact, the BBC and its generous pay rates were a lifeline for Brian as he attempted to establish himself as a writer. Just before the *Irish Times* piece appeared, he received fifteen guineas for a new story, 'My true kinsman', to be broadcast on the Northern Ireland Home Service; it would not appear in print until a few years later, when it became one of his first stories in the *New Yorker*. He earned even more for his final fifty-minute script for *A sort of freedom*, and gleefully detailed plans for spending the fee when he thanked Mason.

> This 50 guineas is to take Anne and myself to Verona, tile the kitchen in fire-brigade red and dazzling white & supply me with a new typewriter. After a week's time, we will submit to writing off some year old bills with it. Anyhow, it's more than welcome.

Annual teacher salaries for married men ranged between £285 and £509, depending on seniority, so the BBC's disbursement of fifty guineas (£52 10s.) equated to more than a month's pay (and perhaps as much as two months') for a trained teacher on the official scale. Mason responded to Brian's elation with amused benevolence. 'Never has fifty guineas been proposed to stretch so far!'

Spurred, perhaps, by the potential gains to be made in churning out radio scripts, Brian assured Mason, 'I am not idling; I'm up to the neck in another play'. This script, *Make vile things precious*, would become *To this hard house*, both titles excerpted from *King Lear*, on which Brian modelled the plot: an ageing teacher with failing eyesight suffers betrayal by his conniving children. His rural school, Meenbanid Primary, is threatened by a bigger, modern institution in a newly developed town nearby, with 'every possible facility you could think of; cinema, swimming pool, milk-bar and do you know what? … a rest-room for the teachers!' As the plot progresses, the new school lures family after family from the countryside into the town, 'poaching' children who have sustained Meenbanid's 200-year history in the area. In a twist that would be echoed decades later in Brian's play *Translations*, the frustrated teacher 'clings tenaciously to the world he knows and is master of', only to learn that his son has been offered principalship of the new school, and that he himself will be forced to retire as a result.

Again, bitterness permeated the script, and again Brian shared doubts about his work in progress with Ronnie Mason.

> The theme is good, I think, but I KNOW I am liable to make a real bloody mess of what ought to be a good play. And the more anxious I become about making a mess of the thing, the more hesitant I get about tackling parts of it … The killing part about it is that I think it could be a wonderful play.

He also wondered whether any of his short stories might work as radio drama.

> I was looking over some older stories I did with a view to trying to dramatise any one or two that could be transposed. I am afraid there's nothing worthwhile among them but something may occur to me later. That has always been the way with me. Anything I wrote over 12 months ago appears pathetic on re-reading & whatever work I have on hands (witness the suppressed enthusiasm about the teacher-play I'm at now!) is always THE BEST, for a short while.

In the decades to come, Brian would indeed transpose stories into theatre – 'The highwayman and the saint', 'Foundry House' and 'A man's world' among them. He continued to mine earlier work for ideas over his entire career, though none of his radio plays draw directly upon his short fiction.

Throughout this crucial early phase of Brian's development, Ronnie Mason continued to serve as guide and mentor. The new script, like the first, exposed family rifts and betrayals in a heavy-handed style – Dan's son takes the principal post, ending his father's career, and Dan's daughter elopes with a local boy from 'one of those get-rich-quick families that most rural areas seem to throw up'. When she tries to console her father over the loss of his school, he rails, 'Take your hand off my shoulder; I'll have none of your transparent affection. You have left me no doubt where your loyalties lie; with everyone and everything that I oppose.' Brian acknowledged that he was a neophyte at playwriting, having never performed onstage nor participated in the life of a theatre, and even as he raced to finish the script, he warned Mason, 'Very probably I will take you up on that offer of calling to see you in your office. I can foresee that my abysmal ignorance of all things dramatic is going to have me trotting & asking far too often.' Mason urged him to follow existing models: the three scripts he had given Brian over lunch, as well as books on the art of theatre. 'How is the reading going? You know that St. John Ervine has written a book – I think it's called "How to Write a Play" – a stage play, of course, and Val Gielgud has contributed something on writing plays for radio.' As radio drama took hold of the listening public's imagination, there were more and more manuals for aspiring playwrights, and in this vein Val Gielgud, the BBC's director of productions from 1929 to 1963 (and brother of the actor Sir John Gielgud), had published *The right way to radio playwriting* in 1948. Mason brainstormed a list of books to recommend to Brian: J.B. Priestley's *The art of the dramatist*, John Van Druten's *Playwright at work*, William Archer's *How to write a play* and Harley Granville-Barker's *The use of the drama*. These were all aimed at stage playwrights, not radio. While Brian was grappling with the art of drama itself, Mason was already encouraging him to expand his ambitions.

Brian certainly felt pulled toward the stage, but his social network of theatrical connections was thinner than his new friend's. In October 1957, as the school year was beginning, he sent Mason his script for *Make vile things precious*.

> You suggested to me once that I should have a shot at a stage play. In the embryo stages of this play, I had that idea at the back of my mind but there were too many difficulties; for example, my ignorance of stage craft. But my big problem was: If I do write this for the stage, where would I send it?

Brian's interest in staging this script had led him to limit the play's action to a single setting, with most scenes taking place in the main character's sitting room, and he apologized that he seemed 'to have made little use of the possibilities of radio'. He again invited Mason to Derry, suggesting that he and Anne would be delighted to host him for an overnight visit, and asked for a quick turnaround on Mason's assessment. 'I am dying to know what you think of it so put me out of my misery as soon as you can.'

Mason ignored Brian's hint about placing the new play with a theatre – likely because he perceived structural problems, especially with the ending, when Dan's daughter, jilted by her upstart beau, returns from London and begs her father's forgiveness. Mason assuaged the writer's ego – 'My personal opinion is that you have written a good, well authenticated, at times moving piece of work' – but he flagged the final section of the play as needing substantial rewriting. 'I am impressed by the characterisation, the dialogue and sound development of the theme right up to about ten pages from the end', when it would be 'dramatically much more acceptable' for Dan to become reconciled to his daughter's marriage.

Mason disclosed his doubts more bluntly to McMullan in an internal BBC memo. 'The play needs heavy cutting ... Altogether the last ten pages are bad, striking too many false notes.' He nonetheless advocated for Brian and requested approval to help him make revisions. 'I am sure Friel is well worth encouraging and I should like a green light to work on this script with the author, who proved himself very conscientious over the re-write of his first play.' McMullan, persuaded, wrote in red pencil: 'agree – it has the makings but there's a lot to be done. accepted.' Two weeks later, Mason wrote to Brian, affirming, 'I like it, and I think we can make a play out of it', but explained that he had other productions to work on first, as well as a trip to London for the BBC. It would be over a month before he wrote again, this time not in regard to Brian's second play but to invite him to view the rehearsals and recording of his first, *A sort of freedom*, which would be broadcast on 16 January 1958. Brian was ill at the time with pleurisy, and Mason's father died unexpectedly in mid-December, but the two men exchanged sympathies and reunited in Belfast for studio rehearsals, as Brian made the most of his 'unlimited freedom' due to sick leave. They planned to discuss *Make vile things precious* after completing the first play's production.

Meanwhile, Brian's humour found an outlet in the *Irish Times*, where his semi-autobiographical features about life in Derry echoed the flippancy and self-mockery of Myles na gCopaleen's popular column 'Cruiskeen lawn'. In one sketch, Brian confessed to anxiety that a neighbour would inform on him to the police, 'not that I have anything to hide – my life is an open book; but I know that someone is going to report something on me, and once they get me inside, once they get to work on me, I'm liable to sign my life away. Putty was my nickname at school.' In another, he recounted the 'complicated theories of economics' that Anne applied to his football pool winnings, and how they might be best put to use. 'Now the point is that I know I'm £13 4s. 6d. in the red – I know that. She can juggle as much as she likes, talk about unearned gratuities and balance payments until doomsday but I will still be certain of that much.' The newspaper published these on an irregular schedule, but they offered a welcome opportunity for experimentation and exposure to a Dublin reading audience.

Brian's second play, however, was facing an uncertain future. The story of the ageing teacher required much more editing than Mason had implied. In its revision, Mason achieved a balancing act between encouraging the novice playwright and holding him to artistic standards, all the while promoting his work to decision makers within the BBC. Mason again travelled to Derry in January 1958, the day after Brian's first play was broadcast, and rekindled his lively conversations with the playwright. (Brian would later write to him, 'Be sure to call in the next time you are in town: my defence of the Pope was not nearly good enough the last night.') Based on their discussions, Brian made several alterations to *Make vile things precious*, cutting a final episode from the script entirely and shortening other scenes. He no longer aspired to placing this play in a live theatre, as he noted to Mason, 'I hope I have cut out all stage directions'. He went to great lengths to verify his story's authenticity, recalling the script from Mason's secretary for revisions after a letter from the Northern secretary of the Irish National Teachers' Organisation (INTO) corrected a plot point.

Mason managed to get Brian's play accepted, persuading the head of programmes that 'It is a better play than his first, and, apart from a few odds and ends, should now be ready for production', but once he had arranged for Brian to receive an increased fee of £75 (nearly 50 per cent over his first playwriting wage), he wrote to the author with details on even more 'final amendments and polishing'. Cuts, he warned, must be extensive. Mason interspersed specific scenes to be trimmed with the artistic rationale behind his verdict.

> The play is too long by 150 to 175 of your lines. I can suggest cuts which have more to back them than the time factor alone ... its identity with Lear and Cordelia is somewhat too obvious to be successful. I personally feel that it strikes a false note here and there ... This all must sound rather devastating at this stage, but I do think that since this is

> your second play you want to have as much polish on it as possible. Read the play in the light of the criticisms which I have made, remembering that there has scarcely ever been a play written which doesn't improve by the ruthless use of a blue pencil.

Mason confirmed the play's rehearsal and recording schedule for late April 1958, perhaps to assure Brian that it would be produced despite its flaws. The ending was still a problem. Mason believed that Brian had introduced an 'unnecessary complication' in the elopement of the teacher's daughter. For his part, Brian had a much longer ending in mind, culminating in the Carlisle and Blake Premium (the same prize Master Friel would win a few years later) being awarded to Dan as consolation for losing his school. Mason ended his comments by asserting, 'The last point is that we are none of us quite happy about the title. A play sells itself to a fair-sized audience on the title alone, and this – even though it is from *Lear* – is not neat enough to be eye-catching.'

Before he received Mason's letter, Brian received the cheque, which may have leavened the criticism. As in previous responses to his radio producer, Brian willingly made the requested edits without protest, though he voiced difficulties with Mason's demand for greater economy of language.

> Here it is again, more grubbier and more grubbier ... I have done the painful business of cutting; 163 lines are gone. You will see that I have worked at the 6 places you mentioned. One section I cut out altogether ... I have no gift for comedy writing and since wholesale cutting was necessary, it had to go.

Brian confessed that in the act of excising so much of the script, he was guided by the producer's judgment, not his own. 'When I got down to the job of cutting, every line, every word seemed absolutely vital and I just could not see how any of it was to be sacrificed!' A further 120 lines were crossed out before broadcast, so that the performance transmitted to listeners was roughly 15 per cent shorter than the version Brian first discussed with Mason in Derry.

One additional change arose from Brian's prescience in naming the fictional town where a new school was to be founded, at a time when the Belfast rural district council was responding to urban growth in Northern Ireland. 'In last Friday's *Telegraph*', Brian reported, 'I saw that a new town is to be opened somewhere next week and it is to be called Newtownabbey! Here's hoping no Clareford [the name substituted in his revised script] is built in a day'. As for the play's title, Brian offered three alternatives: '1. Daniel Stone, Principal. 2. Retirement. 3. The End of a Teacher'. He appended a handwritten postscript: 'Of the three I prefer "The End of a Teacher"' – perhaps an allusion to Arthur Miller's *Death of a salesman*, which had first aired on British television a few months before.

Or perhaps Brian was anticipating an end to his own career as a teacher. He was eager for the opportunity to observe rehearsals after the play was renamed by Mason *To this hard house*. Having already asked whether he could 'look on some day when you are working on it', Brian now explained that he had a greater purpose in learning as much as he could about the art of drama.

> If I can manage to get away from the wanes on Sat. 19th, I hope to get up to Belfast for one of the rehearsals. I want to ask your advice about a stage play I am attempting, and I still have a lot that I could learn by simply watching you and a cast in motion.

Standing in a Belfast BBC studio as his early plays were brought to life, Brian gleaned insights about pacing and characterization that had eluded him in the solitude of writing. After the play's broadcast, he wrote to Mason, 'You set it going at a good rattlin' pace which helped to conceal the heavy documentation. People who heard it here in Derry seemed to enjoy it'. Mason acknowledged Brian's appreciative assessment of the performance and complimented him on his developing skill as a playwright.

> I consider it, pared as it was in production, an advance on your first play. It was much more taut, and the documentation which you mention was cut down, I think, to a minimum. The human element was played up in production so that it became a vital piece of writing. The craftsmanship itself is now on firmer legs, and if your next play is as far in advance of this as this was of the last, then you are well on the way to having a fairly predictable market for your literary products.

In fact, unbeknownst to Mason, Brian's work had just found a welcome in a more distant market, having landed on the new fiction editor's desk at the *New Yorker*.

In February 1958, after a previous story had been rejected by another *New Yorker* editor, Brian's agent sent a new attempt, 'A late child', directly to Roger Angell, touting her client as 'a young Irish writer whose work interests me'. Angell, too, was impressed, and replied that 'the manuscript certainly contains enough promise to make us very interested in him as a writer'. But the *New Yorker* already had a stable of Irish authors in steady publication, including Ireland's best-known short story writer, as Angell explained.

> I kept having the feeling that he was trying very hard to write like Frank O'Connor, and that he just didn't have enough wisdom to achieve the remarkable effects that O'Connor gets with what appear to be simple themes and simple people. I guess this means that I think Mr Friel seems very young, which you have already told me. Nevertheless, I hope you will tell him that we would like to see more of his work.

A fortnight later, drawing upon Brian's indefatigable creativity and prolific output, the agent sent Angell a new story, 'The Skelper'. Set in the fictional Donegal village of Beannafreaghan, it was to be Brian's first sale to the magazine, and his introduction to a new mentor on the far shores of the Atlantic.

CHAPTER 2

Understudy, 1959–60

'I WOULD LIKE TO HAVE HIM EXPLAIN, in a parenthetical clause, just what a Skelper is', wrote Roger Angell, in response to Brian's story about a cattleman who settles in a Donegal village, 'and he should also state what the fine for poaching is'. Angell wanted a new ending for the story, and, in a later draft, a new beginning. And then there was the title itself, still troublesome after revision: 'we gather by indirection that the word is synonymous with a cattle-jobber. However, our dictionaries only give one definition of the word, which is "an extremely large person", adding that this is Scotch dialect. For American readers, I think you should explain whether the man is named for his job or for his size'. There were other edits needed in this vein: Brian's original name for the village was Ardmore, deemed confusing since it is shared by a Philadelphia suburb, and the skelper was initially carefree as 'a schoolboy at hometime', redacted to read 'a schoolboy on vacation'. These were the first of many times that Angell would instruct Brian on reaching American audiences, and far from the most extensive revisions he would coach the young writer to make.

Angell was the son of Katharine White, the stepson of essayist and novelist E.B. White, and a fiction writer himself. He had recently moved from *Holiday* magazine to the *New Yorker*, which was then publishing two or three pieces of fiction in each of its weekly issues. The American short story was at its peak as a high art, and Brian's first stories appeared in the company of work by revered practitioners John Cheever, John Updike, Mavis Gallant and James Thurber. The *New Yorker* was also on the rise, having boosted its circulation during the war years by printing a monthly edition for US troops, many of whom became subscribers as they settled into the suburbs and enjoyed America's post-war economic boom. By 1947, circulation had doubled to 320,000, with many readers outside the New York area, so that in its third decade the magazine was truly becoming 'a national cultural heavyweight'. In its early years, humour and personal reminiscence – a genre the *New Yorker* labelled as 'casuals' – had filled the pages, but under Katharine White's

2.1 Roger Angell in his *New Yorker* office.

editorship as well as William Shawn's, after he took the helm in 1952, literary fiction soon came to dominate the magazine so entirely that the idea of 'the *New Yorker* story' became a byword among critics and aspiring writers alike.

Decades after his retirement from the magazine, Roger Angell disputed the idea that the *New Yorker* sought or shaped fiction to fit predetermined moulds. 'Most people misunderstand editing', he explained, recalling his first encounters with Brian's short stories. 'A lot of writers or literary people who were outside the *New Yorker* thought we were trying to turn writers into *New Yorker* writers. That is not what we were doing. We did not have a type of story that we thought was a *New Yorker* story. It was just trying to get the best out of this particular person. And if they were brand new, so much the better.' The magazine accepted 'serious, wonderful fiction from around the world', Angell pointed out. Multiple subeditors read each story, wrote their opinions and then handed them to editor William Shawn, who was 'deeply involved in the whole process', sifting pieces into '"A" fiction, "B" fiction and "C" fiction', indicating their placement toward the front or back of each issue. 'The Skelper' ran as 'A' fiction, as did most of Brian's accepted *New Yorker* stories. 'It's no great trick to take a submission and turn it into the greatest story ever written', Shawn told his editors, according to Angell. 'The hard thing is to make it into the best story this writer could have written. In other words, you have to edit in the style of the writer.'

In his letters to Brian, Angell was encouraging but firm, and his suggested edits were detailed and far-reaching. 'I was new at this, too', he recalled, speaking from the distance of half a century when we met in his quiet, sunlit apartment, five storeys above Madison Avenue. 'I had been an editor for years at *Holiday*, and another magazine during the war, but I hadn't edited fiction.' In the years to follow, his long career would bring John Updike, William Trevor, Ann Beattie and many other writers to face the scrutiny of his careful eye. 'In the relationship of a fiction editor and a fiction writer, there's a third presence which is the text, and we're trying to get it right, we're both trying, and often get stuck, or something isn't quite right', Angell explained. 'It's the text that unites you'. Brian's story 'The Skelper' was, Angell told him in 1958, 'a very nice little story' with 'an excellent chance of working out for us', but there were significant changes to be made – especially to the final scene, when the skelper lies to the local police to protect his rival, the postman – before it could be accepted.

> Our real reservation on the story is that the ending seems a little too simple and perhaps even too noble to ring true. There has been nothing in the story up to this time to indicate that the Skelper would be likely

to perform such an unselfish act as he does in covering up for the postman. I have a notion that this could be fixed quite easily. Perhaps after the Skelper and the policeman get into the police car, the Skelper could start damning himself for having been such a sentimental and good hearted fool. And perhaps he could add an expression of anger at the residents of the village, calling them simpletons and village louts for having forced him to do such a fine thing. In other words, the Skelper himself is not entirely sure why he has been so unselfish, unless it is because he needs the good opinion of the villagers for his trade, and he is a little annoyed at himself for what he has done. I don't think that Mr Friel needs to explain all of the foregoing in such detail; just a few lines, most of it in dialogue might do the trick. But it is up to him, of course, as to how he wishes to handle this, and he may not agree with us at all.

Brian agreed, and made all of Angell's changes with alacrity. The skelper's motivations were made clearer in the story's opening paragraph, as he now 'decided that it was time he took root somewhere' and 'determined to come to terms' with his fellow villagers in the renamed Beannafreaghan. After losing a salmon-poaching contest to the postman, he accepts the fine (twenty pounds) and complains in the police sergeant's car 'how a man of my caliber can decide to spend the rest of his life with wastrels like those people', just as Angell suggested. In a second round of edits, Angell cut hyperbole and clichés, and he even rewrote the story's final line, replacing the villagers' cries of 'Hip Hip Hooray!' with 'a ragged roar of voices lifted in response'.

Angell's acceptance of the revised story made the summer of 1958 a busy one for Brian. He received Angell's letter on the 5th of May, and then wrote to Ronald Mason on the 9th that he had completed 'THE GREAT IRISH PLAY!' – a comedy verging on farce, titled *The Francophile*. It was his first attempt at writing expressly for the stage rather than for broadcast, and told the story of a middle-aged Derry postman enamoured with French culture. Brian sent Mason one typescript and cheekily informed him that 'The only other existing copy is being posted today to Harold Goldblatt. I hope he appreciates the honour I am bestowing on him.' Goldblatt was a founding member of the Ulster Group Theatre company and had been acting in Belfast for over thirty years. As a young man, he led the Jewish Institute Dramatic Society, which merged with the Northern Ireland Players and the Ulster Theatre in 1940 to become the Group, Belfast's de facto repertory. Brian had met him during rehearsals and recording sessions for *A sort of freedom*, when Goldblatt voiced the part of embittered boss Jack Frazer. Privately, Brian worried that the new play was similarly cynical, as he told Mason, 'I think myself it is in ways better than the two you did but again it is unrelieved and sullen and far too chippy-on-the-shoulder. I hope H.G. doesn't keep me on pins and needles for months.' Little did he know it would be two years before *The Francophile* was produced.

Mason promised to advocate for the new play, 'a good Ulster comedy' in his opinion. His directing work for the BBC brought him into frequent contact with actors who moved between the broadcast studio and the Group's Bedford Street theatre, housed within the nearby Ulster Hall. 'I have Harold Goldblatt in the cast tomorrow – Ervine's "The Christies" – and I shall speak to him about it ... In brief, I like it and shall be surprised if it hasn't a stage future in Belfast.' Mason also shared the script with a rising star in Belfast drama circles, younger even than Brian and himself, who had recently been appointed assistant artistic director of the Group.

> I have had James Ellis of the Group (a director) read it. I have asked him to try and get a reading panel on to it. Confidentially, he likes it very much, but will probably have a few technical things to suggest on it. His decision would not alone be enough, so don't quote me on it.

Ellis, then 27 years old, was the son of an East Belfast shipyard worker and had strong ties to the city's Protestant working class. He had attended the prestigious Methodist College on scholarship, then joined the Dramatic Society as a fresher at Queen's University Belfast. He won Northern Ireland's first Tyrone Guthrie Scholarship to apprentice at the Bristol Old Vic as a director, and joined the Group Theatre after Guthrie himself arranged for Ellis to act in an Ulster tour of *The glass menagerie*. In later decades, Ellis would star in the BBC series *Z Cars* and became a well-known figure on British television.

In August 1958, Ellis and Goldblatt officially accepted *The Francophile*, and the Group agreed to pay Brian 10 per cent of its box office takings. Brian shared the news with Mason in a letter from that summer's rented cottage in Rathmullan, Donegal, which he and Anne had found after placing an *Irish Times* advert, describing themselves as a 'Mildly Eccentric family (two children)' seeking a 'comfortable holiday house on unfrequented coast, Cork to Clare: six weeks, July/August: remoteness an attraction'. Though they ended up much closer to home, the break from Derry allowed Brian to devote his summer to writing, and he was bolstered by the Group's commitment to staging *The Francophile*. He thanked Mason 'for the interest you showed in this play and the encouragement you gave me in many ways before it found a resting place'.

It was the last time Mason would hear from him for a full year. Instead, Brian threw his energies into writing stories for the *New Yorker*, buoyed by the generous cheque he received in July for 'The Skelper'. Over the summer of 1958, he submitted four new stories and a rewritten version of a previous one, recast from first- to third-person narration. All were rejected. Angell gave a range of explanations. One story, 'My fine white boy', was 'pretty contrived and melodramatic – emotion created and recorded just for its own sake'. The next, 'My little girl Joan', was on 'a terribly familiar theme, and a difficult one, too. Mr Friel's treatment of it seems to us to be a little on the obvious side'. Brian's agent pitched his unsolicited rewrite of 'A late child' to a different *New Yorker* editor, but it was ignored, and she followed with a new story, 'The Return', that was judged as lacking 'the strength or conviction of THE SKELPER'. As the summer holidays drew to a close, she sent 'Jimmy Gleeson's cats' to Angell, who responded, 'I'm afraid it falls between two categories. It can't be considered a realistic story, and at the same time it isn't funny enough or surprising enough to be acceptable as a tall story. Please tell him to keep writing, because he isn't missing by much.'

Brian kept writing. He published humour pieces in the *Irish Times* on the oddities of his rental cottage's water tank and the ugly purple tweed he bought after visiting too many pubs in Donegal. He sent *The Francophile* to the Abbey Theatre in October 1958, after it had already been accepted by the Group, perhaps following the example of playwright John Murphy, who sent his script *The country boy* to the Abbey that same month, even though it was already on the Group's performance schedule for 1959. Murphy's play was accepted for the Abbey's spring season, while *The Francophile* was rejected. But despite Ronald Mason's plea for new radio material in late November ('Dear Brian, You can't have retired to life on the income of your playwriting! What's happened to you, and why haven't we heard from you in so long? Have you any ideas, or are you putting anything on paper at the moment?') Brian continued to focus on fiction, hoping to sell another story to the *New Yorker*. At last, in the darkest days of winter, he hit upon a successful formula with the story 'The fawn pup'.

Like 'The Skelper', this new story focused on a village outsider, a wager and a lovable loser. As in *To this hard house*, the central character was a schoolmaster, and, as in *The Francophile*, he was eccentric in his serial obsessions: ballroom dancing, then holidaying in a gypsy caravan, and, eventually, as 'The fawn pup' explained, dog racing. It is the pup who is the lovable loser, a greyhound raised as a household pet but coaxed into training for the Omagh Stakes. In his rural childhood, Brian's family, too, owned greyhounds, as he had recounted in an *Irish Times* column, and they slept under the kitchen stove, as in the story. The tale's humour stems from the juxtaposition of the town ruffians and the boy narrator's genteel but naïve parents, who don their Sunday best for their visit to the muddy field used as a track and ask polite questions about the sport, only to be disappointed when the fawn pup gives up the race. When the boy's mother cheers 'Bravo! Bravo!' for their dog's competitors, she is mocked by 'the whole field ... clapping and calling "Bravo! Bravo!" in falsetto voices'.

Angell liked it, but wanted revisions. 'Most of it is very pleasant and convincing', he wrote to Brian's agent, 'but we all think that the ending is entirely wrong'.

> From the moment when the dog fails to run, the story falls away to a broad and dubious letdown. Perhaps he could fix this by having the dog run a little bit of the race, in a rather amateurish and frantic way, and then become distracted. Then there would be some justification for the mother's applauding him.

Brian took his advice. Rather than end with the fawn pup refusing to run, he crafted a new paragraph full of the story's most vivid imagery, as the impetuous dog sacrifices his lead out of misplaced love for his master:

> The pup, exulting in his freedom from the box, and discovering that there were five other dogs behind him who, unlike those he knew at home, were willing to chase him, flung himself forward in an ecstasy of joy, giving short yelps of happiness ... But when the race was three quarters through, he spotted Father standing with us beside the wire fence. The pup was just looking back to encourage the other dogs again, when I saw recognition light up his face. He faltered momentarily, looked hard at us to make sure he was not mistaken, and then, forgetting the wonderful game he was having, stopped instantly and loped over to us, his mouth wide in a foolish grin, his tail flailing the air in greeting.

With Angell's guidance, Brian brought the story to a comforting close. At home, after he goes to bed, the boy overhears his father reframing the race with admiration for the bookie, his former pupil, whose offices would soon expand across Tyrone and Derry. Angell even added a line of dialogue, uttered by the schoolteacher father: '"He's going to go far, that fellow!" he said. "Always knew he would."' The story's final sentences mirror the final image of Brian's first story 'The Child', published eight years earlier, with the bitterness of rowing parents removed, as the boy falls asleep soothed by the sound of his father's words rather than fighting back tears. 'His voice was strong and confident through the ceiling', the 'fawn pup' narrator tells us. 'I went to sleep as I often did, listening to the heavy drone of his voice and knowing that he was in a good humour again.'

But Brian had by no means cracked the code for *New Yorker* acceptance. As soon as Angell informed him that the revised 'fawn pup' story would be purchased, Brian sent off a series of new attempts. The first was 'The happiest woman in Donegal', which, Angell regretted, 'seemed forced – too much laughter, too many tears, too much folksiness. I have a suspicion that the author has gone in for all this exaggeration in order to make up for the basic deficiencies of the story, which is a fairly dull one. Please tell him how sorry we are.' Next was 'The Giant', rewritten since Angell had judged it 'a little scattered', but the editor now confessed, 'we really don't understand the ending … And finally, it seems to us that the giant's conversation is such a familiar-sounding piece of Irish lyricism that it simply adds to the impression that this is only another Irish set piece.' He did his best to be encouraging, however, confiding to Brian's agent that 'This was a close thing … Please tell Mr Friel that I am most anxious to see more of his work.'

So immersed was Brian in making final changes to the proofs of 'The Skelper' and 'The fawn pup' that when Ronald Mason sent him a second plea, in the summer of 1959, it took him a month to respond. 'Dear Brian,' wrote Mason hopefully, 'It is a very long time since I have heard of you, and, apart from a brief second at the Opera House Finals, I haven't seen you for a very long time. I should like to have heard that you were working on a radio play, or even a half-hour television. Let me know what is happening, if anything.' Brian downplayed his short story acceptances when he responded from Magheragallen, Derrybeg, Donegal, claiming that he was living 'in grand indolence' but that 'for the past 5 months all my scattered energies have been spent on a new stage play which I finished only last week … Apart from that, I was working on a *New Yorker* story which they wanted revised. That is the sum total. When I get back to Derry & the day becomes organised again, I hope to have a shot at a radio play. With all day on my hands here, I get nothing done.' He and Anne had found that summer's cottage through an advert in the *Donegal Democrat*, seeking a 'comfortable bungalow' in a 'quiet locality; beside open sea'. The stage play he was writing may have been *The making of Mark*, a script rejected by the Abbey the following year, though no record of it survives outside the Abbey's submissions ledger. The two men made tentative plans to talk about a new drama for broadcast, but it would be another year before Brian wrote to Mason again.

Instead, as the school term began, the young teacher continued to pour his considerable energies into fiction, sending story after story to the *New Yorker*, craving Angell's feedback, whatever his decision. In September 1959, he submitted 'My famous grandfather' with the request, 'I hope you like it but even if you do not use it, I would value your opinion on it'. Angell rejected it, pointing to 'an error of technique in the whole second half of the story, where he starts to write as an omniscient author' after beginning in the style of 'a tall story'. Similar problems plagued Brian's next submission, 'The king of Knock Island', which, Angell said, 'has some freshness and some real laughs' but 'depends entirely on one tall joke, and as one reads on, this joke becomes pretty thin and stale'. (He couldn't resist pointing out, however, that 'it would make a wonderful script'.) Undeterred – and unsolicited – Brian rewrote 'My famous grandfather' in hopes of correcting its problems of narrative voice. His revisions to 'The fawn pup', adding descriptive sections on dog trainer Lobster O'Brien, the racetrack itself, and the overheard ending, earned him an additional fee for the story of $30, about £10 at the time, since the *New Yorker* paid by the word.

'My famous grandfather' was turned down a second time. Angell pointed out that he had not requested the revision, and he advised Brian's agent that the story's ending 'just seems too wild to us, and almost seems to make the piece into a parody of an Irish story. I have the odd feeling that he started this story off in too exaggerated a tone, and that then there was nothing for him to do but to make it wilder and wilder as he went along.' The story, the tale of the first gramophone brought to Donegal, is written largely without dialogue until it ends with a mêlée in a parish hall, as hundreds of dissatisfied paying concertgoers break up their wooden seats and smash the record player to pieces. They had expected a live rendition of 'The Blind Boy', a recording admired by Brian's parents, as he mentioned in the *Irish Times* during that same spring. He eventually sold the short story to *The Sign*, an American Catholic monthly, whose readers were presumably more inclined to find humour in naïve Irish fishermen anticipating a live 'Blind Boy' to sing to them. Brian must have been disappointed, not only because *The Sign* couldn't match the *New Yorker*'s pay rates but because Angell discounted the more subtle humour within the piece, generated by the mistranslation of record labels into grandiose biographical notes about classical musicians, promoted by the narrator's grandfather, Clarence Parnell Kelly, and then warped a second time by the 'penny-a-line' journalists of local Donegal newspapers.

Brian had written about them, too. In an *Irish Times* column titled 'Friel and Boswell', he described his 'first and only publicity agent', the anonymous small-town reporter who 'proclaimed to the world each new arrival in our household; who knew my hobbies, my fads, my little oddnesses; who has heaped on me a wide variety of academic qualifications which, although I may be worthy of them, I do not in fact possess.' These began when it was announced to Donegal readers that 'Mr. B. Friel, M.A., and his wife are at present holidaying in B—' and progressed, the following year, to 'Mr. B. Friel, Ph.D.' Gradually, as Brian explained, 'I graduated from philosophy to law, from law to science, from science to dentistry, from dentistry to music ... I was in turn "a popular figure," "prominent in Derry business circles," "an ardent sailor," and once, in some frenzy of inventiveness, "fresh from his London success."' The phrase was prophetic, but wildly improbable, and Brian was only too willing to mock himself by guessing at the vagueness of the reporter's claim. 'Had my two-year-old dog, A Lad of the O'Friels, romped home an easy winner in the White City? Was my musical, "The Swim Suit," breaking all records in Drury Lane? ... I remember swaggering round B— that summer, my shoulders back, my keen, grey eyes languid but penetrating, pushing the pram in front of me as lightly as if it were a caddy car.'

In real life, the rejections continued. In March 1960, Brian submitted 'A man's world' to the *New Yorker*, the story of a young boy visiting his five Donegal maiden aunts – Kate and Maggie, schoolteachers; Agnes and Sarah, who looked after the house, the cow and the chickens; and Rose, the youngest, slower and less clever than her sisters in her childlike innocence. '"Rose will always be Rose"', say her sisters, and much of the story centres on her camaraderie with the child narrator, her knack for finding 'a black rabbit in the warren or a pigeon's nest in the wood or a hedgehog along the path beside the burn or a rose tree, sudden and inexplicable, in the lower meadow'. Her revelation of an old love letter from a suitor in Boston, which she keeps hidden above the lintel in the byre, closes the story on a poignant note. Three decades later, these characters would form the raw material for Brian's Tony winner *Dancing at Lughnasa*, but at first glance Angell deemed them derivative, and scolded Brian's agent by proxy:

> I wish you would drop Mr Friel a note (I think this is better coming from you than from me) indicating the fact that he may be hurting himself by paralleling so closely the Frank O'Connor first-person narrative technique. As you know, this kind of story telling is one that O'Connor has been polishing and refining for years, to the point that it almost has become his signature ... I think Brian Friel can write a great deal for us, but I think he would improve his chances if he tried to work out a more personal kind of style.

Brian had laced the story with details that would surface elsewhere in his dramatic work – the 'trunkful of mysteries sent home from Kenya by some granduncle' revealed a sun helmet that would become a ridiculous prop in *Dancing at Lughnasa*, and the necklace 'bought with egg money' by Aunt Rose foreshadowed Gar O'Donnell's secret egg money fund in *Philadelphia, here I come!* But the plot was not strictly autobiographical. The boy narrator is an only child, unlike Brian, and the boy's father, a civil servant sacked for his drinking binges, appears to have little in common with Master Friel of St Columba's, Long Tower. The five maiden aunts have no siblings outside their village apart from the narrator's mother, while the real Father MacLoone of Glenties was survived by a brother in Dublin and a sister in religious orders in Manchester.

Brian's agent, ignoring Angell's request for diplomacy, forwarded the editor's letter directly to her client in Derry. Exasperated, Brian appealed directly to Angell for insight into his losing streak with the *New Yorker*. 'Now, at the very outset, let me apologise for writing. This letter is in no way an attempt to elicit from you a justification for your decision; I have cheek but not that much.' He confessed that he was confused by Angell's comparison of his work to O'Connor's, and saw no pattern to his rejections. 'Within the past year and a half, you have taken two stories of mine – out of perhaps nine submitted and what puzzles me is, why these two and not two others?' He threw himself at the mercy of the editor's guidance, pleading, 'If you can find time, I would be grateful if you would help me. It sounds almost naïve to say that I would like to write more for you. I would give up my present job if I could write more for you! But my problem is that I do not see what you want.' Brian apologized repeatedly for asking such questions, and explained his isolation from potential peers in the art of writing. 'I am not looking for a gimmick or a pill-size panacea for my work. But I do want to learn and you can help me. Derry is in the very northern tip of Ireland and I am cut off from the critical assessment that even Dublin could offer … If you can find time, I would appreciate and be very grateful for whatever advice you could offer.'

Angell responded generously, with a three-page, single-spaced letter, affirming his faith in Brian's talent, and teaching Brian, as best he could, how to write more truthfully in his short fiction. It helped that he had just received Brian's new story, 'The saucer of larks', and liked it – so he used it as an instructional example and 'the best way of explaining to you what we look for'. The story, he said, 'seems excellent up to page 8, where you begin the story about what happened to the German aviator. The introduction of the "wee lassie by the name of Sweeney" seems to us to introduce an entirely false note – one that is sentimental and soft and even, if you will forgive me, "predictably

Irish.'" In Angell's view, with this embellishment, the tale of a Donegal police sergeant who accompanies German officers to exhume wartime remains from a rural cemetery quickly 'went from a realistic and believable situation into sentimentality and a kind of folklore'. The premise itself was one Brian had already reported in the *Irish Times*, in a solemn diversion from his usual domestic comedies. He had described Donegal headstones for foreign soldiers, who, he hoped, 'have come to love the whispering of the sea behind them and the rush of birds across the flat land before them' – the eponymous saucer of larks, a small valley that sheltered a nesting flock. German officers arrived in the summer of 1959 to transport disinterred remains to their official cemetery beside Glencree, in the Wicklow hills, where dozens of Luftwaffe and Kriegsmarine members now repose, many of them washed up on Irish beaches during the Second World War. In the *Times*, Brian voiced an opinion about the dead that he would later assign to his fictional sergeant, the belief that 'in time – if they are left in peace there and not brought away to iron-railed isolation – they will soon rub shoulders with the Gweedore folk who sleep there.'

Angell appreciated the sergeant's perspective, and encouraged Brian to revise the ending in order to deepen it. Cut the episode about 'the wee lassie', he said, because 'the real strength of this story lies in the initial situation of the Sergeant, loving his country and feeling his own death coming on, being moved, to his surprise, to plead with the Germans to let the body stay where it was.' He felt that in the original version, as in other stories, Brian had 'a tendency to exaggerate an initial situation into a tall tale.' While this had worked for 'The Skelper', he cautioned, 'you must be aware of the dangers of sentimentality and eccentricity and exaggerated behaviour that are presented entirely for their own sake'. The story of the gramophone was one such example, as was the rejected story about 'The king of Knock Island'. The criteria for the *New Yorker*, Angell insisted, were 'believability and honesty'. Moreover, the magazine received so much material from Irish writers – O'Connor as well as Mary Lavin, Benedict Kiely and others – that there was understandable pressure on a newer author to stake his originality. Brian's repeated reliance on first-person narration and an 'almost non-fictional' style evoked inevitable comparisons, despite Angell's sympathies. 'You and I know that you imitate no one and that this is only an unfortunate coincidence, but I believe that the problem is more yours than Mr O'Connor's, since he has been contributing stories here for a great many years.'

Frank O'Connor, whose given name was Michael O'Donovan, had sold his first story to the *New Yorker* almost by accident in 1945, when his wife Evelyn sent his story 'News for the church' to William Maxwell, who had started out at the magazine as Katharine White's assistant. Nine years earlier, White and

Maxwell had accepted Brendan Gill's first stories without knowing his gender – they were unable to guess it from his name – and Gill, who later joined the *New Yorker* staff, understood that the editors 'knew little about Catholics' but 'were eager to read about them, as occupying a hitherto largely unexplored field of human conduct.' As an Irish American, Gill obliged, and when O'Connor submitted his own work a decade later, he was fortunate to tap into a growing interest in Ireland itself, as well as an expanding readership among the newly moneyed Irish American middle class. Flights from the US to Shannon Airport had just begun, and, with the establishment of Bord Fáilte in 1955, Ireland seemed more accessible – and more acceptable – to many in the diaspora who were eager to reconnect with their heritage, shedding the stigma of famine and poverty that had driven their ancestors to emigrate.

O'Connor's stories fed this interest, even when they diverged from a romanticized view of the Emerald Isle and exposed taboos such as premarital sex, illegitimacy, parental abandonment and suicide. The *New Yorker* bought a total of forty-five stories from him over twenty years, three times as many as he published in any other periodical in his lifetime – an output that made him an abiding presence in the magazine and effectively recast him as a transatlantic writer in his later years. Selling stories to American readers sometimes meant playing to expectations of quaintness and local colour, as well as raising the curtain on rituals of Catholicism and the cloistered lives of priests and nuns. O'Connor's first *New Yorker* story intrudes on the privacy of the confessional, where a priest with a 'wine-colored' face lectures a lively girl on the error of her 'carnal intercourse' before marriage. A story from 1959, the same year as Brian's first sale to the magazine, opens with Cork-accented dialogue that evokes O'Connor's home city, as two priests plan a funeral for an elder curate, with a long digression into the quality of the whiskey at hand in the parochial house. 'Tisn't much of a welcome we have for you, God knows … Sure, you know yourself what he was like.'

Despite the fact that his stories were drawn from the opposite end of the island and held little in common with O'Connor's choice of subject matter nor with his narrative voice, Brian could see the logic of Angell's position. He accepted that some of his stories were 'predictably Irish', which was, he wrote, 'a lazy habit and one that discipline ought to wipe out. We have the mistaken idea in this country that simply to be Irish is to enjoy international good will and sympathy!' He thanked Angell for his patience and courtesy in detailing his thought process, because 'This – from editors – has disappeared altogether on this side of the Atlantic. It is encouraging to meet with it again.' But he also harboured no intention to write like his more famous countryman. 'I know that I am the last person in the world to judge this but I <u>think</u> that if there seems to be a relationship between O'Connor's and my style, it is accidental'. He promised to take Angell's criticism of 'The saucer of larks' to heart and to submit a revised version right away. In fact he put it into the post only five days later.

Brian's persistence paid off, this time almost immediately. Less than three weeks later, Angell wrote to accept 'The saucer of larks', though he suggested further changes, especially the addition of dialogue as an ending for the story. In particular, he wanted the sergeant to express more anger toward his visitors, Herr Grass and Herr Henreich, and toward the Germans as a people, going so far as to pen a new paragraph in the sergeant's voice. 'They're the glory of the world for power and neatness and getting things done proper, and there isn't a man living in all the rest of the world that doesn't hate them and want to smash his fist into their face.' Brian politely objected. 'I feel that anger is justified all right but somehow the words you have put into his mouth savour of strong racial hatred. Admittedly he is very angry but I believe that his anger is directed against two Germans and not against a nation. In this country, we are too insular to have broad hatreds against other nations (the English excepted!); we usually concentrate our anger against individuals.' Overruling his editor, Brian toned the lines down for the version that appeared in the *New Yorker*. 'Them and their notebooks and their dates and their data – aye, and their well-planned cemetery in Wicklow, with their decent dead laid out like neat herrings on a fishmonger's slab. For Christ's sake, who do they think they are? Even their dead, are they not safe from them?' Neither outburst made it into the story when Brian later chose it as title piece for his first anthology. At that point, he restored the sergeant's sputtering that developers had made an 'arse' of seaside towns near Dublin – Angell and his *New Yorker* colleagues had balked at that word – and excised American expletives like 'Damn!' that never sounded quite right from a career member of the Gardaí.

'De mortuis', Brian's 1959 *Irish Times* column on the same disinterment, had taken a sympathetic view of the Germans and their dead. Though it mentions the German officers, the Irish guards, the public health inspector and the reporter who accompanied them to the grave of 29-year-old airman Werner Bornefeld, shot down over the Atlantic in 1942, Brian's initial focus was on the 'small rounded couples with foreign accents' paying respects at the graves of their fallen sons: the dozen or so 'young men, English, Italian, German, who were carried in on the filling tide between the islands of Gola and Innisman and laid on Magheragallen strand'. The column's title derives from the Latin adage 'Of the dead, speak no ill', and Brian hoped that the bereaved parents, who 'have scarcely enough English to get them to their destination', would be consoled by the beauty of Donegal and would 'store their mind with pictures which they will carry back with them to Antwerp or Aachen or Avignon, where they will soon die themselves'. He mused, 'It is strange to think that these pilgrims are statistically part of our tourist trade'. His fictional character, the efficient Herr Grass, would go home to his plump wife and three sons in Berlin without knowing that a wall built the following year would prevent any return to Ireland for quite some time.

Just one week after accepting 'The saucer of larks', Angell wrote with more good news. *New Yorker* editor William Shawn had approved the acceptance of Brian's latest story, 'The potato gatherers', and the writer qualified for a $300 advance and a chance to increase his pay rate through the magazine's 'fiction bonus' system. Again Angell pointed to the story's ending, and again he wrote several lines of dialogue for Brian to include. Without them, he said, the story 'seems to trail off so quietly that it hardly amounts to a story at all'. The potato gatherers, two brothers, have taken a day off school – risking 'a hammering … Six on each hand' from the teacher – to earn money from a local farmer. They banter throughout the story about what they will buy with their shillings, even though Joe, the eldest, knows their mother will need every penny. For his young brother Philly, the job is 'his first opportunity to prove that he was a man at twelve years of age. His energy was a burden to him.' This was no tall tale: Brian well understood his restless pupils and the economic pressures on their families, and his portrait of the two brothers includes their play-acting as cowboys even as their hands begin to shake from the strain of gathering what the tractor digs up. 'Where *is* this potato territory, Mistah? I want to show you hombres what work is.' But by noon, 'The sun was a failure … They no longer straightened up; the world was their feet and the hard clay and the potatoes and their hands and the buckets and the sacks.' Angell wanted the final paragraph to include 'a very small bit of dialogue near the end', and he wrote a few lines for the working proof, spoken by Philly, laying his head in his brother's lap as the tractor carts them home after eight hours in the field: '"I think you're daft," he said in an exhausted, sullen voice. "Ma won't give us back enough to buy anything much. No more than a shilling. You knew it all the time."' Brian kept the editor's words, both for the magazine and for his first anthology, because 'your little paragraph rounds off the story beautifully; I should have seen that myself'. He was already working on the next.

His own economic pressures weighed on him as he pitched two new pieces to the *New Yorker*. In early June, 1960, Angell explained that with three stories accepted, Brian was 'in an excellent position to qualify for a fiction bonus … a simple plan designed to get as many pieces as possible from writers whom we admire'. The plan's simplicity was debatable, but its rewards were plain: any author who sold the *New Yorker* four stories in a twelve-month period received a retroactive 15 per cent bonus on the fees paid for all four acceptances. (The rate rose to 35 per cent if the writer was lucky enough to land six stories in one year, as Frank O'Connor had done in 1957.) Since 'The Skelper' had been published in August 1959, Brian had two months to submit a successful fourth story and qualify for the annual bonus. 'I think you are in an excellent position to do this,' wrote Angell, 'and I certainly hope you will want to try'.

Brian told Angell he would 'do my damdest to beat the deadline'. Within weeks, he sent two stories, one that was new and one that had, unbeknownst to the *New Yorker*, been broadcast on the Northern Ireland Home Service in 1957 and had already earned Brian fifteen guineas. True to form, Brian favoured the newer effort, a story titled for its central character, a teacher with tuberculosis confined to a sanatorium ward with two other men. '"Barry" is my main hope,' the writer told his editor, 'and I have sweated a lot over it. If you find time, let me know what you think of it, whatever decision you come to about it'. Angell reluctantly obliged, and a week later, wrote to Brian of the 'two main flaws' in the story. It was 'a terribly familiar' premise, and it was told too passively in the form of reported speech. 'All the way through, I kept wishing that more of these exchanges were in dialogue'. The crux of Barry's interior crisis could not be voiced, however, for the narration seems to imply that what he is hiding from fellow patients may be homosexuality. Why is he a bachelor, they ask, on their final night in hospital, sharing confidences as they smoke on a darkened verandah. 'Panic was rising in him. Can I, he thought? Can I? Can I? ... Now. Before the second passes. Now.' Neither the patients nor Angell guessed at any subtext, but the patients' questions are not unlike those Brian put to his friend Ronnie Mason, over their years of correspondence: 'Did you have a good holiday, alone and palely loitering?' and 'Are you engaged or married or even going strong?' It is not clear what Brian intended in 'Barry', but he would later write a 'homosexual scene' in the first draft of his story 'My father and the sergeant', and would openly depict gay liaisons in his 1971 play *The gentle island*. For now, Angell decided simply, 'it is too easy to see that Barry, for all his boasting, is envious of the married life of his two friends'. Though he hinted that 'this has the chance of being a good story some day', he advised Brian not to bother with a revision.

Of 'My true kinsman', Angell was more receptive. He accepted the story for publication, which qualified Brian for the 15 per cent retroactive bonus, though Angell warned that it would likely be delayed going to press. 'This is in no way a criticism of the story, but is due to the fact that we already have some nine or ten Irish stories on hand, and we must space these out in order to avoid the risk of becoming wholly Fenian.' (He said this without malice, unaware of the significance of his letter's date: 11 July 1960.) Brian had confessed that this was his third revision of the story, 'and at this stage, I have not the least idea of its worth'. He was 'slightly stunned and very, very delighted' that Angell bought it – perhaps all the more because it was a first-person tale that could be read as stereotypically Irish: a boy's encounter with his wayward grandfather, who pulls him into a village pub and borrows his ten-shilling note to buy drink. Though neither Angell nor Brian said so, it also echoed Frank O'Connor's 1949 *New Yorker* story 'The man of the house', whose boy narrator goes to buy medicine for his mother (Brian's narrator was similarly sent to fetch iodine for a cut) but returns home empty-handed. The difference between 'My true kinsman' and Brian's prior submissions was the strength of the story's ending, as the grandfather drapes his farm-scented jacket over the boy's shoulders and sends him home in the rain to his disapproving mother. 'The smell was through me and all about me. And I knew that as long as it lasted, I would have the courage to meet my mother and tell her the terrible news – that I had no iodine and no money and that Grandfather had got me.'

The very next day, Angell wrote with more encouraging news. The *New Yorker* wanted Brian to sign a first reading agreement, 'an expression of our confidence in you and of our desire to see everything you write for magazine publication'. In exchange for an annual $100 retainer, Brian would be required to 'give us first look at all fiction, humor, and reminiscence that you write'. In return, his pay rate per story would rise 25 per cent above the guaranteed minimum word rate of eighteen cents per word for the first half of each piece, or first 2,000 words, and nine cents per word for the remainder. In the exchange rates of the day, eighteen cents came to one shilling and fourpence per word, or one guinea per sixteen words, a significant boost over the BBC, and sixty times more than the defunct *Bell* magazine. Angell assured Brian that these agreements were commonly held by the *New Yorker*'s regular contributors, and that overall 'they are very pleased with the arrangement'. Still, it took Brian a few weeks to sign – he was mindful of his 'short, humorous feature' series for the *Irish Times*, which, he told Angell, 'appears irregularly, depending on space, but usually every ten days or so. I am not on the staff nor am I under any contract whatever so that I would be breaking faith in no way by stopping this work, if the First Working Agreement called for that.'

By this point, Brian had authored thirty-five columns for the *Irish Times*, and had gained enough readers to merit listing his name on the paper's front page, occasionally beside Myles na gCopaleen's 'Cruiskeen lawn'. Brian's humour mirrored na gCopaleen's taste for comedy in provincial Irish life, as in the percentage point ratings for Bord Fáilte's newly launched Tidy Towns competition, won in 1958 and 1959 by Brian's ancestral home place, Glenties. 'My mother's people were MacLoones, and their tidiness was a byword in the village. Because of this virtue, the girls in the family were keenly sought after by young men from all over the county. Swains from Carrigart (78% Highly Commended), Buncrana (63% Commended) and even presumptuous boys from Letterkenny (51% Good) vied for their hands, but since none of the suitors could match them in tidiness and since the girls could not marry beneath them in tidiness, only two got wed'. Another frequent focus was the impact of advertising, especially in American magazines sent by a cousin in Boston in exchange for copies of the *Derry Journal*. 'They know how well I would look behind the wheel of a convertible sports car, my cravat tucked casually under my monogrammed silk shirt, my keen face still sunburned after a Christmas in Nassau.' Though he confessed to being a susceptible target, Brian confided that 'Those admen, cute and all as they are, may know my weaknesses, but they don't know my overdraft ... The £6 4s. 6d. in the envelope behind the clock is needed for the first moiety of the rates due next month.' Among these comedies were occasional tragedies, such as the German war dead of 'De mortuis' or the baby coffin in a sombre 'Lunchtime interlude', laid on the floor of a taxi by two young men 'in their Sunday clothes, very likely the same suits they had been married in'. Angell assured Brian that his newspaper work fell outside the bounds of the *New Yorker*'s first reading agreement, and hoped that the contract would mark 'the beginning of a long and profitable association'.

It was certainly more profitable than staging a play in Belfast. Though it was no guarantee of future success, the *New Yorker*'s $100 payment was worth £35, more than double the royalties Brian received for his play *The Francophile*, belatedly produced that summer by the Group Theatre. Though James Ellis and Harold Goldblatt had accepted it in 1958, Brian's first script for the stage fell victim to controversy that erupted when the Group's chairman censored *Over the bridge*, a play by former shipyard worker Sam Thompson. Thompson, known for his ebullience and frankness, would later act in Brian's play *The blind mice*, and, like Brian, he had written for radio – his play *Tommy Baxter, shop steward* was produced under the mentorship of BBC dramatist Sam Hanna Bell just a year before Brian's first play aired. But *Over the bridge* exposed shipyard sectarianism too sharply for the Group Theatre's board, chaired by Ritchie McKee, a well-connected businessman and brother of the lord mayor of Belfast. McKee's opposition was seconded by the Group's vice chairman, H.W. McMullan, the same BBC head of programmes who had approved Brian's fledgling dramas for broadcast. The board viewed Thompson's script as subversive: it centres on religious divides among shipyard workers, and culminates in the killing of a Protestant trade unionist who tries to protect a Catholic comrade from mob violence. When McKee and McMullan demanded the final scenes be cut, Ellis protested by resigning as the Group's artistic director. Goldblatt's resignation soon followed, and caused such an uproar that it was reported internationally in *Variety* in 1959. With Thompson in tow, Ellis crossed the border to see his first mentor, Tyrone Guthrie, at Annaghmakerrig, Guthrie's ancestral estate. Guthrie listened and advised quick action. He encouraged Ellis to found a new company, Ulster Bridge productions, and stage *Over the bridge* in Belfast's old Empire Theatre, a capacious music hall in Victoria Square whose backstage entrance faced the Kitchen Bar. Ticket sales exceeded 40,000 over a six-week run, and many who had never darkened a theatre's door queued to see the show in the early months of 1960. It later played in Dublin, Glasgow and London.

Meanwhile, *The Francophile* languished, a victim of unlucky timing. In late 1959, after Ellis resigned, the Group Theatre's board appointed Englishman Jonathan Goodman as its new artistic director. Goodman sent Brian a new contract in March 1960, confirming plans to produce his play while stipulating that he wanted the title changed. Brian suggested four new ones – *Land of heart's desire*, *The Overseer*, *Velvet and vineyards*, or *Lord Logue, overseer* – but none was right. Goodman dithered over the combination of vowel and consonant sounds, the Chekhovian tones of *The Overseer*, and the evocative potential of using instead a well-known quotation, perhaps from Rudyard Kipling. ('That is,' he wrote, 'if Kipling is recited in Northern Ireland. I don't know.') He conferred with Brian about the cast, reporting that Patrick McAlinney was unavailable for the part of French-loving postman Willie Logue, but promising that the playwright would not be disappointed by his replacement, George O'Prey. (Brian later called O'Prey 'too keen-featured, patently too intelligent for the part'.) Renamed by Goodman *The doubtful paradise*, the play ran for two weeks at the Group Theatre, sold a total of 722 tickets, and earned Brian £16 9s.1d. in royalties. The Belfast *News Letter* reviewed it as a play that 'just avoids bathos' in its attempt to balance the 'caricatured' Willie Logue against his 'embittered' barrister son and his daughter's 'hard glitter'. But the critic conceded that 'The author, an Ulsterman, is trying to say things about us which are not political, not kitchen comedy and yet which are funny and sad at the same time. The play deserves to be seen and discussed, the author encouraged.'

A few weeks before opening night, Goodman announced that he was leaving for a new position in England. He would land on his feet as manager of the Liverpool Playhouse, where he learned of an unsolved local murder and launched a new career as a crime writer, eventually authoring forty books. But his abrupt departure from Belfast, after less than a year with the Group, prompted Brian to write to Ronald Mason that 'I have been at no rehearsals, seen none of the changes, and Goodman is fleeing the country the night before it goes on. It doesn't look very healthy, does it?'

Brian also revealed to Mason his ambition, and his newly solidified plan, to make writing his full-time career. 'Sometime too, perhaps we could have a chat. I am considering leaving teaching. But more when we meet.

Sincerely yours,
Brian'

CHAPTER 3

Off book, 1960–1

THE DECISION TO QUIT TEACHING weighed on Brian for over a year. A few days before Christmas 1959, he sent an optimistic note to Roger Angell, accompanying a rewrite, 'I sincerely hope you like this altered version – if only because I hope to take up full-time writing in 1960 and we can live (my wife, two children and I) for two full months on a *New Yorker* story!' That particular piece, like most of the others Brian submitted, was rejected, but nonetheless, securing a first reading agreement with the magazine emboldened him to take the leap. He also hoped that two more of his plays would soon be produced, and had word that the actor Cyril Cusack was interested in one. In September 1960, he confided in Ronald Mason.

> For better or for worse, I have retired from teaching. I have still to work out my notice but hope to be free on December 1st. I have been assured by all sorts of people who claim to know that I haven't a chance in hell of making any sort of a living out of it, ie. writing. Perhaps they are right. If only out of sheer spite, I would love to prove them wrong. If you too think I am mad, in your reply please just call me courageous or brave or hopeful. Too many people have called me foolhardy. I'm about sick of it.

Mason had been a schoolteacher, too, and had left that stable career for a life in the arts, as Brian himself was attempting. As always, Mason encouraged his friend's ambition.

> The world is full of counsellors whose advice is seldom sound or worthwhile heeding. I think you are extremely wise to give up teaching, and in my opinion you certainly have the ability to carve a much more interesting career for yourself outside of it, besides which your teaching qualification doesn't disappear simply because you stop practising, and it's always there in reserve. With that fact I have comforted myself, and I hope you will do the same. Cosy security isn't the best background

from which to do creative work. I think you will broaden your experience and your writing will gain a new edge.

As he approached his final days in the classroom, Brian appreciated Mason's endorsement. 'Thank you for siding with me against the rest. Let's hope we are right and they are as wrong as could be.'

But Mason's support alone was not always enough, and the start of Brian's full-time career as a writer was marked by several stinging rejections. The *New Yorker* declined his story 'Mr Sing my heart's delight' in September, just as Brian was giving his notice, and less than a fortnight after his last day of work, Mason sent bad news about his latest radio script, *The world of Johnny del Pinto*, a dreamscape play anchored in the perspective of a 10-year-old boy. In it, Brian hoped 'to illustrate the life of a child – and the impinging adult world on it'. The plot conveys Johnny's three hallucinations under anaesthesia after getting knocked down by a car. Mason did his best to advocate for its production within the BBC. He told Brian he saw 'flashes of brilliance in the writing', and his script report argued that 'This is not the usual product of an Ulster writer, and has much charm and ingenuity, and is away from the tired old kitchen genre'. H.W. McMullan's response, however, led Mason to tell Brian that the play 'is going to have something of an uphill struggle I am afraid'. His three-page letter to the playwright outlined six major problems with the script, then closed by confirming, 'Just now at the end of all this I have been on the 'phone to Head of Programmes and his objections remain firm, that (1) fantasy doesn't go down with our listeners and (2) that there is an unsavoury quality about this exposé of surgery. He stands firm, and from listening figures is justified.'

Though Mason would go the extra mile for this play by proposing it to the script unit of Broadcasting House, London, his efforts to advocate on Brian's behalf were for naught. To his London counterparts, he pitched the newly unemployed teacher as 'a Londonderry man, a professional playwright under fulltime contract with the *New Yorker*', and pleaded, 'We have few professional writers over here, and I want to encourage this one. He is writing in a genre apart from that in which most of our local authors work.' But while Michael Bakewell, BBC script editor, agreed that 'this is a writer well worth encouraging', he was unwilling to broadcast the play. It fell to Mason to convey the rejection. As he told Brian, 'I sincerely hope that you won't be so disappointed, or so irritated as to stop writing for radio. I heartily dislike sending this amount of disencouragement to a writer of your calibre'. The play eventually found a home on Radio Éireann, and was broadcast to listeners in the Republic in June 1961. Its *Irish Press* review coincided with commentary on Princess Grace's visit to Ireland that same month, and while *Johnny del Pinto* was criticized as 'difficult to follow' without giving the audience 'a chance of getting to know the boy's inner life', the state radio agency was praised for encouraging Brian as a new talent, especially 'since the market for serious writing in Ireland is so small'.

Brian was acutely aware that his family's livelihood depended on finding ways to transcend that market. While he redoubled his efforts to produce regular columns for the *Irish Times*, he extended his humour writing to the *New Yorker*, offering Roger Angell a 'casual' titled 'NATO at night', snippets of dialogue between Derry girls and foreign sailors overheard from the mews lane beneath Brian and Anne's bedroom window. As always, Brian hungrily sought Angell's advice, avowing that 'your criticism of past stories has been very astute and always accurate and now that my bread and butter depend on this typewriter, I am more anxious for good guidance'. Angell liked the piece, and was grateful for the change of pace. He made numerous edits, especially to the ending, which Brian eventually fixed by describing his bus commute across the Craigavon bridge, NATO ships and crew below, and local girls in the seat before him, pretending not to look down. 'But they do not fool me', Brian wrote. 'I know we are all impatient to get the day behind us, combatants and observers alike, to get cracking at night exercises again.' Angell found it 'fresh and amusing' and encouraged Brian to send more humour. 'I am delighted to find that you can write in this vein, as well as in the straight fiction form. I hope you will let us see more casuals like this, for we badly need them.' Brian's contracted rate under the first reading agreement meant that this 2,000-word sketch merited $450 in payment, or £160, enough to sustain his family through the winter.

As much as Angell enjoyed Brian's work, he, like Mason, frequently found himself sending rejections. Two weeks before Brian's retirement from teaching, Angell wrote an apologetic letter to the writer's agent: 'What I have dreaded ever since Brian Friel decided to abandon all in favor of writing has just happened: We are turning down all three of his recent submissions. I have really tried to find some way to avoid delivering this blow, but I can see no solution. The worst part of it is that none of these pieces is really bad; they all miss by a narrow margin.' He sent Brian a cost of living bonus on behalf of the *New Yorker*, along with a new anthology of short stories from the magazine, and an encouraging note after his string of rejections. 'I hope you will not dwell on this disappointment, which must be a severe one since it comes just at the point when you have decided to give up your other work. I am entirely convinced that you will send us many more stories, and I can also say that I think I can see your writing improving in strength and sureness with almost everything you send us.' He expedited payment for 'NATO at night' and announced a new bonus scheme to Brian's agent, so that 'if we purchase two more pieces from him before June 20, 1961, he will qualify for an additional 20% bonus on his last six pieces. At his rate of production, I have no doubt that he will pull it off.'

News of the bonus cheered Brian. 'Needless to say I will try my damnedest!' he wrote to Angell the day before New Year's Eve, a few weeks into his new life as a full-time writer. Between the BBC's rejection of *Johnny del Pinto* and the three rejections from the *New Yorker*, all was not going to plan. Brian had tried to establish a writing routine, he told Angell, but his young family needed attention, especially when 'Anne, my wife, was sick and ordered to bed over the Christmas time and I had all the housework and two energetic daughters on my hands'. Nonetheless he churned out more 'casuals' for Angell, trusting that he could sell them to the *Irish Times* if not in America. 'Hams versus harmony' was one unlikely title that was swiftly rejected, while another, 'The night the bomb fell', took inspiration from a 1933 *New Yorker* piece by James Thurber, 'The day the dam broke': both described ill-founded panic and a public on the run from imagined disaster. Brian hoped that his story of Derry residents fleeing what turned out to be an unexploded land mine would strike a familiar chord with American readers.

Angell, like Mason, was deeply invested in Brian's success, having bonded with him over three years of correspondence, though the two men had not yet met. In his office above 43rd Street, it pained him to inflict rejection, as he wrote to Brian's agent with bad news about the young writer's latest attempt. 'Now I am really getting worried about Brian Friel. To the best of my recollection we have not purchased a single story from him since he made his decision to do nothing but write ... I couldn't be sorrier.' To Brian, he offered advice. Reminiscences and casuals, he said, 'appear to be a good deal more difficult for you than your fiction ... your stories are so fine that I hate to see you turning away from them.' Angell was 'distressed' to deliver yet another rejection, but pointed out that 'we couldn't agree to your comparison with Thurber's story about the dam breaking, since this reference to a story we published years ago constitutes the kind of self-admiration that we always try to avoid.' It was a frustrating conundrum: Brian's fiction had been rebuffed for being 'predictably Irish', and now his humour was rejected for following an American model. Angell tried to help by sending another cost of living adjustment payment, a privilege due to all contracted writers for the *New Yorker*, and told Brian's agent he was 'keeping my fingers crossed in hopes that his next submissions will be acceptable; his last letters have sounded a little sad, and his wife has been sick'.

Still, Angell couldn't issue acceptances based purely on sympathy for the writer's plight. After 'NATO at night', he rejected six stories in a row. In addition to a never-published story titled 'Obscene, indecent and unhealthy in character', Angell rejected the next, 'Aunt Maggie, the strong one' with a stern message that 'This is one of those stories we must turn down because we have run so many on almost exactly the same theme ... we would not buy another Irish story about death unless it were an absolute masterpiece, which this certainly is not.' Often, Brian sold his losing attempts to Catholic magazines in America, so that several were eventually published in *Ave Maria*, *St Jude*, *The Sign* and *The Critic: A Catholic review of books and the arts*. Others were later included in Brian's two short story anthologies, *The saucer of larks* and *The gold in the sea*. Many – at least two dozen – never made it into print.

Three months into Brian's full-time writing career, Angell found a story that he liked. 'Among the ruins' follows Joe and Margo, young parents who bring their son and daughter to Joe's childhood home, 'Corradinna', at the foot of Mount Errigal in western Donegal, near where Brian and Anne spent their summers. Brian borrowed the names 'Corradinna' and nearby 'Pigeon Top' from his own boyhood home: Pigeon Top marks a Mass rock on the Corradinna road outside Omagh. In the story, walking the 'grass-covered track to the ruins of the house' carries Joe toward nostalgia, so that when he sees the collapsed roof, the holes that were windows, and 'The garden, the path, the gooseberry tree', his childhood voice takes over narration, which shifts into present tense. 'That is our swing. Our father ties the ropes across that branch, and we soar up and out over the laneway.' Angell saw much to admire in the 'genuine' tone and feeling, and hoped that Brian would attempt 'some revisions and some fairly large re-writing' to strengthen the story's ending. 'I wonder if you would consider trying to make some more complex and interesting point here – perhaps one that would connect the father and his own children more strongly ... almost any observations you wish to make about the fascinating business of personal recollections and uses, symbols or otherwise, in our daily lives'.

Brian was so eager for acceptance that he revised and resubmitted the story within a single day. He confessed that 'I go quite stupid and unintentionally obtuse when I attempt a revision. The spirit is very, very willing but the ability never quite a match for it.' He dispatched the story to Angell with 'a completely new ending in which I have attempted to link the past and present more strongly' and told his editor, 'I am very anxious to make a success of it'. Angell was less than pleased to receive the new story so soon. He complained to Brian's agent that 'he did this rewrite very quickly', and advised the writer that he should allow more time before another attempt, expressing the 'presumptuous hope that you will consider laying it aside for a period of weeks or months and then looking at it again ... a delayed reconsideration of a story often allows the author to see it in a new light and to improve it tremendously.' The ending, he found, was 'now clear but strikes us as being essentially a familiar and uninteresting point ... a realization that the past is real and that it contains unhappiness as well as the sentimentalized happiness that we all tend to remember'. He gave Brian another shot at rewriting but urged him not to rush, so that he could come to 'some more complex conclusion'.

Brian found it hard to heed Angell's advice, perhaps fearing how quickly he might run out of funds. In search of royalties, he sent a copy of his play *The Francophile* to Ronald Mason with a hopeful note that 'as far as I remember you were the first to see the script – almost three years ago – and you then wrote to me "speak to me about it for Radio". I am now speaking!' Mason took two months to respond; he was working on television plays, but he pitched *The Francophile* to the head of programmes as 'a well-drawn character with plenty of humour ... a Devlin part'. J.G. Devlin, known to Belfast listeners as Granda in the popular family series *The McCooeys*, lent *The Francophile* his sense of comedy, and Brian agreed to 'cut great chunks' from the script to reduce its running time to just one hour. Mason, keenly aware of Brian's financial needs, advised him to take charge of the radio adaptation, warning, 'You are going to lose money' if another writer were hired. With necessity as his guide, Brian 'lopped great hunks out' and returned the script to Mason with the admission, 'The writing business has its off and on days. But so far, thank heavens, I have not a regret in the world at having a go at it. I suppose you noticed too how quickly one forgets that he was ever inside a classroom.' By the end of the summer, Mason arranged for payment of seventy-five guineas (£78 15s.), so that the radio version of the script, 'thoroughly boned' to half its original length, earned Brian almost five times his royalties for the stage production.

In the meantime, he wrote more columns for the *Irish Times*, increasing his output from once a month to almost weekly features by early 1961. The form gave Brian room to try out new material, sometimes based on his summer holidays in Donegal, where preludes to his later work can be seen. His column 'Down to the sea' reports on an overnight fishing trip with local men, the same premise as his 1965 short story 'The gold in the sea', which became the title of his second published anthology. Local speech patterns and even character names, such as Dan Doalty, the mischievous but thick-headed young farmer later played by Liam Neeson in Brian's 1980 play *Translations*, surface in these newspaper commentaries on rural life. The town of Glenties continued to dominate Bord Fáilte's Tidy Towns competition in 1960, heralded by Brian's triumphant column, 'Glenties Abu!' in which he proclaimed, 'Good on you, my aul delight and joy, my pride and my beauty! You have romped home for a third time in succession with your clean nose in the clean air, and there is not another town or village in the country within a spit or a polish of you.' (In a *Radharc* television programme interview with Dublin priest Father Desmond Forristal, the Glenties parish priest credited the town's extraordinary cleanliness to the annual Corpus Christi procession, for which shopkeepers replaced their front window merchandise with small altars, and he preached that his parishioners should emulate the Holy Family, because 'you can't imagine our blessed Lady being anything else but tidy!')

In the *Irish Times*, Brian's humour shed its bitterness, as he learned to produce satire without spite. He playfully mocked the American media, which infiltrated Ireland through film and television and arrived through Brian's door in the pages of the *New Yorker* itself. The same week that John F. Kennedy won the presidency, Brian published 'Taking one's oil', a comedic critique of an American public relations agency, whose full-page *New Yorker* advert claimed their men could sell castor oil to reluctant children. Remembering his own childhood, Brian was astonished, because 'The plain fact is that kids cannot be interested in castor oil. But if you are determined to interest them – that is, if you insist that they take it – then the man you need is my mother.' Unlike the ad men, her methods of persuasion depended on a 'huge iron ladle' and her mighty right arm. A few weeks later, Brian published 'The game bookseller', imagining that Irish censorship could mean black-market success for the American publication of John Updike's new novel *Rabbit, run*, and that the *New Yorker* might join the Free State's list of banned books. Brian's developing approach to comedy underlies his *Irish Times* review of Patrick Campbell's *Come here till I tell you*, which he admired because the writer 'laughs more at himself than at others and when others are involved, he is laughing more with them than at them ... and, if you insist on getting a moral or in digging up the social commentary, God help you, I suppose it is there, too.'

Brian's attempts to pitch humour to the *New Yorker*, however, too often missed the mark. He continued to assail Roger Angell with submissions, including 'The rest of the four million', a satiric view of a returned Yank, which the editor found 'obvious and forced' because, as he told Brian's agent, 'this picture of an American may be funny to an Irishman, but it doesn't seem very funny to me'. While Brian wanted to show Angell he could take time with revisions, he also needed income, so he rewrote his rejected story about tuberculosis patients and sent it to Angell with a new title, 'Stories on the verandah'. Brian told his editor he had based its main character, the secret homosexual, on a colleague, so now that he was free from school, he was no longer 'too close to draw him accurately'. Sadly, it was another miss – Angell pointed out that 'A good many writers have already dealt with this business of hospital patients who exchange intimacies during their convalescence', and named the Ronald Reagan film *The hasty heart* as an example.

Then Angell lowered the boom. 'I am going to make so bold as to make a suggestion to you,' he wrote, asserting that he normally avoided comment on writers' individual routines.

> Nevertheless, I feel compelled to say that I think you are attempting to write too many stories too quickly. I base this not only on the number of stories that have come to us in the past few months, but on the fact that a good many of them seem to share the same qualities – high technical competence, numerous excellent scenes or passages, and conclusions or basic themes that seem to be insufficiently thought out. Frequently, I have the impression that you have a story completely in hand but that you have not yet arrived at a conclusion that is completely original or that reveals all the elements of character that seem to lie in the situation you are writing about. Since this seems to be a pattern, it suggests a single cause, and the only one that seems logical to me, in view of your great talent, is excessive production.

Angell spoke to Brian as writer to writer, using his own experience to show that sometimes putting a story aside for weeks or months helped him find 'that final last touch that will extract real meaning from the material'.

Brian wrote back two days later. He thanked Angell for his attention, which he knew exceeded the editor's duties, and wrote that he was 'all the more thankful to you not only for your recent help but for your original encouragement. This is not Irish blarney – I mean every word of it.' Angell's comradeship as a writer moved Brian to lay bare his anxieties.

> I am inclined to over-produce (for all I make of it!) and to work too rapidly. Before I begin a story, I have the whole thing perfectly lucid in my mind but in the process of writing very often it slips from me – not rapidly but slowly, as if it were smoke; so that I find myself engaged in a race with a fading image. Then when the job is complete, I discover that the tale I have written very often bears no resemblance to the tale I had hoped to write. Your solution is probably correct: leave the thing for a few weeks and take another look at it then. I shall do that in the future.
>
> I may as well admit to other anxieties now that I have begun a confession: Will I make enough to live on in the next six months? Will

the first reading agreement be renewed? I have been lucky so far; they (i.e. the *New Yorker*) have used so many stories but that has been sheer luck; they will realise that you are out of your depth in the magazine and dismiss you any of these days; you are really not their class at all ... read the last Vivante or McKelway story ... now where are you? They have bought four stories this year so far; could you make a fifth, a sixth within twelve months? Admit that you haven't got it in you; admit that your last three stories were forced or contrived or untruthful. You have an obsession these days with father-son or husband-wife relationships or with the past or with childhood or with death or with the private man in each of us – and you have neither the insight nor the skill to treat of these freshly. And so on ...

You are acquainted with this vacillating yourself; you know how one hovers endlessly around the bright light of despair.

Brian agreed with Angell that producing less might actually increase the quality of his submissions – but he admitted, sheepishly, that he had already sent his agent five new pieces for the *New Yorker* prior to receiving the editor's letter.

Among these was 'Segova, the savage Turk', which Angell rejected with regret: a story about a carnival poster and its effect on a nine-year-old boy. Segova is a sideshow strongman, 'a grand six-footer, broad as the gable of a house', who could 'pull ten railway carriages with his teeth – so the poster said – and kill a full-grown ox with a blow of his right fist'. The boy narrator, fascinated with Segova, studies the hair that 'grew close and thick and luxuriant out of his chest and shoulders and arms' and, after being denied permission to see the show by his parents, resolves to shave the 'fine, white down' from his own skin to make it grow thick as the strongman's. It may have been the first time Brian wrote against the grotesque backdrop of the carnival, but it would not be the last: his 1970 play *Crystal and Fox* showcased a troupe of travelling actors, and his 1979 play *Faith healer*, now regarded as a masterpiece, placed a sideshow poster front and centre as its talismanic prop. Angell found the strongman story 'well written, neatly done, and entirely convincing'. Too convincing, unfortunately, for his colleagues at the *New Yorker*, who 'found the entire scene in which the boy shaves himself acutely painful and almost repellent', and insisted he reject the story as 'a matter of personal taste'.

As a fellow writer, Angell responded one by one to Brian's list of concerns. 'I feel sympathy for the feelings of rage and despair you may be having at this moment', he told Brian, but while he understood these, 'being at least a part-time writer myself ... I think you are being much too hard with yourself'.

> Our purchase of stories from you has not been due to sheer luck; we bought them because they were good stories we very much wanted to print. I think you can only do yourself damage by comparing yourself to other writers. I think that almost every writer must face the fact that he may not be as good as various others he admires. This only indicates the honest beginning of wisdom for it means automatically that you are aware of writing techniques you have not yet mastered and that you are striving toward ...
>
> I can reassure you about one thing. You need not worry about the renewal of your contract. Any writer who has given us as many good stories as you have is in no danger of having his first-reading-agreement terminated.
>
> I am delighted to hear that you plan to hold up the completion or at least the delivery of the next few stories until you are certain they are as good as you can make them. I realize this will require courage, because of your financial position, but I do honestly think that this may increase your chances of success with us.

Unbeknownst to Angell, while Brian pledged to hold back on short story submissions, he was hard at work on a new play.

Throughout the spring of 1961, Brian mapped out notes for a drama about St Columba, the founding saint of Derry and a string of churches and monasteries across Ireland and the Scottish isles. In a blue maths exercise book, Brian jotted historical notes about the saint, his family and his brother monks. He worked out the dates of each turning point in Columba's life, labelled one page for each decade and drew a map of sixth-century Scotland – divided among Gaels, Picts and Angles – on the inside back cover. On his typewriter, Brian outlined a tale of conflict between Columba's spiritual vocation as leader of the Iona island monastery and his loyalty to family in Ireland. He titled the script *King's son of reddened valour* and sent it to the Abbey theatre in early April.

At last there was good news from the *New Yorker*. After rejecting Brian's latest submission, 'Straight from his colonial success', as 'another story that would have been helped by more careful planning', Angell picked up the next, 'Foundry House', and declared it 'the best work you have given us in a long time, and it has so much basic strength that it may develop into the best story you have yet written'. Like 'Among the ruins', it was a narrative of nostalgia, recounting the return of another young father, Joe Brennan, with his wife and nine children to his childhood home, the gatehouse of a wealthy Catholic family who own the foundry in a mid-Ulster town. Many of its details would resurface in Brian's 1979 play *Aristocrats*: the bedridden patriarch, Mr Hogan, emerges from his bedroom only to listen to a tape recording of his daughter Claire, a nun on permanent mission to Rhodesia, on a speaker hooked up by Joe, who listens uncomfortably as the old man shouts his daughter's name and then collapses. Angell felt the story was 'almost right as it is', but he wanted a new ending. The 'contrast between old age and youth' he deemed 'a disappointing and not very original conclusion', and instead, he suggested, 'The social situation – the contrast between Joe and the Hogan family, as they were and as they are – is much more interesting'.

Angell specified the revisions he hoped Brian would make, including 'The idea we have for an ending'. He wanted Joe to return to his wife and nine children without revealing the Hogan family's decrepitude, since their fallen state had 'frightened' him, as Angell understood. Instead, Joe should 'lie to her' and say that the Hogans remain 'a fine, upstanding family', just as he believed while growing up on the grounds of their estate. Joe Brennan's position would later be shared between two characters in *Aristocrats*: local farmer Willie Diver, whose uncle once occupied the gatehouse, and the upstart Eamon (played by Stephen Rea for the original performances), whose grandmother was a maid in fictional Ballybeg Hall. For 'Foundry House', Angell found the ageing father's repeated shouting of his daughter's name 'a little melodramatic' as he heard her play 'The Gartan Mother's Lullaby' on her violin, tape recorded at her Rhodesian convent. The *New Yorker* editor suggested it would be 'more effective if he made a tremendous effort and could only call out her name once' before sinking into his chair, rather than falling onto the floor. Almost two decades later, when Brian reworked the story, complete with lullaby, into a scene within *Aristocrats*, he reversed the editor's decision and staged the name-calling three times, culminating in the old man's catastrophic stroke and ending the play's second act with his death.

For now, Brian toned down the drama, rewrote the ending and dispatched the revised story within a week. Angell was so elated to share good news that he telegraphed the author in Derry: 'PURCHASING FOUNDRY HOUSE. THANKS AND CONGRATULATIONS.' There were still cuts to be made, and perhaps a title change, but within a month Angell sent a cheque for $1,568, which came to £560, more than Brian earned per year as a teacher. He had been right to leave the classroom after all.

But he was far from slowing down. Telegram in hand, he sent Angell a third try at 'Among the ruins', again revising the final scene of the young father remembering his childhood below Mount Errigal. Angell wanted so much to help that he made 'an unusual request'. He proposed revising 'the last four or five pages' himself, cutting and adding a few sentences of his own, 'because you have revised this so often that it must be almost impossible for you to see it clearly'. The editor stressed that these changes would be only 'speculative' and that Brian would have final say – but he also mentioned, a bit hesitantly, that getting 'Among the ruins' accepted for publication quickly would result in 'considerable profit'. The one-year window of Brian's first reading agreement was set to close on 20 June 1961, so reaching a quota of six accepted stories would bring retroactive bonuses of 20% to 35% on all previous payments – a bounteous windfall.

The convolutions of the *New Yorker*'s payment system gave Angell free rein to adjust it in Brian's favour. The six accepted stories he referenced date back to Brian's first, 'The Skelper', in 1958, but somehow the editor was able to promise an additional 20% bonus on that story – and 'The fawn pup' and 'The saucer of larks' – three years later. The magazine's formulas for paying writers were 'notoriously Byzantine', and it was tradition to keep everyone's pay a secret in order to ward off jealousy. As one archivist noted, 'no one really understood their own pay, and so … neither could anyone figure out what the other writers or staff earned.' Years later, Angell described the bonuses as 'esoteric and bendable'. He admitted to Brian's agent that he was 'far from sure' he fully grasped the system. She responded, 'That makes two of us'. Even the June 20th deadline that Angell imposed was mistaken: Brian signed his first reading agreement on 20 July 1960, so he should have had another month to beat the deadline.

But no matter. Brian was 'well aware of the financial side', and after three rejected revisions to 'Among the ruins', he told Angell he had 'much more confidence in what you would do with the ending than in what I might try at this stage'. He and Anne and their two daughters were spending the summer in Kincasslagh, Donegal, from May until the end of August, in a rented house with 'no mod. cons'. He told Angell he was 'not working on a story' and was waiting for 'a great spurt of creative energy' to compel him to start a new one. 'There are times – weeks at an end – when I cannot write even a letter. Then something very insignificant releases me and off I go again.' The change of scenery posed its own challenges, as he found it 'difficult to stay indoors and work' while his wife and children explored the seaside. But the remoteness of northwest Donegal did not fully cut him off from news of the world. While it was tempting to 'go native', he kept up with the US–Soviet space race, and a day after Alan Shepard manned the Mercury 7, Brian wished Angell 'congratulations on your aeronaut. We are delighted for you'.

A scant ten days later, Angell telegraphed. Before receiving Brian's permission, he had 'rashly' rewritten the ending to 'Among the ruins' and submitted it to William Shawn, who approved its publication. Angell justified his 'impulsiveness' to Brian by explaining, 'I believe the story is still yours and follows all your directions and intention'. The changes were 'just simplifications and clarifications of the basic theme'. Despite his 'sizable editing and cutting', Angell trusted that Brian would be happy and relieved. His telegram to Kincasslagh read, 'PURCHASING AMONG THE RUINS WITH ALTERED ENDING. LETTER FOLLOWS. CONGRATULATIONS.' Brian was 'thrilled' – the story's acceptance, and the impending bonus payment, 'not only relieves me of financial worry for many months to come but encourages me greatly.' Angell's two acceptances shored up Brian's faith in himself as a writer and confirmed American readers' interest in stories of memory and nostalgia, a thread that would tie into Brian's Broadway success with *Philadelphia, here I come!* and, much later, *Dancing at Lughnasa*. The ending over which Angell and Brian laboured for 'Among the ruins' came to a gentle close with the story's young father driving away from his childhood home, his sleeping son on his lap, remembering the 'private joy' of finding the boy at play near a rabbit hole. 'The fact that Peter would never remember it was of no importance; it was his own possession now ... Generations of fathers stretching back and back, all finding magic and sustenance in the brief, quickly destroyed happiness of their children.' The 'ruins' of the title, beyond the fallen cottage, are the ruins of childhood and a father's bittersweet nostalgia for its demise.

At last Brian's drought had ended. In May 1961, the Abbey accepted his play about St Columba, and in August Doubleday offered a contract for his first short story anthology, *The saucer of larks*. Brian had sent it to Image Books, Doubleday's imprint for Catholic readers, but the editors thought the work 'better suited to a general public' and issued it under their general trade department. Again, Brian found himself compared to Irish icons: his new editor described his writing as 'John Synge mixed with Frank O'Connor's sure, acid feel for character'. The American publisher's advance, however, was only $750, less than Brian received for a single *New Yorker* story – and the book's sales never earned it back. Years later, even after the Broadway success of *Philadelphia, here I come!* brought a slight sales bump, Brian continued to receive billing statements for the dozen copies he bought himself, and eventually the remaining $2.97 balance was absorbed by his second book. His New York agent reminded him that 'short stories are very difficult' to sell, and in London, Curtis Brown's representative hinted that a novel would be an important next step.

For the time being, magazine publication was more lucrative. Angell's acceptance of 'Among the ruins' brought a cheque for $1,000, as well as a 'fat quantity bonus' of $881.25 paid retroactively on Brian's previous five stories, the equivalent of £675 – more than enough to feed his family for another year. Though they managed to spend every summer in rented cottages in Donegal, he and Anne lived frugally, especially when compared to suburban American families of the early 1960s, or to readers of the *New Yorker*, where Brian's stories were framed by ads for Bonwit Teller cardigans, Cartier diamonds and Bermuda resorts. When editing 'Among the ruins', Angell faulted the incorrect detail of a car's heater working without the engine running, and Brian apologized by explaining, 'I have no doubt that Irish cars are much better than American cars but I have no experience of either! I own a motor-bike without heater, horn or headlights.' The disconnect between US and Irish ways of life was fertile ground for humour, which Brian exploited in his next 'casual' for the magazine, 'Downstairs no upstairs', a 'cheerful and original reminiscence' of household life under the electricity board's 'limiter system' for 'cautious families with modest incomes'. In a vignette that recalled his second radio play *To this hard house*, Brian described a school inspector's visit to his childhood home, which ended disastrously when the electric meter, overloaded, shorted out and caused the inspector to tumble down the stairs in darkness, breaking his spine (Angell revised this to a kneecap) and ending Master Friel's hopes of promotion (temporarily, Angell inserted, to soften the blow) to head teacher in a newly built school nearby. ('This is such a light piece that your tragic notes seem a little out of place', Angell advised.) Though it would not be published for another two years, Angell arranged payment of $560 for this 'light piece' immediately, as well as a cost of living adjustment of $1,198, one of the unexpected benefits of the *New Yorker*'s first reading agreement.

Encouraged, Brian continued to mine the memories of his youth, particularly his primary school years in Culmore, where he grew up in the awkward role of his father's pupil. He wrote to Angell that the acceptance of the electric meter story 'has left me almost wordless', and said he was 'absolutely thrilled' to hear the news. 'I will not pretend to understand your system of payments but they are very generous – almost extravagant by our Irish standards – and have removed the necessity of doggedly producing stuff "for the market" for the next 12 months. If I cannot now write a few good stories I will never be able to write them.' Still, even without financial pressures, Brian kept up a prolific pace. His next story about a schoolmaster, 'My father and the sergeant', was titled for the split personalities of the narrator's father, because 'in the same way as I appeared to be two distinct persons to him, his son and his pupil, so he became two distinct persons to me:

he was my father, kind, silent, troubled by an ambition I never understood until years later, and he was my teacher – the Sergeant, as he was nicknamed – stern, driving, humourless, rigid.' Such duality within individuals preoccupied Brian, as did the roles played by each of us in public and private spheres. He would later explore these contrasts in *Philadelphia, here I come!* – but for now, he limited his gaze to the suffering son, confused by his father's dual selves, so that 'never for a moment was I aware of an overlapping, not to talk of a fusion, of their identities'.

Angell predicted that Brian would find his response a 'familiar' one: there was 'a great deal' here to admire, 'but the story seems to come apart at the end'. The issue was not 'the narrator's attitude towards his father', but rather a 'giant red herring' introduced when a supply teacher, standing in after the schoolmaster takes ill with pleurisy, is discovered to be homosexual. 'This is not at all a matter of taste', Angell attested, but a problem of plotting and a question of pandering to 'shock value'. Brian once again attempted to revise. Angell suggested devising 'some entirely different way' to resolve the ending. At a minimum he begged Brian to 'put this story aside for a month or two – perhaps until you have completed one more story'. Brian tried. As he told Angell, 'I have now come to accept that endings are my weak spot' and promised to 'leave the story for some time' until he could approach it 'completely fresh'. Five weeks later, he sent a new version, with the supply teacher stealing a kiss from a local girl, the narrator's classmate, resulting in his dismissal. Angell was disappointed. 'A pause of a few weeks is usually not sufficient to freshen one's eye towards a story, and the result is all too often a patchwork repair job.' He rejected the story.

This cycle became a pattern of repeated rejections, revisions, and, eventually, editorial exasperation. 'My father and the sergeant' was the first of seven stories the *New Yorker* turned down in 1961, punctuated by unsolicited revisions. Brian continued to falter when it came to endings. At last, at the dawn of a new year, Angell coached him step by step to bring a story to a close that was subtle but satisfying. 'The Diviner' told of the drowning and search for Nelly Doherty's husband, the discovery of his body by a dowser summoned from a neighbouring county, and local villagers' discovery of a shame that Nelly had been hiding for months. In the draft that Angell accepted for the *New Yorker*, the drowned man's whiskey bottle shows a 'bulge in the raincoat pocket', while 'the neck of a brandy flask' is open inside his jacket. The editor objected that 'finding those bottles seems terribly obvious. Even worse, it is a device that requires you to <u>explain</u> the central revelation of the story. It seems to me that this ought to emerge through action or dialogue.' Angell suggested instead that the parish priest, Father Curran, could ask bystanders to search the man's pockets, and that 'the man who was asked, might say, with considerable embarrassment, that they found a wallet and a watch and so forth, and then indicate by his discomfiture that there was something else.' The editor proposed that 'Father Curran, rather stupidly, would not understand at first' but would press for more details until Mr Doherty's secret alcoholism became plain. As Angell put it, 'this way, the matter will come as a revelation to all the characters and to the reader as well'. Brian followed Angell's outline to write a new ending the same day he received his letter. He had just celebrated his thirty-third birthday, and, as he told his editor, 'An acceptance by you is a cause for great rejoicing in this house.'

In March 1962, Brian sent the *New Yorker* a story about cockfighting and the delicate subject of a husband's impotence. 'Ginger Hero', titled for a rooster that becomes 'the champion cock of Ireland' after the narrator and his brother-in-law buy it for seven pounds, marked a stylistic departure as Brian's first story narrated by an adult character that was not a childhood reminiscence. Angell was drawn to the 'convincing and exciting and horrible' fight scenes, but disliked the 'fake and mawkish' unravelling of the two men's friendship. Though he cautioned that William Shawn might decline the story 'because of its violence and bloodiness', he felt sure he could 'do battle' and 'sway him' if Brian rewrote the 'human part of the story', especially the ending. Three weeks later, Brian sent a new version, closing the story with a secret tryst in the back of a van, when the narrator and his childless sister-in-law comfort one another after a brutal cockfight.

Angell squawked in protest. 'I must confess to you that I'm a little irritated over the speed with which you revised and resubmitted GINGER HERO', he wrote, dismissing the new conclusion as 'entirely arbitrary'. The 'few good scenes and vivid moments' were not enough 'to keep the whole business afloat', and Angell was peeved that Brian's rush to rewrite kept this from becoming 'a unified and convincing story'.

> While I am being so unpleasant and so free with unrequested advice, I would like to go further and tell you that I suspect you are writing entirely too fast. You send us more stories than any other contributor I know about, and I think they show the effects of haste and incomplete thought. I am fully aware that you may think it necessary to write this much in order to earn a living, but it might just be that you are injuring and impoverishing yourself in the long run. Most writers have only a limited number of ideas and themes, and it is usually wise for them to conserve these and to spend them, as it were, as carefully as possible ... If you could possibly take the time to brood over each story, to rewrite,

and to go a little deeper into complexities, I think that your percentage of success and your financial return would be higher in the end.

Angell knew he was being 'harsh', but he hoped his friend would heed his advice. To Brian's agent, he explained, 'He's too good a writer to go on hurting himself like this'.

Brian accepted the rebuke and responded with a long, writerly confession.

> You know all about this business yourself: the necessity (only partly financial) to produce: the misery of getting the thing down on paper; the self-delusion that what you have got down at last isn't half bad – anyhow, it's up to the other fellow, the reader, to put up a bit of an effort too, isn't it; the conviction that you're spun out; the certainty of failure; worst of all, perhaps, an impotence induced by extreme scrupulosity. I know that I am writing too many stories. I know that they are not good enough. And – as a result of your letter – I believe that at last I have got it into my thick head that I am damaging myself. So I now resolve to leave a story aside (i.e. a completed manuscript) for at least four months after it is finished.

True to his word, Brian waited five months before sending a father-son fishing story, 'The wee lake beyond', again offering a new stylistic turn, with the entire story in first-person present tense. Angell was 'entirely baffled' by it, though he was 'certain that you are trying for something more profound than what appears on the surface'. After another two months, Brian sent 'Everything neat and tidy', a story Angell gave 'mixed notices', encouraging the writer to try again, as long as he could 'take plenty of time in the revision'. Eventually, three rewrites and nearly a year later, Angell accepted it for publication. Brian responded to each of Angell's rejections by thanking the editor for his meticulous attention, acknowledging that 'It would be so much easier for you to enclose a little "The Editor regrets …" slip'. He invited Angell to use his Marlborough Street house as a stepping-off point for a summer holiday to Europe, and hailed their correspondence as the only literary conversation he sustained, and that sustained him. 'I probably mentioned to you before that there is no-one within striking distance of me with whom I can discuss these things. Occasionally I meet Ben Kiely – maybe for five minutes every six months. Apart from him – nobody. This isolation has its advantages. But its big disadvantage is that there is nobody, apart from yourself, on whom I can rely for fair criticism.'

Angell wrote back immediately, countering Brian's insecurity.

You must not believe for one moment that I am 'sick and tired' of you as a contributor. All those harsh words were not an expression of impatience, but were caused by the fact that I admire and believe in your writing. At the same time, I quite understand the difficulties and self-doubts you encounter because of your isolation and the lack of anyone with whom you can discuss writers' problems. Actually, I know of no real solution to the writer's problem. It is heartening to talk to other writers sometimes, but not really helpful; in the end, one must sit down and do one's best – a lonely and frightening process.

Brian's isolation was soon to come to an end. Doubleday published his first anthology in June 1962, and in August his play about St Columba was staged, at long last, by the Abbey. To see it, BBC producer Ronald Mason made a special excursion from Belfast to Dublin, driving the return trip, 217 miles, in one night. Little did anyone know that another member of the Abbey audience, Sir Tyrone Guthrie, would be moved to write Brian a seven-page fan letter, luring him farther from fiction and toward the bright lights of the stage.

CHAPTER 4

Stage directions, 1961–2

Ernest Blythe had assumed directorship of the Abbey Theatre after two decades in government, including nine years as minister of finance for the Irish Free State. His predecessor at the Abbey, F.R. Higgins, was a convivial, boisterous poet, much loved by fellow writers and much lamented when he died at age 46, felled by a heart attack after a full day of watching rehearsals. Blythe, in contrast, was 'a Buddha in grey plaster' with a 'cantankerous personality': a bald, bespectacled, business-minded man, a 1916 member of the Irish Republican Brotherhood, a hunger striker turned bureaucrat and a staunch believer in the Irish language as the key to national identity. Born into a Church of Ireland and Presbyterian farming family near Lisburn, he went to Dublin as a teenage 'boy clerk' for the British government in 1905, but soon defected to the Gaelic League, where he befriended Seán O'Casey and attended Irish classes taught by Sinéad Flanagan (who later married another of her pupils, Éamon de Valera).

Like de Valera, Blythe had a convert's zeal for the language. In his late-stage career as a theatre manager, he took it upon himself to Gaelicize the Abbey, established scholarships for young actors from the Gaeltacht, and required an Irish-language audition for all prospective performers. In cast lists, all actors' names were Gaelicized, so that Vincent Dowling became Uinsionn O Dubhlainn and Philip Flynn, Pilib O Floinn. Blythe signed his own name as Earnán de Blaghd and shunned Shakespeare as a foreign playwright. One of his first initiatives was to stage annual Christmas pantomimes in Irish, many written by Tomás Mac Anna, appointed in 1947 to a new post, Gaelic producer, which brought Mac Anna's experimental stagecraft into play with European and Irish legends such as *Tristan agus Isialt*, *Setanta agus an Chu* and *Diarmuid agus Gráinne*. The cast of characters for a panto in the late 1950s included Sancho Panza, Don Cichote, Julius Saesar and Isabella, Banríon na Spáinne. The annual Irish-language panto persisted until the late 1960s, making the leap, as did the entire company, to the Queen's Theatre in Pearse Street after a 1951 fire ravaged the Abbey's original building. The Queen's had been built on a grand scale for melodrama in the nineteenth century, when it presented Boucicault and other playwrights to audiences as large as two thousand, nearly double the size of the theatre that Yeats and Lady Gregory had established on Abbey Street. The new house's increased capacity placed increased pressure on Blythe and company, who needed crowd-pleasers to balance the books.

Blythe was unsure whether he had found one in Brian's play about St Columba. His nationalist zeal made him a perfect reader for the script he received from Derry in April 1961, and one might have guessed that his response would be enthusiastic and welcoming. Instead, Blythe wrote to Brian that while the play had 'intrinsic merits' and would indeed be performed by the national theatre, he foresaw that 'the chances of popular success are not very good'. His self-assured business acumen predicted that without female characters, the play was 'not likely to have a long run' unless there were some kind of 'exciting free publicity' like the Legion of Mary's protests during the all-male prison drama *Design for a headstone*, or 'Brendan Behan's special method of personal advertisement' by way of court appearances during his all-male play *The quare fella*. A married and settled father of two, Brian was unlikely to follow in Behan's footsteps; instead, he invited Blythe to visit him while on family holidays in the Donegal Gaeltacht that summer. Blythe sent a contract, a £30 advance (£10 per act, the Abbey's standard rate), and a tentative plan to cast Ray McAnally as Columba, depending on the actor's filming schedule for Melville's high seas mutiny *Billy Budd*. The Abbey's artistic director for English-language plays, Ria Mooney, would take charge of production. Brian modestly reported to Roger Angell that despite Blythe's promise of 'commercial failure', the Abbey's acceptance letter was 'encouraging, especially since I am very keen on drama'.

One point Blythe insisted on was a title change. Brian submitted the script as *King's son of reddened valour*, the saint's honorific from an eighth-century Gaelic poem, translated in the nineteenth-century *Life of St Columba*. Blythe wanted something more modern, but a gifted writer he was not. Late in the summer he sent Brian his list of failed attempts to generate an eye-catching phrase, self-described 'lame starters, or non-starters, in the hope that some one of them may annoy you enough to make you think of something incomparably better'. Among them were ABBOT OF ROYAL BLOOD, IMPETUOUS SAINT, MERCURIAL MONK, IRREPRESSIBLE PRIEST and A SOLDIER UNDER HIS HABIT – none quite right for the Queen's Theatre marquee.

They all fit Brian's characterization of Columba, however. In his script, the saint bounds across the stage, youthful despite his age and brimming with enthusiasm for each new person he meets, each new challenge he encounters. Brian studied St Adamnán's hagiography and set the drama in AD587, a murky phase in Columba's life when he returned from Iona to Ireland for a battle among his cousins, breaking his voluntary exile after 24 years of penance. The playwright intentionally avoided writing about Columba's reputed miracles, prophecies and construction of monasteries, the better to focus on 'the private man'. While drawing upon historical fact for the names of four of Columba's fellow monks, Brian took liberties with their diction in dialogue, and invented a subplot involving an imagined brother and nephew of the saint, heirs to his factual great-great-grandfather, Niall of the Nine Hostages. In his preface, Brian acknowledged his use of 'modern prose', 'geographical alterations' and 'purely speculative' characterization, but he quoted his source, William Reeves' translation of St Adamnán, reminding prospective directors that the monastic era was 'violent and bloody', and that clergy were not exempted from military service until AD804. Adamnán noted that Columba's thirst to join his kinsmen in battle led to 'the grand error of his life, for which he paid the penalty of pilgrimage' and withdrew to Iona to save himself from 'the failing of his nature'. With twelve followers he built a stony island community, where farm work and preaching to the neighbouring Picts were anchored by prayer and penance for 'having fomented domestic feuds' that had killed thousands among the disciples of St Finnian and St Comgall.

Brian's script opens as the Iona monastery becomes a magnet for young Christians from across Britain and the Continent, drawn by Columba's fame. The playwright imagined them 'all looking to him, perhaps idolising him, at times causing him to sin with pride, at times infuriating him. He is a saint because of them and in spite of them.' As other founding monks age and contend with failing eyesight or hearing, Columba remains a pillar of strength, harvesting grain all day alongside his novices. As Brian conceived it, 'Heroic sanctity is not a progression but a series of beginnings.' When the saint enters his stone cell to greet a newcomer from England, Columba speaks energetically, in an Ulster cadence: 'I'm sorry for keeping you but we had to get the field stooked before the light falls'. Privately, riven with homesickness for his native Donegal, he confesses that despite his prayerful life as 'a builder of churches', he cannot overcome 'the inner man – the soul – chained irrevocably to the earth, to the green wooded earth of Ireland!' This outburst is prompted by Gospel verses that the near-blind scribe, Caornan, has spent the day copying. 'Do not think that I come to send peace upon earth; I come not to send peace but the sword. For I come to set a man at variance against his father and the daughter against her mother and the daughter-in-law against her mother-in-law. And a man's enemies shall be they of his own household.' It was this passage that led Blythe and the Abbey board to propose the play's eventual title: *The enemy within*.

Ray McAnally loved the script. A Donegal man and an Irish speaker, he romped across the stage every Christmas in Blythe's Irish-language pantos, and his childhood in Buncrana and Moville gave him close ties to the Inishowen landscape that tugged at Columba's heart. A veteran actor, McAnally was known to Abbey audiences as a young Michael Gillane in *Kathleen ni Houlihan* and as an older Eddie in *The country boy*. But Brian's script, he said, was 'the most beautiful play I have come across in a long score of years'. He had just turned down a TV role in Ibsen's *An enemy of the people* and confided to Brian that he didn't like that play's 'arrogant self-sufficient Liberalistic smug' characters, preferring instead the 'unity and integrity of Columba'. He told Brian, 'your feel for the stage and the theatre is absolutely wonderful. You know when he should speak and when he should be silent, and the ebb and flow of his inner battle is not just merely psychologically possible, but also theatrically true and stated in stage terms'. He asked about Columba's hair and beard – wigs would have to be made in London – and professed faith in the play's importance, as well as its success, despite Blythe's gloomy forecast. 'I am more thrilled about this than I have been about any play for a long time. I hope to God Blythe's prophecies about the public taste are inaccurate; but he is a shrewd old dog when it comes to these things, and I have learned to have respect for his horribly realistic and sometimes very depressing views.' In fact, McAnally said, he hoped to produce *The enemy within* in London, where it would be a tonic against the 'poison' of social dramas then in vogue. 'I wish I had a few thousand quid, – I would buy the rights of this play, and take an option on your next six!'

Ria Mooney, too, effused enthusiasm. Writing to Brian, she thanked him 'for a play that I don't have to reconstruct and which is neither underwritten nor overwritten, a condition which I haven't met with in a play for a great many weary years.' More than three decades had passed since she originated the role of Rosie Redmond in *The plough and the stars*, and the Abbey had lost much of its provocative power in that time. In the 1930s, Mooney acted in Teresa Deevy's plays, among others, before becoming the Abbey's first female artistic director in 1948. She directed over a hundred productions and débuted over eighty new plays, including work by James Plunkett, Denis Johnston, Hugh Leonard and John B. Keane. But she had no Irish, and was less favoured by Blythe and his board than her daring colleague Mac Anna. *The enemy within* was to be her last great success. Though Mooney normally channelled her ideas to playwrights though Blythe, she broke her own rule in the summer of 1962 to send Brian a specific request about 'the endings to Acts II & III. They'll pass, but they are a bit weak. Could you strengthen them? The lines – <u>not</u> the situations – need greater punch to bring down the curtain.' Brian rewrote. At the end of Act II, Columba slaps the new English novice for calling him a saint when he feels anything but. The boy runs away and is not found until the end of Act III, when he returns, hungry and cold, after a remorseful Columba has searched the entire island, forgoing sleep and food and rejecting a final plea from his kinsmen to lead them again into battle in Ireland. For this Columba is cursed and disowned by his brother, yet his final line speaks his renewed commitment to take up the yoke of monastic life, 'to begin again – to begin again – to begin again!'

McAnally's film commitments and Blythe's reluctance to count on a long run delayed production of *The enemy within* for over a year. Meanwhile, Brian celebrated the New York publication of his anthology *The saucer of larks*. Curtis Brown's London agent, James MacGibbon, pressed Brian to work toward a novel and reminded him that 'When we met I talked at great length of the importance of publishing a book. While they are not a novel, these stories will still be a book!' It was a hint he repeated half a dozen times in encouraging letters to his new client. When MacGibbon left Curtis Brown, he joined the staff of Victor Gollancz Ltd, who published *The saucer of larks* in the United Kingdom. It got good reviews, and MacGibbon returned to his argument that 'this situation screams out for you to write a novel. What are the possibilities? Of course we should always want to publish another volume of short stories but what we want to do is to establish you as a writer not only with succès d'estime behind him but with a sales success.'

Brian wanted sales success, too. By 1962, he had published eight short stories and two casuals in the *New Yorker*, and was actively experimenting with fiction and dramatic genres, shifting gears between print, broadcast and the live stage. He was eager to move into television, but Ronnie Mason gave his first TV script, 'Post mortem', a withering assessment:

> If you break it all down the title is off-putting; the opening shot is a cemetery; the exposition and a large part of the development are shrouded in the low key writing of the aftermath of a funeral ... It just doesn't 'come off' Brian. I can hear you ... 'It's not meant to. It's not a pair of pants.'

Mason had begun to travel frequently between Belfast and London, spending weeks in the capital to develop and produce dramas for television. When Brian sent him a second TV script, *Three fathers, three sons*, Mason advised him, 'It has come back I am afraid with a rejection, mainly because we did not see in it enough entertainment value for the wide audience that television has, even regional television.' Brian submitted it instead to Telefís Éireann, where drama director Hilton Edwards cast Ray McAnally as one of three generations to 'repeat the age-old pattern of argument: the son always knows better than the father' for its broadcast from Dublin. Yet Brian's script for a TV series titled *Michael Mannion, proprietor* lay neglected in the RTÉ editorial offices and was never filmed.

Throughout this period of experimentation, Brian relied on occasional publication of his humour pieces in the *Irish Times*, and in April 1962 he landed a steady contract with a larger market: a weekly column for the *Irish Press*. For the first month of this arrangement, his work appeared in both newspapers, and in multiple instances, he recycled a previous column from one with a different title for the other. Sometimes he even used the same title, so that his 1959 *Irish Times* send-up of a *New Yorker* luxury hotel advert was reprinted almost verbatim in the *Irish Press* in 1962, both under the headline 'Haven for the harassed', mocking the advert's claim of prices 'so low that you can't afford to stay at home'. In both, Brian's wonderment that 'the Intercontinental people know by some miraculous and accurate intuition that I owe money to shopkeepers all over the town – that literally I cannot afford to live at home here in Derry much longer' yields to anxiety that his Gweedore summer holiday (in the *Irish Times*) or his gas cooker (in the *Irish Press*) 'has to be paid for by stories I have yet to write and about which I have no ideas'.

The ideas he did have, even those Roger Angell rejected, were profitably repackaged in several columns for the *Irish Press*. 'When the bomb fell on Derry' may have too closely resembled James Thurber for *New Yorker* readers, but Brian's Dublin editors were happy to accept it as one of his weekly tales. 'Downstairs no upstairs', the 'casual' about his parents' electricity limiter system, appeared as 'Old memories' in the *Irish Press* while it was still undergoing final edits at the *New Yorker* – American readers would never know that they were not the first to see it in print. And while Angell scolded Brian for rushing his revisions of 'Ginger Hero', there was plenty of material about rural cockfighting, and night fishing, and dog racing that could be put to use in humorous newspaper sketches as well as in Brian's literary short stories.

As in the *Irish Times*, Brian wrote most of his humour autobiographically, and his *Irish Press* columns from 1962 and 1963 paint a gently self-mocking portrait of his daily life as a full-time writer, husband and father. Two years after leaving the classroom, he told readers that 'I spend the greater part of my working day in a back room at the top of the house. It is a damp, depressing room, and I hate it very much. My wife, with her doubtful gift for putting a nice skin on things, calls it The Study; and if that suggests a large, well-lit, high-ceilinged, oak-panelled apartment, nothing would please her better – or be further from the truth.' He claimed that he faced droughts of inspiration when, he confessed, 'I spend a lot of my time gazing out the window'. Twice a day, he stood at the school gate to meet his oldest daughter Paddy for lunch and hometime, and so 'made the acquaintance of some of her classmates' fathers who, like myself, are not the masters in their own homes that they would like to be. We are a sorry bunch. The very fact that we are on call for this unmanly job indicates that none of us is in steady employment, and we bear the shabby signs of indolence.' He often wrote about money, and introduced himself to *Irish Press* readers in his first column as being '33 years of age, of average height, lean, going bald, married, father of two daughters (aged six and four)' with an annual mortgage of £98 17s. for his 'large, dry-rotting terrace house', a weekly national insurance payment of 14s. 2d. and a yearly life insurance premium of £10 5s. 6d., which would pay Paddy £224 at its maturation in 1975, 'after which time I will be 46 years of age, of average height, completely emaciated, bald as the hairless Mexican, the owner of a worthless, rotted house, and the father of two teenage daughters. The prospect is not warming.'

Brian explained to Roger Angell that 'Readers of the *Irish Press* look on me as the small, ineffectual man who suffers all sorts of misfortunes – hence the general tenor' of his weekly columns. He assessed his newspaper work as 'average in execution & very trivial in content. But, as I told you, this is the image the Irish public has of me – the small, set-upon, comic figure. You can imagine how I love that.' Still, in writing for so many disparate venues in such a compressed timespan, Brian honed the flexibility that would allow him to cross generic and geographic borders and appeal to audiences not only in 'the very northern tip of Ireland' but also in Dublin, and, farther still, in the United States. Readers of the *Irish Press* could safely chuckle at Brian's 'Old memories' of his childhood home's electric wiring, because by the early 1960s the rural electrification scheme was nearly complete, and having to compensate by switching off each downstairs light for an upstairs light switched on was, for most in the newspaper's audience, a thing of the past. American readers, on the other hand, were modernizing even more swiftly, and could read the comedy of 'Downstairs no upstairs' as a quaint portrait of post-war countries less advanced, and, they imagined, less complicated than their own. For both audiences, comedy was key. Brian's mimicry of his father shouting 'Compensate! Compensate!' up the stairs, and his father's eventual downfall on the very day his supervisor came to visit, provide a pathos that allows readers from multiple backgrounds to write themselves (and perhaps their own hapless fathers) into the text.

Crossing from one Dublin newspaper to another brought Brian before a different audience and onto a larger platform. The *Irish Press*, *Evening Press* and *Sunday Press* were the most popular newspapers of their era, with a combined weekday circulation of 267,568 and Sunday circulation of 419,948 in the mid-1960s. The company was managed by Vivion de Valera, whose father had founded the *Irish Press* as a necessary adjunct to his nationalist political party Fianna Fáil in 1926. By contrast, daily circulation of the *Irish Times* had sunk to 33,000 in the early 1960s, as the population of liberal Protestant Unionists, the *Times*' traditional readership, continued to dwindle within the borders of the Republic. (Eventually the two newspapers' positions would reverse, not least because the *Press*' editor Douglas Gageby crossed to the rival *Times* in 1963, reoriented it, and doubled its circulation in the following decade.) Over the spring and summer of 1962, Brian's photograph accompanied each of his columns in the Saturday *Irish Press*, so he was well-known to many Dublin readers by the time the curtain rose on his first Abbey play.

In the year after Ernest Blythe accepted *The enemy within* for performance, he wrote to Brian multiple times to explain delays due to Ray McAnally's absences for film shoots in London and the new Ardmore Studios in Wicklow, or to the Abbey's financial precarity and the need to rehearse each play for three weeks even though it might run for only one. At last, in May 1962, Blythe announced happily that he had solved the all-male problem of *The enemy within* with a plan to alternate its evening performances with an all-female production, *The house of Bernarda Alba* by Federico Lorca, boosting 'publicity value in having all the Abbey men on stage on Monday night and all the Abbey women on stage on Tuesday.' Ria Mooney invited Brian to attend rehearsals 'as often as you can', and she promised a set as true to Iona as possible, in keeping with her longstanding membership in the Society of Antiquarians. Ray McAnally advised Brian to 'find some way of rallying the Derrymen's and Donegalmen's Associations in Dublin to fill the theatre, especially on the first few nights'. Brian and his young family went to Donegal for the summer, as always, but they journeyed together – along with their Lakeland terrier and Anne's eighteen-year-old brother, whom they 'meanly intended to exploit as a baby-sitter' – into Dublin for the week of dress rehearsals and opening night. Brian made the most of the family trip as material for an *Irish Press* column, chronicling a 'day of indescribable wretchedness' in their 'modest car', their meagre roadside picnic, the children's carsickness, and the dog's 'hollow dismal howl' that stopped only when it vomited on the doorstep of their rented house near Phoenix Park. Once at the Abbey, Brian watched evening performances of *This other Eden* by Louis D'Alton, *Mac Uí Rudaí* by Mairéad Ní Ghrada and *Strange occurrence on Ireland's Eye* by Denis Johnston, a courtroom drama which Blythe eventually decided to stage on alternate nights with Brian's play, abandoning the idea of Lorca's all-female cast.

On Monday, August 6th, the curtain rose on *The enemy within*, and after a year in limbo it became an overnight success. Audience numbers during the Dublin Horse Show were strong enough to warrant a second week of performances, and Blythe then decided to run the show for six straight nights, rather than alternating with Denis Johnston. The Abbey was able to rehearse and open a new play by John McCann, *A Jew called Sammy*, which then alternated with *The enemy within* until mid-September. Press reviews glowed: they complimented Brian's script as well as McAnally's 'performance as the brisk saint', Ria Mooney's pacing and direction, and Tomás Mac Anna's set design. 'It's the Abbey's best in a long time', concluded one critic, and Dublin audiences lucratively agreed. Over six weeks, Brian earned £177 6s. 1d. – almost twice his annual mortgage – as royalties at five per cent of the box office takings, which totalled over £3,500 and proved all of Blythe's predictions wrong.

Buzz about the play reached Ronnie Mason in Belfast, and in the third week of its extended run, he petitioned his BBC boss, H.W. McMullan, to fund a scouting mission to Dublin. Mason sensed that the play had a future in radio, or possibly on TV. Of Brian, he wrote, 'He has contributed so much to this region, and may submit a radio adaptation of it. In 1963 this would be acceptable during the Colmcille Anniversary year', fourteen centuries after the founding of Iona. McMullan evidently missed the reference to the saint, but allowed the trip, grumbling, 'What is "The Enemy Within" about? Don't tell me it is more I.R.A.! Let us have a report anyway.' Two days later, on a Thursday morning, Mason climbed into his car and headed south. McMullan offered no BBC money for a hotel room in Dublin, so Mason would make the return journey home again after the show that night. It was a full day's drive, and as he manoeuvred through market towns and rural roundabouts, the summer sun high in the sky, he may have doubted the wisdom of his excursion. At last he arrived at the Queen's Theatre on Pearse Street, where the lobby was bustling with well-dressed men and women who had come to see the summer's most popular play. From a distance Mason spotted Sir Tyrone Guthrie, towering over his fellow theatregoers at six foot five, head and shoulders above the crowd. Guthrie was in Dublin en route from his family's Monaghan estate to Minnesota, where he was overseeing the formation of a new repertory company and plans for construction of a 1,000-seat theatre, soon to bear his name. He was known for his innovative approach to classical theatre and his muscular approach to directing. A former director and governor of the Old Vic, he had founded the Stratford Shakespearean Festival in Ontario, and had been knighted in 1961 for his services to the arts.

Mason took his seat as the lights dimmed and the play began. A hush fell over the audience as Iona's nearly-blind scribe and nearly-deaf cook bantered about Columba's work in the fields and the 'scores of young men from all over the world' drawn to follow him. The bitterness of Brian's radio plays had been replaced by humour and warmth, as when the ageing monks miss each other's meaning, or when Columba tells a joke about the Picts. But the abrupt arrival of a Donegal visitor interrupts Columba's wit. Citing battles Brian had studied in St Adamnán's text, the messenger urges Columba to return and fight alongside a cousin avenging the saint's uncle, Baedan, to defend his kingdom against an army led by a rogue follower of St Comgall. Despite Columba's avowed exile, the messenger provokes him to action by conjuring images of his home place and embattled family. At last Columba catches the man by the throat, shakes him, and explodes:

> I love them, yes, I love them; and every hill and stream and river and mountain from the top of Fanad down to the waters of blue Melvin. And never a day passes but I see the clouds sit down on Errigal or smell the wrack at Gweebarra or hear the wood pigeons in the oaks of Derry. But I am a priest, messenger, a man of God, an *alter Christus* – a poor priest, but still a priest. For the sake of Christ, messenger, leave me alone! Don't wedge my frailties between my soul and its Maker!

The audience was riveted. Here was a saint in flesh and blood who shuddered with self-doubt and shook with anger. After sending the visitor from the room, he 'goes on his knees below the crucifix and prays', then tells his confessor, 'Home is a millstone round my neck'. As a storm breaks and thunderous crashes bombard the audience, Columba caves to the messenger's exhortations and strides powerfully offstage to cast off for Donegal, barking orders as he goes. 'Hoist your sails, Innishowen man, and strip your oarsmen to the waist!' Lightning flashed as the curtain fell, ending a tumultuous first act.

Mason was spellbound. As he later wrote to Brian, 'I was tremendously impressed by its wholesomeness, by the warmth and earthiness of its humour. I found it gripping, and at times deeply moving. I think you have written a splendid play.' At the interval, he shouldered his way through the crowd to greet Tyrone Guthrie, who was equally full of enthusiasm for Brian's script. He and Mason both agreed it was the best they had seen at the Abbey in years. Guthrie would later write Brian a seven-page letter full of 'shrewd, accurate, and vastly entertaining criticism', as the playwright ebulliently reported to Mason. The great director was on his way back to America, but invited Brian to meet him at his home in Monaghan when he returned. For now, as lobby

4.1 Abbey director Ernest Blythe, Fr Edward Daly, and Brian Friel in Derry.

lights flickered for the second act, Guthrie turned to Mason and declared: 'This is the sort of play which makes a National Theatre worthwhile'.

Guthrie wasn't the only one inspired by St Columba's onstage vitality. In Derry, a young priest named Edward Daly, newly appointed curate of St Eugene's Cathedral, heard about *The enemy within* and wrote to Ray McAnally to ask whether it might be staged in the saint's home city. Father Daly would later shepherd dying Jackie Duddy through the Bogside on Bloody Sunday, and, later still, would become bishop of his war-torn diocese, but in 1962 he was trying to lighten the lives of his impoverished parishioners by bringing concerts, bingo and theatre into their midst. He had come to Derry from Castlederg, where he arranged weekly dances that drew up to 800 young people from the surrounding countryside. His new superior assigned the young, energetic priest to organize social events at St Columb's Hall, which had been built in the 1880s and could seat an audience of 1,000 in its main auditorium. In the early twentieth century, the parish used the hall as a cinema, but with the advent of television and stiffer competition to show first-run films, ticket sales were lagging. To keep the building open, Father Daly needed to draw parishioners to activities that would 'counter-balance' the 'often harsh realities' of life in the overcrowded Bogside. A play about Derry's founding saint seemed providentially purpose-built.

Ernest Blythe was amenable, though the Abbey had never travelled beyond Belfast – but he and Father Daly came to terms, and in mid-October, the curtain rose on the national theatre company's first of three performances in the maiden city. Press photos show the grinning young priest in conversation with the Abbey's elder statesman and the local teacher-turned-playwright. Bow-tied and bemused, Brian posed in his suit jacket with the cast, a notable standout amid the bearded monks of Iona in their habits. He and Anne invited Blythe to their house for dinner, while the teetotalling Father Daly scrambled to find a host for an impromptu cast party: the play's opening night was a Sunday, and all pubs in the Six Counties were closed.

More regional performances followed. Dozens of Catholic schools and seminaries across Ireland, the United Kingdom, United States and Canada requested amateur rights; the all-male cast was, as one rector explained, 'perfectly suited to the seminary situation (which sets great limitations on the selection of a play)'. Brian's name circulated among priests touring Ireland from La Crosse, Wisconsin and Sioux City, Iowa, building upon his nascent short story readership in Catholic American magazines. In 1963, Ronnie Mason directed the Lyric Players Theatre for ten performances of *The enemy within* in their Belfast studio on Derryvolgie Avenue – founder Mary O'Malley's converted garage – with seating for forty-five people. Mason submitted the script to London BBC for television, pitching its timing: '1963 is the millennium-and-a-half, or something of St Columba! I think the play would adapt. It's a wholesome, funny and at times moving treatment of the theme.' But he was later dismayed to report that London was 'unenthusiastic' about the project, and instead, commissioned Brian to adapt *The enemy within* for BBC radio in Northern Ireland. Radio Éireann's television department was just a year old in 1963, when a producer asked to see Brian's script, but nothing came of it – and Ray McAnally did his best to pitch to Granada TV in London, to no avail, after failing to convince an English stage manager to take it on. In the meantime, likely at Guthrie's prompting, the Ballymoney Literary & Debating Society picked up amateur rights to perform it at the Grand Opera House, Belfast, where Gate Theatre director Hilton Edwards adjudicated the Ulster Drama Festival in May 1964.

4.2 Brian Friel with cast of *The enemy within*.

Brian was beginning to make his name in theatre. But his breakout success with *The enemy within* was muted by the Abbey's rejection of his next play, *The hero of Thian-Hee*. Months before Columba and his ancient monks materialized onstage, Brian submitted the story of a modern-day priest, also sainted by his local community, also exiled, also flawed. This one would be a much tougher sell. It was based on material Brian had been trying to write in various genres: the plight of the returned missionary for whom Ireland has become a foreign land. In childhood, he had seen his uncle, Father Bernard, beatified by the people of Glenties, exalted by a saintly funeral in Raphoe – but, older now, Brian wondered how his countrymen would react to a long-exiled priest who lost his faith while overseas. As a seminarian at Maynooth, he had surely seen copies of *The Far East*, monthly journal of the Missionary Society of St Columban, also known as the Maynooth Mission to China. Tales of martyrdom abounded in its pages. The first Columbans went to Asia from

Ireland in 1920 and weathered persecution, arrest and torture during successive waves of Chinese revolutions: Sun Yat-sen, Chiang Kai-shek and Mao Tse-tung all regarded foreign missionaries with suspicion. *The Far East* spun tales of Irish priests who withstood months of interrogation and illness 'by going through the prayers of the Mass each day and meditating on hymns'. Dysentery was no match for faith and ritual: one imprisoned priest, Patrick Reilly, 'was allowed to buy grapes because of illness, but used the juice and steamed bread to say Mass' in his cell. Other *Far East* stories told of harrowing public humiliations, as when Bishop Patrick Cleary of Nancheng and four fellow Irish and Chinese priests were harshly interrogated for two hours, then paraded through a crowd of high school students who pelted them with mud and spat on them.

Rather than sing the praises of persecuted missionaries, Brian instead drew a direct line between Chinese political brutality and Northern Irish mob violence, which looms menacingly offstage throughout *The hero of Thian-Hee*, later renamed *The blind mice*. The script opens as Father Chris Carroll's family fend off an onslaught of well-wishers, reporters and customers for their public house in the wake of Father Carroll's release by the Chinese government, who captured and imprisoned him for five years during the rise of the Communist regime. The Carrolls' home is as stifling as those in Brian's radio plays, and family members are locked into similar roles: Lily Carroll fusses over tea and social conventions, Arthur Carroll cares only about money in the till, their daughter Ann rebels by dating a young trade union leader, and their son John, a doctor, hopes his priestly brother's notoriety will land him a coveted hospital post. When Father Chris eventually appears onstage, one-third of the script has gone by without him, and the audience sees his brokenness in his haggard face and unkempt beard. In Brian's stage directions, 'His movements are jerky, unsteady; he might be discovering movement for the first time'.

But the Carrolls, as characters, are not written with warmth. Watching *The enemy within*, the audience could laugh tenderly at the monks of Iona and feel genuine grief, as does Columba, when his aged scribe dies; but *The blind mice* characters have cynical desires – Arthur, to fill his pub with customers, and John, to get 'that hospital job' off his brother's fame. Only Chris' confessor, the tippling Father Rooney, is remotely sympathetic; other characters are mere mouthpieces for political or personal ideologies, and the audience can do little but sneer when, for example, John rails against his faltering brother and explodes, 'You blighted my childhood. And now in my manhood you have ruined my career.'

Roger Angell saw similar problems for a similar story, 'Bark mats for the Toners', which Brian sent to the *New Yorker* that same summer. In this version, the priest is Father Casimir – Brian's confirmation name – who, upon returning to Ireland, '"bought" his way into the homes of fellow missioners who worked with him in Africa'. Angell and his colleagues agreed it was 'an excellent subject for a story, but we all experienced a feeling of disappointment at the end'. The priest character was marred by 'petulance and egocentricity', and 'he is so sorry for himself and occasionally so dishonest that he doesn't seem entirely real'. Angell found the story 'a trifle slick and shallow' and discouraged Brian from revising, because 'a new Father Casimir means a new story and that is a lot to ask a writer to try on speculation'.

Brian tried nonetheless. He pounced on Angell's 'slender encouragement' and, a few months later, sent him a new version, retitled 'The perfect gentleman'. Both the original and revised stories are absent from the archives, so we may never know exactly how Father Casimir was reshaped into a newly imagined Father James. But Brian was hopeful because, as he wrote to Angell, 'I am convinced there is a story in this returned missioner set-up and I think that perhaps I have captured it this time'. Sadly, again, Angell disagreed. The new version, he told Brian, 'does not seem to us to be much of an improvement. The trouble with this one, as we see it, is that the story never penetrates the events you describe here.' As in *The blind mice*, both the priest and those around him seem so 'cold, controlled', and 'inhuman ... that one cannot care much' about their troubles. As Angell put it, 'I was constantly irritated by my wish ... to get some tiny flash that would show them to be human beings'.

It would be thirty years before Brian succeeded with the 'returned missioner set-up' in the character of Father Jack, who totters in the background of *Dancing at Lughnasa* until his apostasy gradually reveals itself in his conflation of indigenous Ugandan animal sacrifices with a Catholic Mass. Likewise, in *The blind mice*, the Carroll family discovers that their celebrated son, far from consecrating bread and grapes in his prison cell, instead abandoned Catholic beliefs during his dark night of the soul. London newspapers report a signed renunciation of faith, flaunted by the Chinese government following Father Chris' release. Brian's script centres on the weakened priest's confession to his only confidant, the buffoonish Father Rooney, to whom he describes the slow psychological damage wrought by five years in solitary confinement. Like the missionaries exalted in the pages of *The Far East*, Chris began by reciting Mass, pacing his cell to the rhythms of the Latin prayers. 'They were manna to me ... I lived on them ... I battened on them ... for a year or so ...' but after so much time alone, he lost his connection to Christ. 'He was slipping from me – I was losing Him. He is the God of life, and there was no life to tell me about Him; not a voice, nor a laugh, nor a smell, nor a mirror, not even a sin. He was becoming an act of the intellect, a mental theorem; and what I wanted was the abiding Saviour, the Christ within me.' Recognizing that he had committed the sin of despair, Father Chris surrendered to the Chinese government: he signed the document that sent him home to Ireland, where he could make a true confession and be absolved.

Father Rooney, like everyone else in the play, fails to understand. 'No torturing? No brainwashing? No questioning?' But at least he attempts to absolve Chris, reminding himself all the while, 'Don't judge, don't judge. There is too much judging.' The townspeople have no such scruples. When word gets out that their local hero has in fact betrayed the Catholic church, their veneration turns to rage. A stone crashes through the family's front window as a mob gathers outside. Father Chris' sister Ann puts out the lights, while his brother John rushes to phone the police, only to find that the line has been cut. The family interrogate Chris in the darkness while a single spotlight shows his face. As they fire demands at their broken brother, Brian's underlying message shapes their words. 'There's going to be a riot! I said that all along!' 'A great day for Ireland! An hour ago it was the triumphant entry; and now – now we're infused with "holy anger"!' 'I could hear some of Devlin's louts screaming, "He's a traitor! A traitor!" just to show the Protestants what good Catholics they are!' Poignantly, mother Lily asks why the police must be called. 'Protect us from what? From our Catholic neighbours? Is this Ireland we're in? Are we Christians at all?'

Though Lily's voice is drowned out by others amid the chaos, Brian made it clear to his friend Ronnie Mason that her question reveals his central point. Chris' confession, he wrote, 'merely triggers all the action & allows the theme to build: i.e. that the N.I. Catholic community succeeded in driving this man mad when the Chinese failed'. Madness, the individual, and the demands of faith were common threads in Brian's work during this time. For his Doubleday book jacket, he pencilled an author's bio to explain that 'at 17 I presented myself at Maynooth as a candidate for the priesthood. 2½ years later I left + ever since I have a feverish nightmare in which I watch myself being ordained'. Brian understood the finer points of Catholic doctrine, and he also knew the power of communal condemnation.

So did Ernest Blythe, and every other director who came in contact with *The blind mice*. The Abbey wouldn't touch it, despite Brian's opinion that it was his best play yet. His Doubleday editor enjoyed it, and his New York agent sent it to the US Steel Hour television show, but no one picked it up for production. Eventually Phyllis Ryan staged it in her Eblana Theatre, which occupied the basement level of Busáras, the terminus station for Bus Éireann, just north of the Liffey.

It was hardly a glamorous setting, but Ryan was a respected figure in Dublin theatre, having débuted at the Abbey as a child actor in Denis Johnston's *The moon in the Yellow River*, cast by Johnston himself and directed by Ria Mooney. As a teenager and young adult, Ryan acted in more than sixty Abbey plays, but Ernest Blythe dismissed her soon after his appointment, explaining that she 'would need to become versed in Irish history and language' and could return only after 'a lengthy sojourn in the Gaeltacht'. She had attended Alexandra College, where classmate Máire Mhac an tSaoi's mother taught Irish until Catholic bishops denounced all parents who participated in Protestant schooling, and though Ryan loved the language, she would not be 'bullied' by Blythe into learning it. To her, Blythe was a 'ruthless politician', a 'dictator' who 'had no time for creative people, unless they shared his tunnel vision and Ulster Protestant righteousness'. In her memoirs, she called him an 'old bigot' and 'an absolute disaster' as a theatre manager. She eventually decided to found her own company, and in 1957 launched Orion Productions in the Gas Company Theatre, above the Dublin Gas offices in Dun Laoghaire, where 'The audience came in downstairs through the showroom and were greeted by an array of gleaming gas appliances.'

The Eblana Theatre may have appeared to be a step down, since it was below the city centre bus station, but it was a step closer to the heart of Dublin, whose theatres – the Abbey, the Gate, the Gaiety, the Olympia – were increasingly frequented by the rising middle class. The Eblana was built as a 'News Cinema, where people waiting for buses might spend an hour or so', but while this idea had been popular in London, it never caught on in Dublin, and the space was redesigned as a performance stage for an audience of up to 237 people. Ryan described it as 'a lovely little theatre, intimate and comfortable' despite having no wings for the actors and a lighting box that had to be entered by climbing over 'formidable railings'. She and her two theatre companies, Orion and, later, Gemini Productions, spent more than twenty years below Busáras, launching many new playwrights and hitting it big with new plays by Hugh Leonard, whose *Da* became a Tony award winner on Broadway, and John B. Keane, whose script for *The Field* was unearthed by Ryan (on a tip from poet Brendan Kennelly) and débuted at the Olympia with Ray McAnally in the lead role of 'The Bull' McCabe. It was Keane's director, Barry Cassin, whom Ryan chose to stage Brian's *Blind mice*. Belfast actor and playwright Sam Thompson, who had caused so much controversy with his shipyard play *Over the bridge*, was cast in the role of Father Rooney, the drunk but kindly confessor.

Ronnie Mason, ever loyal, believed in *The blind mice*. He saw the Eblana production and told his superiors it was 'a moving play, written with skill and sensitivity, and one which I should like to commission'. He urged Brian to rewrite it for radio, because 'to allow anyone else to adapt it was to throw money away, since you would be perfectly capable of doing it in so short a time yourself'. Brian cut two minor characters and did his best to refashion the script, although he admitted that 'Once a play has been on the boards it is impossible, I find, to visualise the characters in fresh casting; so that I keep seeing all these characters as they were first portrayed in the Eblana – and in many cases the fossilised memory is not one bit happy'. Eventually Dublin actor Donal Donnelly would be cast as the radio version of Father Chris, replacing the 'Ulster Presbyterian' Derek Young, who had played the troubled priest on stage. Brian cut much of the play's opening exposition and replaced it with American and Chinese news reports about Chris' release, to be read with authentic accents by actors recruited and recorded in London. Once the script was ready, Mason launched it toward the BBC's national drama office, with a note from the head of Northern Ireland programmes reminding his London counterparts that 'It is by Brian Friel, who is, of course, our new coming playwright'. Still, H.W. McMullan appended a note of warning. 'My only concern is whether this would be very offensive to a Roman Catholic audience. I think it will not be understood by the Protestant audience who may resent it also, but its merit as a play would override that thought.'

The London BBC drama producers agreed to give *The blind mice* a commission. They had, after all, drawn a large listening audience to another religious play, Sam Thompson's *The Evangelist*, the story of a 'hotted-up, sub-Billy Graham style transatlantic Gospel spieler' who comes to spread the Word in Northern Ireland. It was left to Ronnie Mason to work with Brian on his *Blind mice* script, and to spell out some of the finer points of its Catholic plot twists. McMullan, as Mason's boss, wanted some 'cleaning up of the motive behind the whole thing', particularly Father Chris' signed renunciation of his beliefs. 'As a hardened Protestant I cannot understand how, in fact, he did this in the context of his faith and apparently got away with it.' Brian, accordingly, added a few lines of dialogue to help the uninitiated understand the doctrine behind the plot. He admitted that 'one very easily forgets that his first job is to communicate', but explained that 'Short of writing in a theological paragraph – which nobody wants – I don't see much chance of getting out of the problem'. By this point, he was far more interested in the Northern Ireland Catholic community's hysteria and its damaging effects on Father Chris as an individual. 'And I think Papes & Proddydogs are all capable of understanding that'.

It is clear that in *The blind mice*, Brian was trying to write psychological drama. He spends pages of dialogue describing the effects of solitary confinement on Father Chris's mind and 'the torture of despair' he suffered. Unfortunately, words alone do not translate into visually compelling action. In his radio adaptation, Brian conveyed stronger psychological undercurrents by layering sounds of the Chinese prison – 'marching feet in an echoing corridor; a cell door opening; sharp commands in Chinese' – while Father Green, the parish priest, questions Chris about his ordeal. Later, after the stone through the family's window, the prison sound effects are 'superimposed on the distant sound of the mob'; and they surface again on the script's final page, as Father Chris breaks down. Brian explained to Mason that he wanted to 'correlate' the 'Communist technique' to the 'grilling' Chris receives from his local community, and his resulting 'insanity' or 'crack-up'. Over and over, as in *The enemy within*, Brian tried to depict the mind and its workings, pushing the theatrical envelope to project a character's inner life as well as his external actions.

As *The blind mice* closes, Father Rooney convinces Chris that he has been absolved. Childlike, Chris takes his father's hand and implores him to 'Say a prayer for me, Father. I am starting life again, and I need the prayers of all good, ordinary, sensible, uncomplicated people like you'. Like St Columba, Chris hopes to begin again – but he cannot, for his mind has been permanently shattered by the private torments of his imprisonment. He limps offstage, leaning on his younger brother, singing the nursery rhyme 'Three blind mice' in place of his forgotten prayers. As in *The enemy within*, Brian has drawn a conflict between faith and family, a priest with a worldly brother, a confessor, and a community that is ready to beatify the hero, or to stone him. Both plays confront religion; both plays question the power of the individual versus society. But only one caught the attention of Tyrone Guthrie, who would bring Brian across the Atlantic Ocean, the widest border of them all.

CHAPTER 5

The giant of Minneapolis, 1962–3

'MY RESOLVE TO GO TO THE US for a year is now practically a fixation!' wrote Brian to Roger Angell in the summer of 1962. Whether he had finally succumbed to the *New Yorker*'s luxury brand advertising, or got caught up in the excitement of the space race, America was drawing Brian into its orbit. *The saucer of larks* was garnering good reviews, and he was persuaded that 'US critics are much more open-handed in their compliments than are critics over here'. The book brought together seven *New Yorker* stories and ten that Angell had rejected, a handful of which were published in other American magazines such as *Argosy, The Sign, St Jude* and *Ave Maria*. Privately, Brian acknowledged that the anthology was 'very uneven', but he thanked Angell 'for making the collection possible because without you there would never have been a collection. Indeed had it not been for you & the *New Yorker* I would still be teaching. I will always be in your debt.'

Two days later, he divulged to his *Irish Press* readers that he and Anne, 'exhausted looking for a holiday house each year', had bought a two-room cottage near Kincasslagh, Donegal, with a view of 'Errigal, Gweedore, Rannafast, Innishfree, Innishman, Gola, Tory lighthouse' from its 'kitchen/livingroom/lounge/drawingroom', where a hearth fire provided heat for the adjoining family bedroom. On their first night, young Mary, too frightened to sleep in an upper bunk, crawled into Brian and Anne's bed, so the writer swapped places with her, only to tumble all the way to the floor at three in the morning. Brian christened the house 'Friel's Folly' and mused that 'the ugly, swollen contour of my financial status' would be exacerbated by the cost of the cottage, despite its charms. 'The more I think of the mess I have landed myself in, the more I am convinced that I need a place like this to escape to'.

Although Angell remained supportive, acceptance by the *New Yorker* was never guaranteed, and 1962 was another lean year for publication. Brian continually mined the vein of childhood memories that had brought him success with 'The fawn pup': he sent Angell story after story about dour, dissatisfied fathers – often schoolmasters – and their perplexed, lonely sons. In 'Pearls in the Strule', the father fantasizes about oyster farming in Omagh's local river; in 'The first of my sins', the son agonizes over his first confession; in 'The wee lake beyond', the son becomes a father himself, and reminisces about a failed fishing trip to Donegal. Angell turned them down with such regularity that Brian 'feared he would be cast out' from the magazine's list of authors holding a prized first reading agreement.

Over eleven months the editor rejected nine of Brian's stories, yielding only when Brian sent him a 'strange' story just before Christmas, 'Everything neat and tidy', about a Derry taxi driver's conversations with his mother-in-law as he ferries her to electric shock treatments at a psychiatric clinic. Angell liked it. The 'idea for this story is a really original one', he said, and 'it might turn out to be one of your very best'. The gradual revelation of the young man's 'moods and reactions played out in counterpoint' to his depressed mother-in-law was 'particularly suited to fiction' in Angell's opinion. 'So often, "mental health" requires such a deadening of true feeling that one must ask oneself whether emotions have not become too much of a burden for us to carry in this hard, changing world.' All the same, he told Brian, 'your handling of the story is entirely wrong'. This time, he felt, 'Too much information is withheld' so that 'as a result, this is almost a trick story, with a flip, last-line ending'. As before, he asked his friend to 'take plenty of time in the revision', reassuring him that 'The situation is so good that all its meaning will emerge if it is told right'.

Brian was already on to the next project. He promised to put the story away, but in the meantime he was making plans that would take him far from Derry – far, even, from the *New Yorker* – and closer to theatrical inner circles. In December 1962, four months after the Abbey curtain fell on *The enemy within*, Tyrone Guthrie returned from Minneapolis and invited Brian to visit him at Annaghmakerrig, his family estate in Monaghan. Over the coming year, Guthrie's emphasis on theatre in the round, theatre as ritual, and the power of physicality and experimentation made direct impact on Brian's development as a playwright. Most importantly, Guthrie's gospel of bringing repertory theatre to provincial audiences set Brian's compass toward a path that would eventually lead him to co-found the Field Day Theatre Company in Derry.

Like St Columba, Guthrie had embarked on a mission of faith. American producer Oliver Rea had enlisted him, along with technical director Peter Zeisler, to form 'an alliance and a plan' toward a theatre project to counter Broadway's commercialism and the constraints it created: economic pressures, frustrated young actors, and trade union rules that amounted to 'tyranny', as Guthrie saw it. Most of all, Guthrie was seeking a new audience. In New York, he lamented, 'audiences are composed of very rich, elderly people, of tourists and of business men and women entertaining other business men and women on expense accounts'. They were 'not content with moderate success' nor with plays that were anything less than the 'super-smash hit' that each season grew 'gaudier, more garish and more deadly'. Instead, Guthrie believed that theatre must be 'a shared experience, and that the audience, unlike the audience for movies and television, has an active part to play'. He believed that 'Artists are ministers' and 'The theatre is a temple'. The director's role was akin to 'the abbot of a monastery' as well as 'foreman of a factory' and 'superintendent of an analytic laboratory', with 'the patience of a good nurse, together with the voice and vocabulary of an old-time sergeant-major'. In Guthrie's high-spirited fervour, he and his actors aimed to 'bring healing and knowledge' to the world.

Over breakfast at the Plaza Hotel in March 1959, Guthrie, Rea and Zeisler had shared their dissatisfactions with Broadway and begun to brainstorm alternatives. But Guthrie 'could not talk seriously nor think clearly in New York – too many distractions, too nervous an atmosphere'. He invited the two Americans and their wives to travel to his Monaghan family estate 'in the depths of very remote country; and there, in quietude, try to formulate a plan'. In misty midsummer, amid the genteel but bohemian environs of Annaghmakerrig, they held 'Long talks over the ruins of breakfast; long talks crouched over the fire at night; long talks up to the neck in damp raspberry canes or bent double over the chickweed; long talks hacking at the overgrown rhododendrons'. Gradually, the younger men succumbed to Guthrie's 'missionary zeal' and agreed on 'some kind of a theatrical project aimed at those parts of the United States into which Broadway's influence did not penetrate'. When they returned to Manhattan, they explained their ideas to *New York Times* theatre critic Brooks Atkinson over lunch at the 46th Street restaurant Dinty Moore's. Atkinson arranged for the project, a 'permanent company that would perform classics' in a city 'relegated' to 'provincial status', to be announced in the *Times* drama pages on 30 September 1959. The next step was to solicit proposals. While Rea placed long-distance phone calls to Pittsburgh, San Francisco and Ann Arbor, Guthrie and his wife prepared for a whirlwind tour of the United States to preach the power of theatre.

Like Columba, Guthrie in his sixties had energy to spare. That same autumn, he adopted another project: the Irish Farmhouse Preserves co-operative jam factory, which aimed to resuscitate Monaghan's rural economy. After the last freight train had rolled through Newbliss, near Annaghmakerrig, that summer, the village's emigration rate 'reached catastrophic proportions', as Guthrie later told the *New York Times*. A local development committee approached the director for help to renovate the railway station into a production line for rhubarb and ginger jam and bramble jelly. The signal box cabin above the tracks became an office; the passenger waiting room became a test kitchen. Guthrie became not only a board member but an enthusiastic publicity agent, giving interviews to newspapers and television presenters about the venture, and writing to his fellow directors in New York and London to use Newbliss jam jars as props whenever possible. He pitched his product everywhere he directed, so that eventually the jam would be sold in Dayton's department stores in Minneapolis, Bloomingdale's in New York, and select stores in Toronto, marking a trail that followed Guthrie's theatre projects over his career. When James Ellis and Sam Thompson visited Annaghmakerrig for advice about the *Over the bridge* controversy, Guthrie sent them home with armfuls of flowers, fresh eggs and Newbliss jam as parting gifts.

Born in Kent to an Ulster Scots mother and Scots Presbyterian father, William Tyrone Guthrie – Tony, to his friends and family – was educated at Wellington College and Oxford, where he played the Welsh prince Owen Glendower in a student production of *Henry IV, Part I* under the guidance of Irish director James B. Fagan. Guthrie later wrote that 'It was a felicitous piece of casting because in this part many of the qualities which prevent my being a real actor became assets, not drawbacks. My overwhelming height, cutting voice and an incurable tendency to emphasise the grotesque and farouche – all these were a help in making something striking and dominant' of a minor Shakespearean role. Much more interesting was 'watching the play take shape' as Fagan orchestrated the student actors as well as the costumes, scenery, props and stage lights, 'all ingredients which have somehow to be fused together into a single work of art'. Young Tony Guthrie was hooked. For the rest of his life, he worked and reworked the raw material of classic scripts – Shakespeare, Molière, Chekhov – and he stretched and reshaped the role of director to suit his towering talent.

Soon after completing his degree, Guthrie landed a job with the BBC and was sent to Belfast, where he cut his teeth as a director of radio drama. For two years, he explored the 'ugly, fascinating city' of his forebears, and soon became 'militantly provincial' in his fondness for local culture. He arrived in 1924 to find that the linen warehouse destined to house BBC Belfast was not yet ready, so, with time on his hands, he took bus trips up the Antrim coast, through Co. Down, and along the shores of Strangford Lough. Stormont was under construction, and hundreds had been killed in sectarian violence, but the landscape was beautiful and intriguing to the young Oxford graduate. He roamed the streets of Belfast on long September evenings, a curfew pass in his pocket, and came to love the city despite its being 'a theatrical Sahara'.

Years later, Guthrie would write that Belfast was where he found his 'vocation'. As radio talks officer, his duties included choosing scripts and rehearsing plays, and he soon found that his 'professional attitude', learned from Fagan, helped him with the BBC's local actors – amateurs who held day jobs 'as commercial travellers, in the linen business, the shipyards, the ropeworks or as teachers'. He could tell that the actors were 'happy' and that his rehearsals 'went with a swing'. Toward the end of his second year at the BBC, the Ulster Literary Theatre invited him to direct their live productions, offering a move from studio to stage. Within a few years, Guthrie was summoned from Belfast to Glasgow, where he directed the Scottish National Players, then to Cambridge, where he directed the Festival Theatre, then to Montreal, where he directed radio plays on Canadian history, and eventually – after marrying his childhood friend, Judith Bretherton, at Annaghmakerrig – back to London, where he rose to the attention of the Old Vic Shakespeare Company and was appointed its producer. Throughout the 1930s, Guthrie directed rising British actors who were soon to become household names: James Mason in *Twelfth Night*, Alec Guinness in *Hamlet*, Laurence Olivier in *Othello* and many other plays. In 1937 Guthrie staged a production of *Henry V* to mark the coronation of George VI, from which, he was pleased to point out, Olivier borrowed 'one or two little notions and wheezes' for his Oscar-winning film about Britain's boyish king.

In every theatre, including the Old Vic, Guthrie encountered the traditional proscenium, which he traced to Italian opera, where scenes and action were framed by a gilt border that firmly separated actors from audience. Despite his success at the Vic, he recounted, 'it became clear to me that trying to put Shakespeare's plays into the conventional framework for opera was wrong. The plays had been written by a master craftsman for a theatre of altogether different design.' It would be a decade before he could construct his own open stage, thrust forward into the audience seating, so that actors faced their viewers on all sides. His opportunity came at Edinburgh in 1948, the second year of the Festival: Guthrie chose to stage the sixteenth-century *Satire of the three estates* in the Kirk Assembly Hall, where his own great-grandfather once preached. Guthrie, a self-described 'mongrel Scot', rejoiced in the resulting effect of theatre in the round – not only on the actors, but on the audience members, too, whose background scenery was 'dimly lit rows of people similarly focused' on the stage. In real terms, they were '"assisting" as the French very properly express it, in a performance, a participant in a ritual.'

The open stage worked, and Guthrie wanted to build a theatre around it. In 1952 the Canadian town of Stratford, a hundred miles west of Toronto, invited him to establish a Shakespeare festival, so he again ventured into the provinces, this time into the heartland of North America. He brought along a few comrades from the Old Vic, among them Scottish-born actor Douglas Campbell and designer Tanya Moiseiwitsch, who had started her career as an apprentice scene painter at the Old Vic before designing sets and costumes at the Abbey Theatre, Oxford Playhouse and Covent Garden, where she expanded the stage for Guthrie's production of Benjamin Britten's opera *Peter Grimes* in 1947. Moiseiwitsch had moved from there to Stratford-upon-Avon, where she modelled scenery on drawings of Shakespeare's circular Globe Theatre, creating multi-level sets for *Richard II*, *Henry IV parts I and II*, *Henry V* and *Henry VIII*. Reunited with Guthrie in Canada, she designed a five-sided stage under a tented roof, and a sweeping crimson coronation robe for Alec Guinness in *Richard III*, the Stratford Shakespeare Festival's inaugural production. The goal of theatre, Guthrie later explained, was not mere two-dimensional illusion, but fully formed, full-blown ritual.

Guthrie believed not only in the participatory ritual of the open stage, but also in the 'spiritual life' of repertory theatre. As a young man, he had experienced the 'monastic simplicity' of living among fellow actors in a house attached to the Festival Theatre in Cambridge. Now, writing for the *New York Times*, he penned a manifesto for the power of a permanent, professional company performing classic plays, 'masterpieces' such as *Hamlet*, *The Miser*, or *The cherry orchard*, plays that 'demand the collective expression of a group'. For its actors, such a project would 'guarantee each season material security with spiritual adventure'. And, like a religious community, it would build a 'collective life of the company which passes like an emanation from the stage to the audience'. Guthrie acknowledged that such ideas diverged from Broadway commercialism. But a repertory company could offer advantages that outweighed its modest box office receipts: young actors could count on playing a range of roles as they developed their craft; older actors could build 'an extraordinary sense of professional solidarity'; and audiences could enjoy 'at least three or four classical masterpieces' per season, not to mention that 'the public's chief dividend would derive from a higher morale within the profession' of the stage.

These were Guthrie's articles of faith as he, his wife Judith, and producer Oliver Rea travelled the United States, meeting with committees in seven cities who had responded to their proposal for a provincial repertory. They boarded a plane for Boston, where Brandeis University had just received a bequest for a new theatre building, then flew to San Francisco, where they visited theatre owner Louis Lurie in his 'penthouse with Chinese décor', then flew to Chicago, where 'the temperature was zero', then took a helicopter to 'another airport in another part of the forest', where their next flight departed for Minneapolis, a city where 'the temperature was not zero but thirty degrees below zero, and the snow was thrice as deep'. They met the mayor, the governor, the president of the *Star and Tribune* newspaper, and the University of Minnesota's drama professor Frank Whiting, who drove them to their hotel 'in brilliant starlight sparkling upon snow like a child's dream of an iced cake'. They flew from Minneapolis to Cleveland, to Milwaukee, to Detroit, before the Guthries returned to Ireland to spend Christmas at Annaghmakerrig. The travel was a strain. Guthrie succumbed to a sinus infection and then had a heart attack while in hospital, so for three months he was 'no more than a sleeping partner' in the provincial theatre project. By the time he returned to New York, this time by boat (under doctor's orders) via Liverpool and Halifax, Rea and Zeisler had revisited their top three cities to make the choice.

In the end, Minneapolis won out over Milwaukee and Detroit when the T.B. Walker Foundation, originally funded by a lumber tycoon, donated a building site adjacent to its art museum and committed $500,000 toward the project. Guthrie demanded 'artistic control over the interior design' and insisted that the house capacity be restricted to no more than 1,000 audience members, preferably closer to 900. Zeisler and Rea had to 'proceed very cautiously' in persuading the director that this might be 'a little unrealistic business-wise'. In the final design, Guthrie conceded to seating just over 1,400, and the Minnesota Theater Foundation, formed to oversee fundraising and construction, enlisted Minneapolis architect Ralph Rapson to work with the director on bringing his vision to life.

Rapson did his best to follow Guthrie's creed. Working toward the director's vision of 'an intimate actor-audience relationship', he drafted plans that arranged seating for the 'Walker Theater-in-the-round' along a 200-degree angle, nearly encircling a six-sided stage. Thanks to a 'steeply raked orchestra' section, no seat was more than fifty-eight feet from centre stage, and there were no more than fifteen rows on any side. To 'eliminate the distinction' between higher- and lower-paying patrons, the balcony was fused on one side 'into one unbroken slope' with the lower house. Cast members affectionately dubbed this 'The Alpine Climb', but Guthrie preached 'the desirability of making an audience feel that it is a unity' by 'not allowing' balcony seat holders 'to feel that they are only second-class citizens'. Custom-manufactured seats were each upholstered in one of ten colours, a spectrum 'ranging from orange and violet to shades of green, blue and yellow', to heighten the audience's

5.1 Sir Tyrone Guthrie amid Guthrie Theater multicoloured seats, 1963.

anticipation for each performance. The exterior had to be similarly eye-popping. Guthrie, Zeisler and Rea rejected the architect's initial drawings of a glass-fronted façade that looked as anonymous as 'a Howard Johnson motel or a new high school in Scarsdale'. Eventually Rapson designed a two-storey geometric screen to surround the structure, marking it as 'a model' for other repertories, a building that proclaimed 'a theatrical revolution'.

Guthrie intended the new theatre to be 'revolutionary' in more ways than one. Not only would its open stage democratize the ritual of theatre for actors and audience, but the building and the company were controlled entirely by a non-profit organization 'whose purpose is to serve the community'. Instead of profit, the new theatre hoped to generate 'a pattern, a purpose and possibilities new to this continent'. Guthrie was so enrapt in the spirit of egalitarianism that he considered turning down the knighthood offered him in 1960, initially confiding to Oliver Rea, 'Don't think I should take it. The people of Minn. might be put off by grand title.' But of course he enjoyed his investiture, and was 'deeply impressed with the show. As a director, it was a real revelation to me to see how the Queen managed it all. A perfect artist!' Alec Guinness, who had himself been knighted two years before, now addressed his old friend as 'fellow Knight Bachelor' and japed, 'Have you paid £150 for a coat of arms yet?' As both men knew, the title conferred a valuable seal of approval upon performances so evanescent they often seemed 'writ on water'. Though Guthrie said he wanted only to be 'remembered by a few and for a while with warmth and joy', he embraced publicity and shared it with magnanimity. He demurred at being called 'Sir Tyrone', but henceforth addressed all letters home to Judith as 'Lady Guthrie'.

In the autumn of 1962, those letters were mailed from the 'airless + cheerless' Concord Motel in downtown Minneapolis, where Guthrie debated the theatre's design with the architect and attended dinners with 'bank presidents from Bismarck, N. Dakota, and stuff like that', as he wrote to Lady Guthrie, 'who are to be NUCLEI in many a far-flung nook, and arrange for busloads of citizens to bump and grind over dusty miles' to performances of Shakespeare and Chekhov. Jessica Tandy and her husband Hume Cronyn had signed on to anchor the cast – she would play Gertrude in *Hamlet*; he would play Molière's *Miser* – and Guthrie had brought Douglas Campbell with him from the Stratford, Ontario project to be his assistant director in Minneapolis. The two men spent the summer of 1962 auditioning actors in New York. They had decided on *Hamlet* as 'an indication, we hoped, that the audience was being regarded as fully adult' and 'not being condescended to ... merely because Minneapolis has the misfortune to be so far from Broadway'. Along with *The Miser*, it would open the inaugural season, followed a few weeks later by Chekhov's *Three sisters* and *Death of a salesman* by Arthur Miller. Guthrie intended these selections as 'a clear, if implicit, statement of policy; three indisputable masterpieces from three widely different cultures and three widely different epochs; each directed in a markedly different style from the others' alongside a contemporary American play he judged to be 'a very strong contender for eventual classical status'.

They had no trouble fielding a cast. As Guthrie recounted, 'Literally hundreds of actors and actresses applied, amongst them many whose names are well known'. He and Campbell interviewed each hopeful candidate before auditioning them onstage 'so that we could form some opinion about their power of projection', crucial for a theatre in the round. Seeking a Hamlet with 'intelligence, wit and humour', they decided on young George Grizzard, then playing Nick in the original cast of *Who's afraid of Virginia Woolf?* by Edward Albee. To this day, it is unclear exactly how and when Grizzard came to Guthrie to audition: did he break his contract with *Virginia Woolf*, or was he cast as Hamlet before it premiered? In Guthrie's account, the actor contacted him 'uninvited', which was a 'surprise' since he was still appearing nightly on Broadway. Forty years later, Grizzard's *New York Times* obituary said he 'stunned his associates' in the Albee play 'by announcing that he was leaving to go to Minneapolis' – but the paper soon published a correction, stating Grizzard's 'departure was expected' because he had a contract with Guthrie before *Woolf* opened. Whatever the circumstances, Guthrie and Campbell were charmed by the actor. 'He was small, lithe, elegantly put together, obviously rhythmic', which was key. 'He could suggest a prince. He would obviously give his eye teeth to have a shot at Hamlet.' They filled out the rest of the cast, including African American actor Graham Brown as Horatio and young Ellen Geer as Ophelia. After a few weeks in Minneapolis, where, as he wrote to Lady Guthrie, 'The building begins to look exciting', the director returned to Annaghmakerrig for Christmas and invited Brian Friel to visit him at home.

Brian was hoping for luck in the new year. *The saucer of larks* had sold 1,584 copies in the US, and was slated for publication in the United Kingdom. Edna O'Brien sent a fan letter, calling the stories 'deft, skilfully written, funny and quite often breathlessly sad', and she praised Brian's creation of 'a world as real and poignant as Chekhov or Camus'. But Doubleday sent statements showing an unearned balance against the author's advance, and zero royalties. Brian continued to write weekly columns for the *Irish Press*, and his agent sold 'Ginger Hero' – the cockfighting story Angell had rejected – to the *Saturday Evening Post*. He broadcast a Christmas Eve story on the Northern Ireland Home Service, for which the BBC paid him £5 5s. All the while, as he told his *Irish Press* readers, his daughters, aged seven and five – like 'two inexorable dwarfs' – wrote secret requests to Santa that he feared might not match the 'cheap' plastic roller skates and 'reduced' price scooter he and Anne had bought them as presents.

Into this uncertainty Tony Guthrie's invitation landed like a lightning bolt. Brian drove to Monaghan in the week between Christmas and New Year 1963, where Guthrie 'charmed my heart away immediately we met'. The 'six-foot-five-inch man who hops easily from Greek tragedy to West End comedy' welcomed Brian's enthusiasm for theatre and the United States, and together, he and the young playwright hatched a plan. As Brian eagerly reported to Roger Angell,

> Very briefly the idea is to go to Minneapolis, work there, and at the same time learn the craft of the theatre there at the new Tyrone Guthrie theatre. Sir Tyrone – I was with him last week at his home in Co. Monaghan – is hopeful that he can fix up a job for me; and if that can be arranged I will then be able to watch him at work in his theatre. If the job falls through (it is on some Minneapolis newspaper) then the whole scheme will be upset. If it does I will be very disappointed, and so will Anne & the children. We are all looking forward to seeing something of the USA.

The newspaper job failed to materialize, but Brian and Anne pressed forward nonetheless. As Anne recently recalled, 'We had no income. All our finances went into this trip. We were foolish, probably. Young.' *The blind mice* opened in the Eblana below Busáras in February, and *The saucer of larks* made its UK début that same month. For its publication, Brian received a £100 advance. Months later, after the book sold 1,267 copies in Britain and the colonies, he received a royalty cheque for the total of 15s. 9d., the equivalent of £20 or so today.

The trip to Minneapolis required a leap of faith for the entire family, as Brian explained to Angell after Guthrie's attempt to find him work at the Minneapolis *Star and Tribune* came up empty. 'I am not going out to a job (in the Tyrone Guthrie Theatre my standing will be less than menial – an unpaid hanger on!) and I will have to live somehow by writing.' Would the terms of his first reading agreement still stand if he were able 'to get myself some sort of American correspondent job for, say, *The Observer* or *The Guardian*?' Angell assured him they would. Ten days later, Brian wrote again: 'there are a million complications at this end: no visa as yet; my wife is expecting; one of the children is sick etc. etc.' The trip was going forward regardless. 'We are all madly excited and not a little nervous and quite certain we are totally reckless and improvident.' Brian invited Angell to stay in their vacant Marlborough Street house if he ventured to Ireland over the summer.

Rehearsals at the Guthrie Theater were due to start March 11th, and Brian was determined to watch them. Cast members found living quarters in 'not-too-elegant apartments and rooming houses' around Minneapolis, and Sir Tyrone and Lady Guthrie rented a flat at the Oak Grove Apartment Hotel near the Walker Art Center and its adjacent theatre, still under construction. The Guthries moved in at the start of February; George Grizzard arrived later that month to begin pre-rehearsal discussions and training for his role as Hamlet. Each morning, Grizzard went to Guthrie's apartment, where he and the director read through the play together and parsed 'each scene, each speech, each sentence' to bring their interpretations of the script into accord. Guthrie insisted that actors should hone their vocal techniques and physical movements, so each afternoon, Grizzard fenced with Douglas Campbell, who choreographed the play's final duel in exacting detail. Campbell took the lead on directing the company's second opening production, *The Miser*, which rehearsed on alternate days with *Hamlet*. Since the theatre was not yet completed, the First Unitarian Society, a short walk up an icy hill behind the building site, loaned its basement as a rehearsal hall.

On 26 March 1963, Brian packed his typewriter, his newly issued visa, passport and chest X-ray, and, with the word 'IMMIGRANT' stamped on his ticket, boarded a plane for New York while Anne, two months pregnant, stayed in Derry to nurse their younger daughter Mary through the chicken pox. Brian made the most of a few days in Manhattan, sightseeing at Rockefeller Center and the United Nations, and at long last getting the chance to 'meet those people who correspond with me'. Top of the list was Roger Angell, who took Brian to dinner and introduced him to Carol Rogge, a fellow *New Yorker* staff member soon to become Angell's wife.

Brian booked his next air ticket at a New York travel agency and flew to Minneapolis, through 'lots and lots of thunderstorms', to observe Tyrone Guthrie at work. He brought with him a script in progress called 'The ballad of Ballybeg', which he had been struggling to write, as he told the *Belfast Telegraph* before departure. 'I don't know whether this one will ever be completed. I've been working at it for six months and so far my characters aren't moving.' He still held an ambition to write the 'great Irish play', one that would appeal to a broad audience, 'one where the author can talk so truthfully and accurately about people in his own neighbourhood and make it so that these folk could be living in Omagh, Omaha or Omansk'. He was toying with the idea of internal monologue, as in his *Irish Press* column on 'Brian Friel's secret thoughts' at a meeting of the anti-war Peace Pledge Union in Derry. 'Drinks on the house? And tea later? Very nice! Very, very nice! No, don't clap, you fool! No one else is clapping! And stop grinning! Sit up straight in your chair and let yourself be seen in case that man who is taking the orders should miss you. That's it.' He also brought the taxi driver story Angell had rejected, and notes for a new one he hoped Angell would like. On his own in Minneapolis, 'mentally marking time' until Anne and the children would join him, Brian moved into the Oak Grove Apartment Hotel, where the Guthries were already in residence, a sedate brick building with a fountain in its foyer. Each day he walked half a mile along Loring Park, past the city's Episcopal cathedral and its Catholic basilica, to observe rehearsals for opening night.

Guthrie's work was well under way. The cast had rehearsed enough of *Hamlet* to do a run-through of Acts III and IV a few days after Brian arrived, and it was evident that the actors had caught 'the feeling of creative joy' that marked Guthrie's 'unabashed delight in working on a scene'. Rehearsals started at noon and continued late into the night, partly because of the 'hammers banging and painters whistling' during the day as the stage and seats were readied for their début in early May. At night the company could try out the theatre's numerous tunnels and trap doors, designed by Guthrie and Moiseiwitsch to allow for inventive staging of scenes both major and minor. Brian watched, for example, when 'Guthrie started experimenting with the comic possibilities of the pit' for the graveyard scene in Act V, as the First Gravedigger sang unseen and one hand, then two, then four playfully threw objects from the plot newly opened for Ophelia. Guthrie 'seemed to enjoy this game, like a kid with a new toy', noted Alfred Rossi, who played Rosencrantz. 'So did the actors.'

Horseplay, physicality and humour were hallmarks of a Guthrie production, as were touches of modernity even in Shakespearean drama. In his *Hamlet*, actors stood under wet umbrellas for Ophelia's funeral and carried electric torches to hunt Hamlet through Elsinore after he murdered Polonius. 'New work must have something interesting, not necessarily solemn, to say and must say it in theatrical terms', Guthrie explained. 'I was, and still am, a sucker for jokes and horseplay, and for great moments, however corny'. He opposed the Method school of acting and had little patience for psychologizing: when the actor playing Laertes asked why his character would be motivated to surrender a weapon, Guthrie told him, 'Because it says so in the script.' Rossi wrote in his journal that Guthrie aimed 'to make absolutely clear what is going on, chiefly by vocal and physical means, and, in so doing, to *show* the play to the audience'.

Guthrie knew that all audiences, but especially provincial audiences, came to theatre 'to participate in lavish and luxurious goings-on', a phrase that stuck with Brian. The director insisted that actors learn the vocal and physical techniques of classical acting, 'how to manage great rhetorical speeches and how to swish about effectively and without embarrassment in the finery of other epochs', as only the great playwrights – Shakespeare, Molière, Chekhov – could demand. Guthrie understood that 'people who normally have to be frugal' wanted the 'price of their ticket' to buy them 'something largely, loudly, unashamedly luxurious'. And they wanted not just to see it, he wrote, but to 'participate' and share in the ritual.

Brian wanted to share in it, too. The day after he arrived in Minneapolis, he pitched an idea to Angell: 'It occurred to me, too, that you might be interested in a Profile of Tyrone Guthrie. What do you think? I understand that doing a Profile is practically a life's work; and whether I would be competent to write it, even after a life's work, is another matter. But if you think the idea is possible, let me know.' Angell instead helped Brian place a profile in *Holiday* magazine, where he had worked before joining the *New Yorker*. It ran under the title 'The giant of Monaghan', playing on Guthrie's towering height, outsized personality, and his 'castle', Annaghmakerrig, a 'huge rambling house overlooking a lake' in remote rural Ireland – a nod to readers seeking travel destinations in *Holiday*'s pages, where the article followed an ad by the Irish Tourist Board. Brian quoted liberally from Guthrie's autobiography *A life in the theatre* throughout his description of the director who 'comes to rehearsal usually in shirt, baggy flannels and navy tennis shoes' and 'charmed' all his actors with his 'baffling combination of English reserve, Irish exuberance and Scottish astuteness'. As Brian observed, 'there is not one Guthrie but half a dozen or more Guthries', an idea that continued to preoccupy him as he brainstormed his still evolving 'Ballad of Ballybeg'.

Meanwhile Brian continued to revise 'Everything neat and tidy', his story about the Derry taximan accompanying his mother-in-law to shock treatments. Within a week of arriving in Minneapolis, he mailed Angell a revision with an accompanying note that 'What you wanted was right, I know, and I hope I have got close to it this time. I have a great fault of understanding – I think that's what damaged the story originally.' Unfortunately, Angell's response followed a familiar pattern. The revision, he wrote, 'does not strike us as being much of an improvement over the first'. Brian had followed his editor's suggestions to the letter, so much so that 'This version seems dogged and unimaginative.' Angell's advice was the same as in the past. 'I hope you will put it aside again, write another story (if you have time), and then come back to it fresh in a few weeks and write an entirely new version, concentrating on mood and feeling and trying to let most of the information come out in a less rigid fashion.' Moreover, Angell suggested, 'there may be too many scenes now between Johnny and the old lady. Perhaps if you could cut these down to two or, at the most three scenes between them', the story would flow more smoothly. Despite such prescriptive advice, the editor stressed that 'This must be your own story, and if you can write a wholly new version you may find some entirely new scenes and events that will appear and demand inclusion.' Brian, alone in Minneapolis, where 'The weather has me hopelessly confused – one day roasting hot, the next snow', lamented, 'It's always the same with a rewrite: I know exactly what you're getting at; I have the best will in the world to do it; but nothing moves for me.' He was writing a new story about a police sergeant and an unexploded mine on an Irish beach, based on an incident at Ballymanus, near Brian's Kincasslagh cottage, that killed eighteen young men during the Second World War. He assured Angell in the meantime that 'I'll leave "Everything Neat & Tidy" aside and pray that God enlighten me!'

After Easter, Brian returned to New York for a few days to greet Anne and Paddy and Mary, who had recovered from chicken pox, and bring them out to Minneapolis. As the weather warmed, they settled into a routine that Brian described to Angell as 'a very quiet life here: Rise about 10:00 AM; go to the theatre; work in the afternoon (if I can persuade Anne & the children to go out & give me peace); read at night.' At the theatre, Guthrie and company opened each rehearsal with recitation of Psalm 118, 'This is the day which the Lord hath made; we will rejoice and be glad in it.' Brian sat 'in the gloom of the auditorium' and watched as Guthrie, with infectious energy, conducted the men and women to deliver alternating lines. 'The company is enthused, and each rehearsal is a vibrant, exciting adventure, never dull for an instant', actor Rossi wrote in his journal. Rehearsals continued six days a week, with Mondays off, and daily practice in fencing and dancing. 'I attend dutifully', Brian confided to Angell. 'Sometimes I'm sure I'm wasting my time, other times I convince myself I'm "absorbing" deeply. The trouble is that I don't know what I'm looking for (I had a nice little formula that covered the whole confused expedition before I left home) but I know for sure that I'm very glad I came.'

On 5 May 1963, the Minnesota Theatre Company recited Psalm 118 for its dedication service, 'a singularly inspiring event' led by a Lutheran minister, Jewish rabbi and Catholic priest, with hymns sung by a Lutheran choir, accompanied by the theatre's resident trumpeters and tympanist. A *Life* magazine photographer shot 'a couple of hundred photos' of the cast in Moiseiwitsch's modern costumes. He wanted to pose Jessica Tandy as Gertrude in her ivory wedding dress among the theatre's multicoloured seats, but Guthrie objected, arguing, 'The gown was made to look regal, and Jessie to be regal in it. Sitting like that would make her look dumpy.' The following day, *Hamlet* previewed to an invited audience of local hospital staff, cab drivers, and the theatre construction crew, and Rossi and his fellow actors performed with 'a great feeling of pride and *esprit de corps*' which 'has built all during the week' of final rehearsals. They took their bows before an 'an emotional audience that wanted to applaud as appreciatively as possible for this realization of a magnificent dream'. It was a feeling Brian would no doubt remember later, when he and Stephen Rea launched the Field Day Theatre Company in the Guildhall, Derry, in September 1980, not long after it had been bombed a second time by the Provisional IRA.

Meanwhile, Brian struggled to revise his short stories, including his 'new one', he told Angell, 'that should be lovely if only I could catch it'. The editor sent reassuring letters to Minneapolis.

> I do not share your glooms and despairs about your limitations as a writer. I think, as I said, that you are only going through a complex process of self-discovery that is bound to occur when a writer has completed a first group of stories he finds within himself and that he writes mostly by instinct and out of sheer exuberance. I think you are now in the next phase, when writing is more calculated and more intelligent, and depends more on one's art. In other words, you are becoming a professional and you are learning the hazards and difficulties of your profession. I am quite certain that in the long run this knowledge will lead to greater self-confidence and to many fine stories.

But would they be stories for page or stage? As Brian worked on the unexploded mine story, he confided to Angell that 'it's as stolid as dough, and I'm getting it down painfully sentence by sentence, and I have a feeling I've lost it long ago. At the same time I think that all I need is one afternoon of joy and – hey presto! – there it would be'. He received Angell's letters, and proofs of the comic casual 'Downstairs no upstairs', with gratitude if not joy. 'I only hope that you are right, that I am moving into another phase. If I am, all I can say about it is that it is a hell of an unpleasant one.'

Theatrical events gave the writer a welcome diversion. *Hamlet* opened on 7 May 1963, and according to Guthrie, 'Everyone who was Anyone in the Twin Cities was present in full regalia' as were 'hordes of newsmen and women with their satellite photographers'. The weather was unseasonably hot for Minneapolis, and Guthrie began to regret presenting Shakespeare's script mostly uncut, with a running length of nearly four hours. A few minutes into the action, the director watched, dismayed, as 'Society Ladies began fidgeting with their scarves and admiring their own rings and necklaces' while the intricacies of the play unfolded. 'At this point', he later wrote, 'I realised with painful clarity just what a risk we had taken by opening with *Hamlet.*' The actors were nervous, as were the audience, and the presence of so many journalists – critics as well as gossip columnists – skewed the reactions of most in the house. 'It was miserable', Guthrie admitted, 'but then, Openings, or any way, Openings of important and difficult plays, which demand something more than that the audience be excited or amused, always are miserable. I guess the misery must be endured in order to achieve the Sense of Occasion.'

Still, the audience gave a standing ovation, 'more for the entire venture' as actor Rossi recalled, 'than for the production or any one actor's performance'. Undaunted, the company premiered *The Miser* the next night, then turned to rehearsals for Chekhov's *Three sisters*, which would open in June with Jessica Tandy as eldest sister Olga. Brian now saw the process from its beginning, as Guthrie launched his cast into action. For first rehearsals, there were 'no comments from Guthrie about the production, no discussion of the play with anyone, no reading of the play; in fact, no comments, discussion, or reading of the first scene of the play, which was put on its feet immediately'. Guthrie was confident that Chekhov would resonate with Minneapolis audiences, and he worked to emphasize the playwright's 'humour, which is never expressed in wisecracks or gags, but springs solely out of character and is the complement of pathos'. On the other hand, pathos could not be allowed to take over. In the performance of tragedy, Guthrie argued, dramatists 'must aim higher than at an audience's susceptibility' to raw emotion. 'The full impact of great tragedy is not immediate; it takes effect slowly. It lies in wait on the fringe of dreams. It wakes one with a start in the small hours.' He believed that Chekhov, as a writer, had long been 'ahead of his time': far from being 'a difficult, oblique author who said one thing and meant another', whose characters seemed almost 'schizoid' because they appeared 'at one moment plunged in abysses of "Russian gloom" and, at the next, carrying on with an extravagant gaiety', he was now a playwright whose complex characters and understated inner conflicts spoke to contemporary audiences.

Brian was still striving to reach his own audience. He sold his self-deprecating 'American diary' columns to the *Irish Press* and the Chicago Catholic magazine *The Critic*, generating a bit of necessary income as he described 'the adventures and bafflements of a frightened, over-sensitive visitor to the United States' for the amusement of both Irish and American readers. But Roger Angell balked at his description of a beleaguered police sergeant and the mine explosion that killed 'The flower of Kiltymore', young men whose loss gave Brian a title for the story he had been writing all spring. 'I am especially grieved at this rejection', Angell wrote, 'because I know the special effort and high hopes you have put into the story'. Even though the writing was 'first rate', the sergeant's ultimate calm 'just strikes us as a psychological fabrication'. As much as he wanted to send better news, in the end, the editor wrote, 'I'm afraid there's just no hope and we must reject it'. He warned against submitting a revision, and Brian, breaking his pattern of relentless rewrites, did not attempt one.

That same week, good news arrived: the Arts Council of Ireland awarded Brian the Macaulay Fellowship, a national prize of £1,000, funded by a former ambassador. It was a grant for 'young Irish writers, painters, sculptors and composers', and Brian was the first to win it for playwriting. He had published more widely – and far more profitably – in fiction, but, as his publisher James MacGibbon prophetically observed, 'I am a little sorry that this wonderful fillip you have had for writing plays may keep you away from novels and short stories for some time to come!'

The fellowship also gave Brian needed funds to return home. For Anne, at five months pregnant, Minnesota's summer weather was 'Hell!' as Brian described it, '86° at the moment & very humid'. They departed the day before *Three sisters* opened, spent ten days in New York, then boarded a ship from Montreal at the end of June. As a family, they had experienced so many new things – 'squirrels, escalators, sherbet, radishes, apartment living' – that one of the girls declared that she 'doesn't want to go home!' Brian even considered staying for a job at *Holiday* magazine, but Angell counselled him that the wages offered wouldn't support a growing family in New York City. Instead, he and Anne sailed for Derry, their two little daughters in tow, a new baby expected in the autumn. In Brian's suitcase were notes for his new script, an emigration story set in fictional Ballybeg, of a young man who – like Chekhov – seemed to show a split personality, and – like Hamlet – felt desperately loyal to his father, but struggled to be true to himself.

CHAPTER 6

Waiting in the wings, 1963–4

ON THE DAY Brian and his family embarked from Montreal to return to Ireland, John F. Kennedy stood before the lord mayor at Dublin Castle to accept the Freedom of the City. During Kennedy's four-day visit to his ancestral homeland, well-wishers crowded the streets of Wexford, Cork, Galway and Limerick for a glimpse of the youthful president in his convertible Cadillac, American flags fluttering from its fenders. Granted honorary degrees by UCD and Trinity, Kennedy gamely promised to 'cheer for one and pray for the other' if ever the two universities met on a Gaelic football pitch. His glamour and vigour raised Ireland's profile on the international stage as reporters and photographers followed his roving tour of the country, a sidebar after his visit to Europe and impassioned speech against the Berlin Wall. Kennedy's statement 'Ich bin ein Berliner' would be etched into history, but in the summer of 1963, his address to Dáil Éireann resounded across Ireland. 'This has never been a rich or powerful country and yet, since the earliest times, its influence on the world has been both rich and powerful. No larger nation did more to keep Christianity and Western culture alive in their darkest centuries. No larger nation did more to spark the cause of independence in America and around the world. And no larger nation has ever provided the world with more literary and artistic genius.'

At home on the streets of Derry, everyone Brian met assumed that he had made his mark on America with his own artistic genius. His final column for the *Irish Press* bemoaned the stereotypes that greeted him as a so-called returned Yank. 'It is useless to protest, as I have been doing, that I made no millions out there, not even a cent, that I am currently a few degrees above need, that I enjoyed myself immensely. No-one believes me. I must have a stack stuck under the mattress, or else I was brought home, steerage, on my poor mother's hen-money.' He was not the typical emigrant, but it was true that his travels had taught him the bittersweet taste of homesickness, 'the most treacherous and most unpredictable of emotions', every exile's price to pay in the voyage to the New World. In the few weeks Brian had spent on his own in lonely hotel rooms, first in New York and then Minneapolis, he learned to 'side-step' the pain of solitude by 'busying myself in thoroughly practical jobs, like washing clothes or boiling potatoes in the coffee percolator'. But it ambushed him one night in Manhattan, as he recounted to *Irish Press* readers. 'I didn't cry. I didn't want to take the next bus out to Idlewild and the first plane home. But for the whole of an evening I was so wretched with homesickness that I just lay in bed and stared at the ceiling. No washing; no cooking; just wallowing in self-pity.'

He would tap these emotions as he finished his play about Gar O'Donnell's last night at home before emigrating to a hotel job in Philadelphia. But first there was work to be done. Ronnie Mason had visited New York as well, and had met Tony Guthrie there while the director took a break from Minneapolis. While the BBC hesitated over a proposed television version of *The enemy within*, they said yes to a radio broadcast, which first aired in Northern Ireland while Brian and his family were still in Minnesota. Now Mason wanted to broadcast *The blind mice*, and he paid Brian to write the radio adaptation as the Friel family settled back into their Marlborough Street house. Brian and Anne invited Mason to Derry for the Twelfth of July – he didn't come – and then they took their annual holidays in Kincasslagh, encouraging Mason to join them at their cottage, although, as Brian warned, 'If you can make it down here all I can guarantee is a welcome: incidentals like food & weather are unpredictable'.

Brian was riding a wave of confidence after publishing *The saucer of larks* and winning the Macaulay Fellowship, and he was 'still on a Guthrie high' after his time with the great director. As Anne packed the girls' clothes for their summer holidays, Brian gathered the onionskin notes he had typed and handwritten in Minneapolis and tucked them into a manila envelope so he could continue drafting his new play. Ever a maths teacher, he had listed scene ideas using Greek-lettered variables – $\alpha, \beta, \gamma, \delta$ – and on the outside of the envelope, he wrote himself a reminder: '1. There must be reactions of <u>hearty</u> (from the heart & belly) laughter. 2. There must be sadness – people must cry for grief.' He borrowed these gut-level extremes from Guthrie himself, whose 'directing is aimed primarily at the heart and the belly, not the brain', as Brian had written for *Holiday*. Guthrie didn't believe in 'Little journalistic plays' which, he said, 'generate a little and limited acting style'. Installed in the Kincasslagh cottage, writing with pencil in a feint-ruled notebook, Brian shed the bitter social commentary of *The blind mice*, *To this hard house* and *A sort of freedom*, and instead gave free rein to playfulness and humour, tools he had sharpened over six years of his wry columns for the *Irish Times* and *Irish Press*, and occasional 'casuals' for the *New Yorker*.

Brian layered the script with physical comedy, whose communicative power he had observed on the rehearsal stage in Minneapolis. As the curtain rises, Gar O'Donnell 'marches' onstage, so 'ecstatic with joy and excitement' at the prospect of leaving for America that he sweeps Madge, the family housekeeper, into his arms and swings her about the kitchen in their Donegal home. Moments later, alone in his bedroom, he mimes a jet pilot who 'nosedives, engines screaming, machine guns stuttering', then swiftly transforms into a footballer taking a free kick using his bundled shopcoat as a ball, then stands at military attention, saluting an imaginary judge who cross-examines him about 'leaving the country of your birth, the land of the curlew and the snipe, the Aran sweater and the Irish Sweepstakes'. Brian noted that Gar 'goes through all sorts of contortions, gyrations of face & body: winking & squinting: cocking snooks; listening at keyholes. Dancing. Conducting. Goose-stepping. Making mad insane eyes. OR if he is in company & cannot speak his mind his Alter Ego does these things for him.' Every internal emotion has an external manifestation, for just as Guthrie had taught his actors, the audience needs to experience the play by vocal and physical means.

From Guthrie, Brian had also learned to take a light touch to tragedy. In the final rehearsal for *Hamlet* the director coached Graham Brown, who played Horatio, 'Don't go for the easy tear and pathos' in the play's closing speech. Tragedy was more than sentimentality, and wordless grief could crack a noble heart. Traces of the bitterness that tinged Brian's radio plays lingered – flaring, for example, when Gar lashes out in his final meeting with his former sweetheart Katie Doogan, now Mrs Doctor Francis King: 'All this bloody yap about father and son and all this sentimental rubbish about "homeland" and "birthplace" – yap! Bloody yap! Impermanence – anonymity – that's what I'm looking for; a vast restless place that doesn't give a damn about the past. To hell with Ballybeg, that's what I say!' But for most of the script, Gar's sense of loss is unstated, and he deflects his loneliness into antics and jokes. As Brian explained, 'I have heightened the comic element because the situation is essentially tragic'.

At the heart of that tragedy lies the gap between Gar and his father, Sean Bernard (S.B.) O'Donnell, a man of few words and fewer emotions, nicknamed 'Screwballs' by his son just as pupils called Master Friel 'Scobie' out of earshot. Father and son work side by side in the shop attached to their house, but they sit down to dinner in near silence at the end of Gar's last day at home. Brian asserted that 'This is not another "American wake" story' but 'a story about growing-up, and the inarticulate love between a son and his father' on a night that represents 'the distillation of all his boyhood and growing-up and young manhood'. The two men tread well-worn paths through every conversation: Gar anticipates every word his father will speak and reflexively assumes 'a surly, taciturn gruffness', according to the stage directions. 'He always behaves this way when he is in his father's company.' And yet Gar wishes Screwballs would 'make one unpredictable remark' or 'Say, "Gar, you bugger you, why don't you stick it out here with me for it's not such a bad aul' bugger of a place."' In a line deleted from the final script – perhaps too sentimental, by Guthrie's measure – Gar promises, 'Say it, and I'll stay! I'll stay!'

Gaps between father and son, between the spoken and unspoken, are mirrored by gaps between memory and reality, just as in Brian's short story 'Among the ruins', when a father revisits his abandoned childhood home and wonders whether his young son will remember the games he plays. In a 'Self-portrait' for BBC Northern Ireland radio a few years later, Brian recounted a similarly vivid 'moment of happiness caught in an album', a memory of walking with his father, singing, fishing rods over their shoulders after a rainy day on a Donegal lake. But 'The fact is a fiction', Brian revealed, because the road he remembers borders no lake, and the walk could not have happened. 'For some reason the mind has shuffled the pieces of verifiable truth and composed a truth of its own.' Gar, too, harbours a truth of his own, a memory of fishing with his father amid a rain shower that prompted them to share a coat, a hat, and a few bars of a song, sung by Screwballs because 'between us at that moment there was this great happiness, this great joy – you must have felt it too – although nothing was being said – just the two of us fishing on a lake on a showery day – and young as I was I felt, I knew, that this was precious, and your hat was soft on the top of my ears – I can feel it – and I shrank down into your coat – and then, for no reason at all except that you were happy too, you began to sing'. The scene recalls the wayward grandfather's shared coat in 'My true kinsman' as well. But the song, and the moment, are nothing his father remembers when Gar finds the courage to ask him in their final conversation. As it turns out, Screwballs has his own memory: Gar in a sailor suit, climbing behind the shop counter and refusing to leave for school because 'I'm going into my Daddy's business' – and this, too, is his memory alone. Madge the housekeeper knows 'He never had a sailor suit', and in an early draft, Brian asked of these private memories, 'did both of you imagine them?'

In the truest sense, it didn't matter. Imagined or not, the memories are real, and they guide Gar and his father, and Madge, and all the other characters who enter Gar's thoughts the night before he leaves for America. *The ballad of Ballybeg* – renamed *Philadelphia, here I come!* once Brian began drafting scenes in his Kincasslagh cottage – stages ideas that Brian had delved for years in his fiction and newspaper columns. He originally planned Gar's fishing memory as a physical tableau, acted by a boy and man with their backs to the audience, seated in an onstage boat, but such technically challenging props were not needed to illustrate the power of the image in Gar's mind. Brian had written in the *Irish Press* 'that the ideal lake, the lake you dream about, doesn't exist in Donegal or in Ireland or anywhere on the face of this globe; and that no matter what lake you fish you will always imagine that the one beyond the next hill would be much better.' Whether this intentionally echoed de Valera's speech extolling 'The ideal Ireland that we would have, the Ireland that we dreamed of', it undeniably speaks to the power of memory to inspire or mislead, to fire our ambitions or stoke our impossible dreams.

Before he settled on Philadelphia for Gar O'Donnell's destination – before he even determined that Gar was an only child, or that his mother was dead – Brian knew he wanted both halves of Gar's inner and outer consciousness in full view on stage. The divide between public and private had long fascinated him, and psychological drama had long preoccupied his writing. In his radio play *The world of Johnny del Pinto*, Brian attempted 'to illustrate the private world of a child' through anaesthesia dreams. In *The enemy within*, St Columba struggled with his inner conflicts while bounding across the stage or falling to his knees. In *The blind mice*, Father Chris, the broken priest, sat static on stage, and it was only through radio sound effects of Chinese interrogators and distant footfalls that Brian would manage to convey his torture in isolation. In his new play, Brian wanted to show 'the private man in each of us', which had become an 'obsession', as he had told Roger Angell in 1961. He later cited Eugene O'Neill's *Strange interlude* as a model in its use of 'lengthy asides' to reveal each character's inner thoughts. But he may also have gained inspiration from an experimental radio comedy – *The disagreeable oyster* by prolific BBC playwright Giles Cooper, first broadcast on the Third Programme in August 1957, as Brian was studying the art of radio drama, and re-broadcast for a tribute series to Cooper in October 1962, the week after *The enemy within* played at St Columb's Hall in Derry.

The disagreeable oyster used two actors' voices to portray the inner and outer personae of mild-mannered accountant Mervyn Bundy, who takes advantage of a failed business trip to splash out of his humdrum existence. Bundy hasn't slept away from home in twenty-two years, but his inner voice goads him into splurging on a hotel, pub, and even a prostitute (until Bundy loses his nerve) by repeating, in rhythm with the railroad car that carries him, 'I've got thirty-four pounds! Thirty-four pounds! Thirty-four pounds!' as Bundy grows ever distant from his wife and home. His inner voice, Bundy Minor, speaks of 'Passionate Bundy! Crammed to the gorge with primeval urges! I'm a gorilla! I snort and paw the ground!' while his outward persona trembles before the women he meets at a late-night café. When Bundy signs a hotel register, he recites his dreary details – 'Mervyn Bundy, British, of 44 Prunella Road, Haddington, London'– upon which Bundy Minor expands: 'England, Europe, the Western Hemisphere, the world, the solar system, the universe ... space!' After Bundy is somehow stripped of his clothes, but before he stumbles into a private nudist colony, he studies the houses that surround him, wondering, 'Is it like this at home? Does my house crouch in the half-dark?' allowing Bundy Minor to extend the question: 'As though it had eaten me in the night and was now digesting?'

Brian followed a pattern similar to Cooper's in plotting the contrasts between Gar O'Donnell and his 'Alter Ego'. In his notes he drew two columns.

1. Gar is an individual of two people: the private Gar & the public Gar: Gar & his Alter Ego.

GAR	Alter Ego.
Is morose to his father.	Loves the father.
Silent with his mother } Dead?	" " "
Quiet	Garrulous.
Obedient.	Riotous.
A 'good son'.	A Rebel.
Considerate.	Selfish.
Chaste.	Lewd.
Humble.	Proud.
Dull.	Quite mad.
Loves his country ⎱	⎰ Loves his country.
Hates his country ⎰	⎱ Hates his country.

He must primarily be himself, highly individual, but he is also <u>THE IRISHMAN</u> who appears to conform – and does – but who leaves.

Each of Gar's two selves was to be played by a separate actor. In the script, they are labelled 'Public Gar' and 'Private Gar', or in shorthand, 'Public' and 'Private'. Private is visible only to the audience, though he can be heard by Public; as Brian's notes to the published script point out, Public Gar 'never sees him and never looks at him. One cannot look at one's Alter Ego.' The rest of the characters onstage are unaware of Private Gar's existence.

The division transforms Gar's near-silent dinner with his father into a comedic illustration of the repression and routine that characterize their life together. In this scene, Gar utters only one word aloud ('Aye') while his Alter Ego keeps up an interior monologue of steady chatter.

> PRIVATE And now for our nightly lesson in the English language. Repeat slowly after me: another day over.
> S.B. Another day over.
> PRIVATE Good. Next phrase: I suppose we can't complain.
> S.B. I suppose we can't complain.
> PRIVATE Not bad. Now for a little free conversation. But no obscenities, Father dear; the child is only twenty-five.
> S.B. *eats in silence. Pause.*
> Well, come on, come on! Where's that old rapier wit of yours, the toast of the Ballybeg coffee houses?
> S.B. Did you set the rat-trap in the store?
> PUBLIC Aye.
> PRIVATE (*Hysterically*) Isn't he a riot! Oh my God, that father of yours just kills me!

The split between Private and Public allows Gar's inner self to sneer at memories of his lost romance with Katie Doogan, whose bourgeois parents represent 'the new Irish ... moneyed, seekers' in Brian's notes, as they urge her to marry a medical student instead of Gar.

> PUBLIC (*Softly*) Kate ... sweet Katie Doogan ... my darling Kathy Doogan ...
> PRIVATE (*In the same soft tone*) Aul' bitch. (*Loudly*) Rotten aul' snobby bitch! Just like her stinking rotten father and mother – a bugger and a buggeress – a buggeroo and a buggerette!

Brian's notes to himself, typed, annotated, underlined, gave constant reminders to 'Keep the humour high. <u>Keep it vulgar, because vulgarity keeps sadness at bay.</u> Everybody is confused, those who stay behind, he who goes.'

The play quickly took shape around each character's repressed desires. In Brian's initial notes, Gar is heading for a hotel in Chicago or California, and while he believes himself a 'late' child of his mother, who was twenty years younger than his father, he initially had an older brother who died, and two older sisters, already married and out of the house. Early in the writing process, Brian stripped these away, distilling Gar's family to himself, his widower father, and Madge. Brian wrote it out for himself in block letters:

EVERYBODY
WANTS
SOMETHING

TRIES TO STATE IT.

CAN'T.

Gar's father wants his son to inherit his shop; Madge wants to marry Gar's father and has been waiting twenty years for his proposal; Gar's friends want women; his American aunt Lizzy wants a sense of home; his old teacher wants to be treated with respect; his lost girlfriend still wants Gar; and Gar wants, Brian wondered, 'what? peace? escape?' While Gar and his alter ego worked on finding an answer, the audience was to be volleyed between laughter and tears. The play, as Brian envisioned it, was 'a comedy besieged by inevitable tragedy'.

Brian knew from the start that the Private / Public division would be a challenge to stage. In his notes, he wondered 'how to establish the two characters' for the audience: 'Could the young Gar be identified by a cobeen, an Australian cap, something bizarre – otherwise there will be confusion'. In his first draft, he brainstormed potential introductions for the Private / Public dichotomy, including three possible prologues which were eventually discarded. In each, Private Gar addresses the audience alone, either noting that his character has been omitted from the program, or pointing out that there are two actors listed for the role of Gar O'Donnell, or introducing the set and cast of characters. Meanwhile Public Gar is offstage, salting pollock in his father's shop, as Private explains, 'I have no physical identity of my own … I don't think anyone in this village knows that I exist – they see the Public Gar and they imagine that what they see is all there is.' And yet, he argues, 'I am really the part of him that matters most … I must get back to him because I am all he has'. Despite the inevitable difficulties of staging, Brian held fast to the dual-personality premise, convinced that on the night before Gar's departure for America, 'a time is reached when he is beaten to a stop – You can't keep up this <u>private</u> façade endlessly.'

Initially, to mirror the prologue, Brian bookended the play with an epilogue, bringing all the characters onstage to look skyward as Public and Private Gar board the airplane to America. While Public sits with a drink in one hand and the other covering his eyes, a medley of music from previous scenes fades, and Private carries on a monologue assembled from lines spoken by others during Gar's preparations for departure. Private then launches into Gar's internal plans for his first letter home: 'I'm in great form and love my work and everything's grand and Con and Lizzy are very good to me and maybe I'll have enough money saved to go home in 3 or 4 years time.' In Brian's notes, 'his Alter Ego keeps up an endless stream of meaningless talk while Gar just sobs & sobs & sobs'.

Brian knew there was something special about this script, and he hoped it would have a broader reach than any of his previous work. In his profile of Guthrie for *Holiday*, he divulged his thinly veiled hope that 'should some dramatist in some remote country write a play that throbbed with love and fun and sorrow and joy – and with a dash of horseplay thrown in for good measure – then the giant from Monaghan would leap across seas with a resounding "Whoop!" and pick up the script, and, if necessary, stage the show in a garage.' The garage he had in mind might have been Belfast's 45-seat Lyric Theatre, then housed behind founder Mary O'Malley's house on Derryvolgie Avenue, where Ronnie Mason directed *The enemy within* in early September 1963. By then, Anne was eight months pregnant, so although Brian initially planned to stay for opening night at Mason's flat, where, Ronnie told him, 'A bed is ready and aired for you', the playwright instead drove back to Derry after watching his play's performance. With only weeks until delivery, he explained, Anne was understandably 'nervous at being left alone'.

The Belfast premiere was a success, and Brian had every reason to feel encouraged and hopeful as he drove home afterward in late-summer twilight, climbing the Sperrin Mountains and descending toward his somnolent native city on the banks of the river Foyle. The next day was Sunday, but at eleven o'clock on Monday morning, 9 September, he carried three copies of his new script, *Philadelphia, here I come!* to the Marlborough Terrace post office near his house. He mailed two to Curtis Brown agents in Covent Garden, London and Madison Avenue, New York, and the third to Tyrone Guthrie in Minneapolis. Postage to America, plus insurance, cost nearly a pound for each parcel, at 18*s*. 2*d*. That night, Brian's radio adaptation of *The enemy within* aired throughout the UK on the BBC Light Programme, thanks to Ronnie Mason's efforts, with Ray McAnally reprising Columba, the role he originated at the Abbey. The *Radio Times* billed Brian as 'one of the most successful of our young Irish writers', as had Ronnie's programme note for the Lyric Theatre production. Mason was happy to report that 'The broadcast seems to have gone down very well' and that he and his secretary fielded multiple phone calls and requests from amateur societies to perform the play, which Brian happily granted at a fee of five guineas for rights, plus ten shillings per script, '(the price I pay to have a copy made here in Derry)'. Toward the end of September, he received his royalty cheque from the Lyric, which at ten per cent of box office takings came to £12 2s. for its ten-night run.

And then, he and Anne waited. For the baby, for the agents' responses, and for Guthrie. The director returned from Minneapolis in late September, after an energetic summer of alternating all four repertory plays – *Hamlet*, *The Miser*, *Three sisters* and *Death of a salesman* – in nightly rotation, with a matinée of *The Miser* and evening performance of *Hamlet* to close the final day of his company's inaugural season. Ensconced once more at Annaghmakerrig, he dashed off a brief note to Brian. 'Hope the baby has arrived + all OK. Thank you for your v nice letter + the script. Have read it fast – at a single gulp + with many tears – it's horribly moving. And will read again more slowly. And write my impressions; or else suggest a meeting so that we could talk. Very preoccupied here with jam + blackberries + trying – in between – to write a "light" book about the M'polis adventure.'

A few days later, Guthrie sent a typed critique and suggested numerous revisions, all of which Brian made. Most importantly, he advised Brian to soften the edges of his satire, so that characters presented in a negative light be allowed at least 'one single, solitary redeeming feature'. He loved the housekeeper Madge, whose characterization was 'so true to life, as lived in the Northern latitudes of our puritan isle; so just exactly like the women who have formed my own life, and therefore so endearing', but Gar's father, he thought, should show the audience 'subtly and not a bit sentimentally, that he is missing the dead wife and is as lonely as Gareth.' Likewise, Gar's friends were 'just ripped apart', in Guthrie's estimation; he wanted the script to suggest 'the effect of their being unable to face Gar's departure'. Regarding the local priest, Guthrie asked, 'why do you devout Papes have to take the hell out of your clergy?' And he cautioned that Katie Doogan's parents' 'Bourgeois prudence ought not, in my humble, to be regarded merely with contemptuous loathing'. Overall, Guthrie sent 'heartfelt and humble congratulation; and much affection for the sympathy and heart's blood you have poured into it. Just get to work and pour a drop or two more of heart's b into the characters you don't like very much.'

'Now for it', Guthrie wrote, bracing himself – and Brian – before plunging into his most potentially damaging assessment: 'I can't decide whether the dodge of having two actors to play Private and Public, Ego and Alter Ego, is justified. I guess it ought to be tried.' He was bothered by insufficient contrasts between Gar's private and public selves, and he felt the casting of two actors for the same character would be problematic. An initial stage production might reveal whether it could be better to use just one actor, employing 'some leger de voix' for Gar's inner commentary, or whether to stick with 'the possibly too elaborate device of the two personae'. In the same vein, he called the play's epilogue 'a mistake' because 'It adds nothing, and would look, I believe, a little pretentious in performance.' Brian cut it. In terms of production, Guthrie warned, 'I somehow think that neither English nor American managements will want to do it. Too "Irish" they'll say; and I think maybe they'd be right.' Possibly the Abbey could do it justice, but, as Guthrie now opined, 'Honestly I wasn't that much impressed with the hand they made of The Enemy Within.' For a first attempt, it was best to aim higher, and he told Brian that 'you're doing the right thing in letting Curtis B hawk it around London and N.Y.C. But don't break your heart if no fish bites'.

The Friels' daughter Judy – christened Judith, after Lady Guthrie – was born just a few days later, '10 harrowing days overdue' as Brian reported to Roger Angell, 'and we haven't quite got over that yet' although both he and Anne were 'very thrilled with this late child'. He was 'all through-other' for a week, he told Ronnie Mason, as he looked after Paddy and Mary before Anne and the baby came home from hospital. Still, as soon as he could get back to his typewriter, Brian set to work revising *Philadelphia* to address Guthrie's concerns, and noted to himself that 'I carried out all his suggestions'. As he told Angell,

> I like it still, although in a few months time I'll probably detest it. But at the moment I think it is good theatre; it is funny and sad and bawdy and moving and it has soaked up a lot of my sweat. The only worthwhile criticism I've had of it came from Tyrone Guthrie who thinks it's good but too 'special', too limited in appeal. He says that he can't see London or New York managements breaking their necks to get it. And he's a pretty shrewd man. I know I can get a Dublin production easily enough, but I've got to the stage when I'm not content with that.

Little did Brian know that two full years would pass before *Philadelphia* would reach audiences beyond Ireland. For now, reviewing and revising his creation in the autumn of 1963, he confided to Mason, 'I'm very excited about this play: nothing I've done so far is comparable'.

But responses from his agents were mixed. Curtis Brown's London agent found the play 'extraordinarily well written. The characters are alive and the dialogue is marvellous.' On the other hand, he worried that it might be too 'static' and explained, 'If you asked me what it was about, I should have to say it was about a boy who plans to go to America – everything is fixed for him to go to America – and then he wonders whether after all he should, but in the end he decides he will.' He also warned that in England 'Most commercial managements are chary of Irish plays', and an emigration tale would be an unlikely business proposition. Instead, with guarded enthusiasm, he planned to approach the state-subsidized English Stage Company, who had premiered John Osborne's *Look back in anger* in 1956. Guthrie's critique opened the door to enlisting 'the great man' in the effort to put the play up. 'Would he ever be free to direct it himself – and would you agree to that?' the agent asked Brian hopefully. Above all, he advised Brian not to 'settle' for a Dublin production until he could shop it to London managements, with a 'commendation' from Guthrie as endorsement.

Brian finished a revised script of *Philadelphia* in late October and brought it with him on a trip to Belfast for radio rehearsals of *The blind mice*, Ronnie Mason's new project. He spent a day in the studio while Mason directed the Dublin actor Donal Donnelly in the role of Father Chris, the missionary released from a Chinese prison. In the BBC office, Mason's secretary made stencilled copies of *Philadelphia* for Brian, who explained gratefully that 'I don't want to let myself in for an expense over a play that may not come to anything'. He mailed the new version to his agents in the UK and US, as well as to Ray McAnally in Dublin, who responded the very next day asking to play Private Gar (though Brian's agent feared the 37-year-old actor was overaged for the part). Back in Derry, Brian mailed his third revision of the story 'Everything neat and tidy' to Roger Angell with a confession that 'I have attempted the rewrite so often that I'm damned if I know what sort of a job I've made of it this time. Maybe it's a terrible hash – I honestly don't know.' His energy and enthusiasm were focused entirely on the new play, as he told Ronnie Mason. 'Remember the play I told you about – PHILADELPHIA, HERE I COME!? My agent in London now appears to have the idea that he will interest some management over there. Things are still very vague; no one has yet been approached; but his optimism is infectious, and I'm trying to keep my excitement down.'

In the meantime there was good and bad news from New York. With 'Three cheers!' Angell elatedly accepted Brian's story, 'which seems infinitely better in this form than in any of its previous versions'. It was Brian's first *New Yorker* acceptance in two years. 'I am really delighted that we shall have you back in the magazine again,' Angell wrote, 'and I hope this is only the beginning of a long series of new successes for you'. On a personal front, the editor announced his own happy news, 'that Carol and I were married three weeks ago, that we went off for a fast two weeks in Paris and London, and that we are now ensconced in our new apartment on 94th Street, and that, from our corner of the world at least, all is happiness and joy.' He apologized for not visiting Derry on their honeymoon, and informed Brian that 'Carol has given up her job here – just too much family, in my case, on this one magazine; it would look like the Kennedys'. Angell gladly sent a renewal of the first reading agreement at an increased rate of $300 for 1964, and he confided to Brian's agent, 'I am really pleased that he is writing well again'.

Brian welcomed the income and the *New Yorker* contract while the wait dragged on for news about *Philadelphia*. As he told Angell, 'Maybe I'm unduly nervy and depressive, but I keep telling myself that this year you won't renew it, that my output has been meagre and indifferent, that my always weak invention has dried up completely, etc. So, for the Agreement, and the money, and the confidence, thank you.' But Curtis Brown's agent in New York took nearly two months to write back after receiving the *Philadelphia* script, and when he did he voiced doubts about 'directorial problems' he foresaw. 'The theme of "breaking the tie that binds" is an admirable one and should certainly find an audience', he wrote, but he doubted that its first viewers should be American. 'I firmly believe that this play must be first produced in England. I think then, and particularly if the production was a success, an American producer would snap it up.' He may have worried that elements of the script could make it difficult to sell to American audiences, notably dialogue voiced by Gar's aunt Lizzy, when she returns to Ballybeg with her husband and an American friend, Ben Burton. Guthrie loved Aunt Lizzy; he found her scene 'the most revealing and alive in the whole play – brilliantly satiric and, as all good satire ought to be, madly sympathetic and touching.' But in Brian's notes, these characters are 'Vulgar. Negro haters, Jew haters' worthy of Gar's 'attraction' as well as his 'revulsion' when they arrive, 'well lit', on the day of Kate Doogan's wedding and invite Gar to live with them in the United States. In one draft, Lizzy turns to Ben Burton and says, 'You got your own problems with them Niggers + Puerto Ricans + stuff like that'. Although Lizzy's racism was toned down to 'You got your own problems to look after' in the final script, there was a risk that American theatregoers might not pay at the box office to see themselves caricatured as crass. Still, the agent wrote, if a British producer underwrote the premiere, 'I have little doubt that the show, if successful before the public over there, would be brought over' to the United States, especially if Guthrie were on board to direct it in New York or Minneapolis.

As time wore on, Brian began to have doubts. In late November 1963, he sent Ronnie Mason one of his only spare scripts, 'a (scruffy) copy of PHILADELPHIA, HERE I COME!', and sought his advice. He never divulged the whole of Guthrie's assessment, nor even the whole of his sentence about having two actors play Gar ('I guess it ought to be tried'). Instead, Brian laid bare his misgivings and tried to marshal his resolve.

> The play has now been written for about two months, and I have had time to think about it, and I am beginning to have wee stirrings of regret that I split Gar into two physical entities. The success/failure of a stage presentation will depend so much on success/failure of this method of approach. Guthrie says: It ought to be tried. I'm clinging hopefully to that. Someone has suggested re-writing the play, making the two Gars into one. But to hell with that: the thing was conceived as Public and Private. I'm not going to start into a new play – and that is what it would mean.

Mason, Brian's earliest drama producer, remained his steadfast supporter. His response to the writer's anxieties was heartfelt and admiring. 'I began reading at one o'clock this morning and went on until after three, and have been finishing it and studying it today. I have no desire to minimise what I want to say or what might appear to be extravagant praise, but outside of Joyce I have never read a more deeply moving, sensitive and profound study of a man's dilemma than this.' Mason acknowledged the technical difficulties of staging Public and Private Gar, but with careful casting and direction, he felt that 'sophisticated' London audiences would understand. He promised to talk with Martin Esslin, the BBC head of drama, about an eventual television production, but first, he declared, 'It must be staged'. Above all, he told Brian, 'You must continue to have implicit faith in this play'.

Brian appreciated Mason's support and thanked him for the letter that 'gave me great, great pleasure, and assurance, and gratification, and restored a measure of confidence'. He trusted his friend's assessment of the London scene because 'As you know, I have no experience of theatre outside Ireland', and he confided his anxiety – and the tumult of his emotions, much like Gar O'Donnell's – over securing a British producer. 'God, you've no idea how I sweat over this problem! Sometimes I think: I'll settle for a Dublin production – now – no matter who does it. And the other times I think: by God it won't go to Dublin until, as Guthrie advises, London rejects it. So you can imagine the vacillations. One minute on top of the world; the next in depths of despair.'

Mason's faith in the script moved him to advocate tenaciously for its radio broadcast by the BBC, which was set in motion months before any stage production was confirmed. After sending Brian his encouragement, he contacted his superiors in BBC London, proposing a production of *Philadelphia* for the Third Programme. Not everyone at the BBC shared Mason's enthusiasm. In particular, John Tydeman, the London script editor (who eventually succeeded Mason as head of BBC radio drama), gave a lukewarm assessment. 'Well it's not that good – not up to Ibsen etc. – but then it's not that bad. Division of Gar into Priv. & Pub. couldn't be wronger ... The beginning is poor, the end indifferent and the whole thing utterly lacking in shape. I feel the bad language gives a false vitality & should be eliminated. God knows what to do with it – commission it for Monday night, I suppose (bad lingo withdrawn it isn't really 3rd) & hope the author will rewrite.' The objectionable language was Gar's frequent use, both public and private, of the words 'bugger' and 'bloody', in keeping with Brian's belief that 'vulgarity keeps sadness at bay.' Vulgarities punctuate the script's opening pages, as Gar chuckles that 'by God I lashed so much salt on those bloody fish that any poor bugger that eats them will die of thirst' while he is 'Up in that big bugger of a jet, with its snout pointing straight for the States ... and then away down below in the Atlantic you see a bloody bugger of an Irish boat out fishing for bloody pollock'. The BBC asked Brian to revise, and eventually he did, in such a way that Private and Public could be played by the same actor to avoid confusing radio listeners with two different voices. He did little to excise the profanity.

In mid-December, Tyrone Guthrie mailed his copy of the script to Brian from Annaghmakerrig, where he had just returned after directing *Coriolanus* as the inaugural production of the Nottingham Playhouse, with a young Ian McKellen in the cast, an event that devolved into 'skirmishes over the sandwiches' when Guthrie protested the scant buffet at the civic reception. The director did his best to bolster Brian's hopes for *Philadelphia* and reminded him that 'I praised it extravagantly – & sincerely' in addition to his critiques. Guthrie's diary, as usual, was a whirlwind of activity, including commitments at Queen's University Belfast, where he had just been appointed Chancellor – hoping that 'N.I. is changing fast & radically & the University ought, & perhaps can, be a liberal and enlightening voice' – so he demurred at Brian's invitation to pay a visit to Derry. 'Off to Belfast tomorrow for 3 days of idiotic CHANCELLOR junketings in cap & gown! ... And the demands of JAM grow & grow. So I see little chance of getting to Derry or Donegal. Can you come here? See me?' A few days later, after Brian made 'the drive back home in the dark', Guthrie travelled to Dublin 'on jam business' to lunch with John Ryan, editor of *Envoy* magazine and, like Sir Tyrone, a man with multiple enterprises, among them Monument Creameries and The Bailey restaurant in Duke Street. Guthrie appraised him 'a nice chap with more aspirations than taste or experience', but encouraged Brian to send the well-financed editor a copy of *Philadelphia*, his 'much-sought opus', for possible backing. Meanwhile Lady Guthrie, in her own attempt at promotion, gave Sir Alec Guinness a copy of the story 'The saucer of larks' – the actor said he 'would dearly love to make a short film of it'. Guinness drafted a screenplay titled *The lark's nest*, with Brian's permission, but production never got off the ground.

At last, word arrived from Curtis Brown's London office that Oscar Lewenstein, a founding member of the English Stage Company, would pay £100 for a six-month option to produce *Philadelphia, here I come!* His proposed venue was not the ESC's Royal Court Theatre, as Brian had hoped, nor any other London stage. Instead, Brian's agent reported, Lewenstein planned to launch *Philadelphia* at that year's Dublin Theatre Festival, which 'would give it an interesting send-off to sympathetic audiences, and of course he would have cast it and directed it in such a way that it would be to a standard which would make a transfer to London practical.' The agent described Lewenstein as 'most sympathetic to the whole thing and this in spite of his realisation that it is difficult to find a following here for an Irish play' in England. Guthrie crowed, 'Splendid! Warmest congratulations! Never rains, does it, but it POURS; and now & again, like this, with GOLD.' It took two months for Lewenstein's terms to be negotiated, since potential film rights were involved, but in the meantime he granted permission for Ronnie Mason to begin work on his planned radio broadcast of *Philadelphia* on the BBC's Third Programme.

Luckily for Brian, his story 'The widowhood system' won acceptance at the *New Yorker* while he waited out Lewenstein's contract. 'Mr Shawn likes this story very much, and so do I', wrote Roger Angell. The new first reading agreement paid Brian a twenty-five per cent bonus for every story. Angell also liked *Philadelphia*, which Curtis Brown had sent him. He praised it as 'wonderfully alive and, by turns, touching and extremely funny and most sad. I have a feeling that it may be a great success, and I wish it well.' Brian was delighted. 'I've been so long out of the pages of the *New Yorker* that I was beginning to think my story days were over. And of course the money will be very welcome.' The story, centred on pigeon racing, 'did not give me much trouble: I loved all the people in it, and they emerged as I wanted them to emerge. You know how seldom that happens.' If only his play's future could be as smooth. 'Naturally I would like it to be a success (if it ever gets on the boards). On the other hand – and surely this is stupid – I don't care a lot. What is most important to me is that I wrote the play that was measurably close to the play I wanted so much to write. How's that for arrogance!' He would need all the self-assurance – and perseverance – he could muster over the coming months, as *Philadelphia* travelled a tortuous path to production. For now, on the threshold of a new year, the fledgling playwright confided in Angell with the air of a prophet. 'You're very lucky not to be involved in the theatre business. I <u>love</u> working at a play, but once the script leaves your hand then all the troubles begin'.

CHAPTER 7

Broadway, here I come!, 1964–6

O<small>N HIS THIRTY-FIFTH BIRTHDAY</small> in January 1964, Brian told Roger Angell that he was 'wildly optimistic' about Oscar Lewenstein's option on *Philadelphia, here I come!* 'If the play does well in the West End there is every reason to hope for a New York production, and this is something I would love. However, I'm jumping the gun. I'll let you know how things go.' A few days later, he flew to London for his first meeting with the producer.

Lewenstein, a leader of the New Wave in British theatre and cinema, had gained critical and commercial success when his upstart English Stage Company premiered John Osborne's *Look back in anger* in 1956 after it came in over the transom in a script contest. He was a shrewd manager, but his origins in theatre stemmed from his commitment to socialism, not profit. He had co-founded the ESC as 'a Playwright's theatre', dedicated to new plays and those by 'foreign writers we considered neglected in England', including Arthur Miller and Bertolt Brecht. He was the first to stage Brecht's *Threepenny opera* in England, which in 1956 became ESC's fourth production. In 1960, while still involved with ESC, Lewenstein founded his own smaller company, with Osborne, director Tony Richardson and two American investors as his board. Their first production was *Billy Liar*, adapted from Keith Waterhouse's bestselling novel of 1959. The stage version starred Albert Finney as the title character, a young Yorkshireman with an exuberant inner life. Like Gar O'Donnell, Billy escapes his dreary job and stifling family in flights of imagination – in his case, to an invented kingdom called Ambrosia, where Billy is prime minister and major-general of the armed forces, a decorated war hero beloved by all. *Billy Liar* ran to packed houses in London for nine months, and continued for another nine even after Finney yielded the lead role to his understudy Tom Courtenay, who went on to star in a successful film adaptation with Julie Christie in 1963.

Lewenstein pursued 'a steady policy of presenting productions that criticise the status quo and show how the other half live'. He had spent his childhood in and out of that other half, a self-described 'Russian Jew born in England' whose father made and lost money easily, so that Lewenstein moved among grammar and boarding schools as fortunes rose and fell. His father was also his mother's uncle, a 'taboo' topic among the family, and for much of their marriage he was absent, either for work or affairs with other women. For many years Lewenstein's paternal grandfather lived with the family, but as the children spoke no Russian, Yiddish, or German, communication with him was impossible, and he remained 'a distant, even mysterious figure', an orthodox Jew who prayed daily in Hebrew, 'another language we didn't understand', as Lewenstein later recalled. When his father eventually went broke, Lewenstein spent a final term in the Central School in Hackney, but left at sixteen without exams or qualifications. He and his siblings moved with their mother into two rooms of her parents' basement in North East London. Lewenstein joined the Young Communist League in the early 1930s, and, after clerking in the British army during the war, became secretary of the Unity Theatre Society, whose charter was 'to work for the betterment of society' by 'truthfully interpreting life as experienced by the majority of the people'. He soon became manager of the Glasgow Unity company and shouldered its mission of staging Scottish and Irish plays, including *Juno and the Paycock* in 1948, which kindled a lasting friendship with Seán O'Casey.

Philadelphia must have resonated with Lewenstein on multiple levels: Gar's unspoken love for his gruff, distant father, his stunted future prospects, his ambivalence about emigrating from Ireland and leaving it all behind. Brian's agents, meanwhile, were counting on Lewenstein to cast 'stars' in *Philadelphia* and boost its box office appeal. Lewenstein had recently joined Woodfall Films, the production company founded by Osborne, Richardson and Canadian producer Harry Saltzman, and was associate producer of Woodfall's blockbuster *Tom Jones*, starring Albert Finney in the title role. Irish actor Micheál MacLiammóir voiced the film's Narrator, overlaying the young hero's adventures with rich tones of irony and indulgence. *Tom Jones* had opened to wide acclaim in late 1963 and, while Lewenstein's negotiations with Brian's agents were still in progress, it would win Academy Awards in four categories including Best Picture, beating *Cleopatra* and *How the West was won*.

Brian was disappointed by Lewenstein's proposal to launch in Dublin but understood that he and his play had to earn their passage across the Irish Sea. Throughout the early months of 1964, he worried and waited while his agents wrestled with Lewenstein over final wording of the film rights in his contract. Brian confessed that patience was 'by no means my brightest virtue' and reached out to Roger Angell for reassurance. 'So far our winter has been as gentle as spring, but I'm sort of depressed myself, and not working well, and concerned with great questions about Truth and Life and Religion – isn't that stupid? Nothing like thinking in abstractions to depress you thoroughly – and make a real phony of you.' He channelled those great questions into his latest *New Yorker* submission, 'The death of a scientific humanist', the story of a returned emigrant uncle who announces on his deathbed that he has rejected religion, sending his family into a quandary when the village canon refuses to bury him. Brian was similarly steadfast in his beliefs about his emigrant play. After meeting Lewenstein, he instructed his agent to be 'quite firm' about two key points: 'the necessity for 2 people to play Gar', and consideration of Tyrone Guthrie as director. 'I think he could do a <u>wonderful</u> job of PHILADELPHIA'.

Lewenstein agreed, and both he and Brian wrote to Minneapolis in early March, inviting Guthrie to direct *Philadelphia* in the Dublin Festival that October. But Guthrie was in the midst of rehearsals for *Henry V* and *Saint Joan*, counting down to his second repertory season, and it was impossible for him to get away. Brian tucked St Patrick's Day shamrock into his letter as inducement, which 'arrived a week late & totally dehydrated – hay!' as the preoccupied director informed him. His cast were the same actors Brian had observed, and Guthrie ruefully confided that 'there isn't quite the thrill of the first year – a slight feeling of it's all been done before – not too bad, but perceptible'. His theatre needed $50,000 in upgrades and repairs, including new carpeting and plaster in its foyer due to a pipe that froze and burst over the winter. His friend Frank Whiting, who had championed the city's campaign for the new repertory, had delayed his sabbatical from the University of Minnesota so he could assist as Guthrie directed *Six characters in search of an author* in the fall semester (with 'a stoodent cast', Guthrie told Brian, 'a needful bit of liaison twixt Professional + Academic'). Most importantly, Guthrie lacked time and sufficient contacts among young Irish actors to do the 'careful casting' that *Philadelphia* would need. With regret, he mailed Brian a list of actors who might be suitable, and apologized for declining Lewenstein's offer to direct. 'I <u>wish</u> this letter could have said YES with the enthusiasm which I feel.'

St Patrick's Day 1964 brought good luck nonetheless. Roger Angell, who reported from his *New Yorker* office that the holiday was 'going on outside, if not exactly in my heart, with dozens of Mick bands tootling and blaring under the windows here' in the city's annual parade, announced that he and his colleagues 'all absolutely love THE DEATH OF A SCIENTIFIC HUMANIST and that we are gobbling it up for our pages. I think it is the best thing of yours in a long time – maybe the best ever.' Brian had told him in mid-February that 'For some reason <u>I</u> don't understand I've got a great spurt of energy for stories again. I know you tell me that I write too many as it is, but when I have the energy and the ideas it would be wrong to turn my back on them.' In this spirit Brian sent another, quickly, the story of a debt-burdened young father asking his bachelor uncle for £500, a venture called 'The Barney game'. Unfortunately Angell found it 'far too obvious and not really believable. Even a stupid man would not have asked Barney for money at just that moment'. It was rejected.

St Patrick's Day also marked the date of Lewenstein's signature on his contract for *Philadelphia*, which promised Brian royalties on a scale of 5% for the first £1,000 in weekly box office receipts, 7½% on the next £400, and 10% on all weekly ticket sales above £1,400. If Lewenstein managed to import the play to Manhattan, a similar scale would pay Brian 5% on the first $5,000, then 7½% on the next $2,000, and 10% on weekly box office receipts over $7,000. These may have seemed unimaginable sums: throughout 1963 and 1964, Brian continued to receive semiannual statements from Doubleday that he still owed them $25.24 for buying gift copies of *The saucer of larks*, and his advance of $750 was still $69.41 short of being earned out.

In April 1964, Lewenstein broached the idea of removing *Philadelphia* from the Dublin Festival and waiting until Guthrie became available to direct. Guthrie, now in dress rehearsals and 'fighting flu', demurred, insisting, 'I want to make it perfectly clear that this is not due to lack of interest in the play, which I like very much', but due to commitments in Minneapolis through the end of 1965. Instead, Lewenstein enlisted Phyllis Ryan to work with Brian on finding another director. Just a year before, Ryan had rescued *The blind mice* from the Abbey's rejection by staging it in her Eblana Theatre below Busáras, but, as Brian admitted to his agent, 'From then on neither of us has been fully at ease with the other'. While Ryan liked the *Philadelphia* script, calling it 'extravagantly different and difficult, and splendid', she felt strongly that changes were needed. She invited Brian to Dublin and told him she was 'Looking forward to almighty argument – the script deserves it and demands it'. Her analysis declared that 'The Private and Public Gars work well only when other people are present on the stage with them' and were 'dramatically unacceptable alone'. Private Gar, she argued, was 'constantly overwritten', while 'The minor characters are underwritten', which could pose problems for casting high-profile actors in minor roles. While she believed that 'the play could be made work on its dual level in spite of the difficulties', she warned that 'The ending is sentimental and trite'.

Most significantly, Ryan disagreed with Brian as to possible directors, and their difference of opinion fuelled a row that threatened the entire trajectory of *Philadelphia*. In May 1964, just five months before the Festival, the playwright visited Ryan at her Palmerston Road home, where they talked through changes to the script and possible lead actors. Brian still wanted Ray McAnally to play Private Gar, and, according to his impressions, 'I thought we agreed on most points'. That changed when they turned to the question of who would direct. With Guthrie unavailable, Ryan argued for Barry Cassin, who had directed *The blind mice*, but Brian would not consent. He and Ryan debated the 'idiosyncrasies' of director Jim FitzGerald, who was fresh from success with Hugh Leonard's *Stephen D* in Dublin and London and would later found Project 67, which evolved into the Project Arts Centre. But when Brian conveyed Phyllis Ryan's opinions about FitzGerald to Oscar Lewenstein, he set off a disastrous cycle of accusations. Ryan found the playwright's letter 'misleading and harmful', and protested that 'what you have stated is libellous, and should never have been put on paper'. She was angry enough to break her company's association with *Philadelphia*, writing to Brian that while she wished him and the play good luck, 'We too have a reputation to consider, and we have always worked with people who had confidence in us and we in them'.

Lewenstein scolded the playwright. 'Apparently your letter of the 14th May to Phyllis Ryan had a traumatic effect on the lady and she has written to me to say she doesn't want to do the play. I am afraid this places me in some difficulty and I haven't yet resolved how to proceed.' Three scathing letters from Ryan had left him 'reeling' and 'baffled and dismayed'. Brian pleaded his case. 'Phyllis & I did have our differences of opinion but I thought we parted on good terms. To put it mildly, it seems I was wrong.' In late May, he drove to Belfast to watch the Ballymoney Literary and Debating Society perform *The enemy within* on the Grand Opera House stage, to popular acclaim and first prize in the Ulster Drama Festival, adjudicated that year by Hilton Edwards. But the victory did little to distract Brian from *Philadelphia*'s predicament. 'This whole business has distressed me deeply', he wrote to his agent in London, 'and I have been very troubled about it all'. To make matters worse, the *New Yorker* rejected his story 'The highwayman and the saint' that same week, his second failed submission that spring. Roger Angell explained that 'The writing is good, but the story is far too obvious – just another Irish mother-in-law who dominates her house and destroys the groom.' (It later became Act Two in Brian's 1967 play *Lovers*.) Ronnie Mason did his best to buoy Brian's spirits by commissioning the radio adaptation of *Philadelphia* at double the BBC's usual rate: two guineas per minute, for a total of 180 guineas, or £189. In Mason's view, it was 'all the more important because of this fuss with Phyllis Ryan that it should be a resounding success on the Third'. Brian remained inconsolable. 'I have long ceased to have any coherent thoughts about the whole business', he told his agent. 'Theatre is just HELL'.

Brian worried that Lewenstein might abandon *Philadelphia* altogether, and self-doubt sapped his energy for writing. 'I have no idea what Miss Ryan has told Oscar about me, and I prefer not to think about it', he wrote to his agent.

'I would love to be started into a new play, and I have excellent resolutions, but until this mess clears itself up I just can't bring myself to begin.' Desperate to regain momentum, he sought advice from mentors who seemed all too distant from Derry when he needed them most. 'What about a <u>cheap</u> flight to these islands?' Brian asked Angell, with a reminder that 'you are welcome to have this shabby house or the cottage in Donegal at any time'. His recent *New Yorker* rejections had further stalled his work, and the summer was not shaping up to be a productive season.

> At the moment I'm not actually <u>writing</u> a story but am flirting unhappily around two or three themes. The great burst of energy and enthusiasm of two months ago has leaked quickly away. For someone as undisciplined as myself I now think that the trick is to work like hell when one has the energy and enthusiasm, for 18 hours a day if necessary, because these periods of industry are so short lived and they are inevitably followed by slow winters of debility.

With Ronnie Mason's encouragement, Brian spent the next few weeks on the tedious task of rewriting *Philadelphia* for radio, grappling with the difficulty of conveying Public and Private Gar without visual cues, but, as for the script, he confessed, 'I'm about tired of it'.

In early summer, with the Dublin Festival approaching, a sequel to Brian's dispute with Phyllis Ryan triggered a series of events that saved *Philadelphia*. Seeking a new production for the Festival, Ryan rebounded from her falling out with Friel and outbid Gate Theatre director Hilton Edwards on a controversial script, *King of the castle*, which had just won the Irish Life Assurance Award. Rooted in Monaghan's stony grey soil, *King of the castle* told the story of an ageing, impotent farmer who conspires with a younger man to impregnate his wife. Its author, Eugene McCabe, had sent it to Edwards months earlier, and though one Gate staff member deemed it 'an unpleasant, even repellant, play', Edwards found it 'a very strong, if grim and unpalatable, work' and wanted to direct it. Its dialogue was 'poetry and sheer genius. The language is authentic, simple, minimal and genuinely realistic and yet it conveys so much more than is <u>said</u> by its allusions, imagery and, above all, by its peculiar ebb-and-flow rhythms.' In late May 1964 Edwards invited McCabe to dine with him at his favourite haunt, Jammet's French restaurant in Dublin, to discuss script revisions with a plan toward eventual production. In particular, he proposed that the playwright relocate a challenging central prop – a threshing machine – offstage, but overall, as he told McCabe, Edwards felt that 'Your play seems as good a way as any other of my being banished forever from these shores'.

Despite his centrality as 'Dublin's senior producer', Edwards had long occupied several potentially liminal spheres as a gay transplanted Englishman in post-revolutionary Ireland. He grew up in London, began his acting career in a touring Shakespeare company in 1921, and joined the Old Vic as a stage assistant and sometime actor the following year, appearing in bit roles in almost every play by Shakespeare by 1925. He then joined another touring group, the Intimate Theatre Company, whose founder, Anew McMaster, recruited Edwards on short notice to replace an alcoholic actor arrested for disturbance of the peace. McMaster brought Edwards to Ireland, where his company was playing the Enniscorthy Athenaeum before stops in other small towns across Munster. Another young actor, Micheál MacLiammóir, volunteered to help the new cast member learn his lines. So began a lifelong marriage of true minds, as Edwards and MacLiammóir bound their personal and professional futures to the shared dream of starting their own theatre company, a dream they realised in 1928 when they founded the Dublin Gate Theatre Studio. In the decades that followed, they staged experimental European and Irish plays, weathered financial crises, and continued to work in other theatres – Galway's Taibhdhearc and London's Old Vic among them – to support themselves and the Gate.

By 1964, Edwards and MacLiammóir had spent nearly four decades establishing the Gate at the centre of Dublin's theatrical world – a brash, experimental counterpoint to Ernest Blythe's starched-collar nationalism at the Abbey. Edwards served as the inaugural head of drama at Telefís Éireann from 1961 to 1963, but then 'reverted with relief to the theatre', the better to devote himself to directing. As a member of the Dublin Theatre Festival committee, Edwards well knew its inner workings and precarious financial state. Though London theatre critic Harold Hobson called it 'the best and most exciting of all theatre festivals', at least one American critic described it as 'nuts': the Festival annually showcased '10 new productions of plays, seven of them premieres, all opening in a 10-day span' in a city that boasted only four full-size theatres: the Gate, the Gaiety, the Olympia and the Abbey, still housed at the Queen's Theatre though its new building was at last under construction. The brainchild of actor and director Brendan Smith, the Dublin Festival began in 1957 with funding from Bord Fáilte, and its original focus was solely to showcase Irish plays – as *Variety* noted, 'That's the gimmick that makes Dublin stand up and stand out' among the international festival circuit: 'It's the home team all the way'. Still, Irish critics worried how much ground their capital had lost to Edinburgh, whose annual theatre festival launched a full decade earlier, 'while we wasted our energies on An Tóstal, which had no message for the world'. Others complained that the Dublin Festival itself was 'killing Irish drama' due to its 'ever-increasing emphasis placed on finance and its value as a magnet to draw visitors to this country'. The frenetic fortnight risked robbing oxygen from other productions throughout the rest of the season, leaving Irish theatre 'lifeless'. By 1964, the Festival was in its second year of a three-year Bord Fáilte grant but received no other government subsidy. Funding from the nascent Arts Council, 'the tundish through which State patronage flows to the arts', went mainly to visual arts exhibitions, the Dublin Grand Opera Company, and amateur music and drama groups throughout the country.

Confident that McCabe's play would stir both controversy and admiration, Edwards pitched it to the Festival board and secured an envied spot in the programme: it would open the second week of the Festival at the Gaiety Theatre, with the guarantee of an additional week if ticket sales warranted. Meanwhile, McCabe's agent had offered the rights to Oscar Lewenstein, who had known Edwards for many years: in 1955, Edwards designed the lighting for Lewenstein's West End production of *Moby Dick* starring Orson Welles. The two men agreed to collaborate on *King of the castle*, which they hoped to transfer to London after the Dublin Festival ended. But McCabe's agent also shopped the play to other producers, and among them, Phyllis Ryan offered a higher bid as well as a promise to cast Cyril Cusack as the embittered Monaghan farmer. Ryan nabbed the first week in the Festival calendar to stage the play in the Gaiety. Disappointed, Edwards complained that he had been 'embroiled in a sort of Dutch auction – a position that I always do my utmost to avoid', but Lewenstein seized the opportunity to substitute Brian's play into *King of the castle*'s Festival slot. He sent Edwards the *Philadelphia* script in early June with instructions that 'If you like it perhaps you would (a) like to have a word with Brian Friel and (b) drop me a note. If you don't like it, drop me a note and don't have a word with Brian Friel.'

Edwards liked it. He phoned Brian on the eve of departure for a month in Italy, 'very enthusiastic, saying he would love to do it, etc., etc.' as Brian reported to his agent. After months of uncertainty, arrangements for the Dublin Festival snapped into place at dizzying speed. Enterprising Brendan Smith wrote a 2½ per cent royalty for the Festival into his agreement with Edwards, and opening night was set for the 28th of September in the Gaiety, 'a beautiful elegant theatre with great atmosphere' as Brian described it, relieved, though he was still wary of the Dublin scene. 'As ever,' he wrote, 'I'm opposed to the Festival and agree to it only because Oscar wants it. His obvious purpose is to see how a try-out will go; then, if he likes it, he will talk about the West End. And what I dread is that, in the catty, competitive, hysterical atmosphere that the Festival always seems to engender,

PHILADELPHIA won't get anything like a <u>balanced</u> reception. I refuse to accept that it will get its week run and then die – and that could so easily happen.' Edwards was about to depart on a working holiday with Gate actor Patrick Bedford to write about dance and drama festivals at Nervi and Spoleto for the *Irish Times*. After losing out on McCabe's play, he was 'in no mood for work and I hereby give strike notice for one month as from the 16th June. My marching slogan is "The universe is unfair to Hilton."' He promised Brian that he would study the *Philadelphia* script during his sojourn on the Italian coast of the Mediterranean.

The rocky coast of Donegal was less serene, and unsettled weather mirrored Brian's state of mind as he and Anne and their three daughters began their annual holidays in Kincasslagh. 'At the moment the weather here is VILE – storms and rain and boats disappearing all along the coast', he wrote to Ronnie Mason. 'Mails here are erratic and uncertain.' He and Anne hosted the BBC's John Boyd and his wife Elizabeth for the Twelfth of July, and Brian invited Ronnie to come along. 'It would mean a camp bed in the living-room, but you'd be very welcome.' Mason declined, but Boyd proved a valuable listener for Brian's fears and advised him to stay the course. After he left, Brian opened a new notebook and recorded his thoughts.

> This is nothing more than a revving up of the engine to prevent it from stalling completely, an antidote to total paralysis.
>
> Exactly 3 months since I wrote anything at all; and in the interval panic has gathered its focus & attached with increasing strength. But there is no total depression, no mental air-block; just the inability to focus sharply, incisively on a single theme (at least 4 are rattling around in my skull like dice, & occasionally when I sit down with a blank page & a pencil I hope that a 6 will come up. It never does.)
>
> Perhaps the play is the great unsettler. I think about it constantly. And most times I decide calmly &, I believe, correctly that I will write a <u>much</u> better one some day. There are also financial worries: I should have a story for the *N.Yorker* within a month from now – but I won't; I should be working on a *Holiday* piece – but I don't think I will; etc. And there are nagging personal worries. But, as John Boyd advised, the thing is to keep writing. Hence this.

Looking across the bay from his cottage window, Brian toyed with a story idea based on a First World War shipwreck nearby and weighed which genre would suit it best: fiction, journalism, or drama? It would later become an alluring motif in his story 'The gold in the sea', but for now, Brian stalled and fretted about the best way forward. 'On the other hand, perhaps this is my greatest fault: a tendency to hoard, when I should be prodigal. But, I reply to myself, you are not inventive, and the raw material is not easily come by.' Letters to his new London agent, Suzanne Finlay, hinted at despair. 'Absolutely no news about the Dublin Festival. I haven't even met Hilton Edwards yet. We'll be here until near the end of August. Vile weather. Not working.'

Finlay's rousing response from London was immediate. 'If you wait for sunshine in which to work, your total output as an author in this country will be very limited indeed. Besides, surely vile weather is the time to be working. By the way, when you emerge from that mysteriously named Irish hinterland where you are presently in retreat, I think it would be a good idea for you to march upon the Gaiety Theatre and introduce yourself to Hilton Edwards.'

There was no need. The long wait had ended. Edwards telegraphed Brian in Kincasslagh upon his return from Italy, and in late July, the director drove to Donegal with Patrick Bedford, a young actor who travelled with Edwards as his 'cook, chauffeur, nurse, and *confidant*', as Bedford would later explain, though it was an open secret that he also infringed on Edwards' sexual relationship with MacLiammóir. Less than a decade later, in his play *The gentle island*, Brian would describe the arrival of a similarly urbane pair of visitors, a 'plump, balding, middle-aged man' and his companion, twenty years younger, both 'dressed in summer slacks and open shirts' when they land on fictional Inishkeen to the wonderment of local islanders. Patrick Bedford had played many roles in the Gate and would ultimately be cast in *Philadelphia* as Public Gar. For Private Gar, Edwards wanted Donal Donnelly, who had started his career at the Gate and met Brian while playing Father Chris in *The blind mice* on BBC Radio, Belfast. Over tea in the Friels' cottage, Edwards showed Brian 'all sorts of plans & drawings' for the *Philadelphia* set by designer Alpho O'Reilly, with whom Edwards had worked during his tenure at RTÉ. 'He also requested some minor changes in the script, which I have since done', Brian explained to his agent. 'The weather is still vile + I'm still not working. But both things will right themselves simultaneously.'

Eventually the weather won out. The Friel family cut short their holiday and retreated to Derry in early August 'when a 60 m.p.h. gale just knocked the bejasus out of us and we were forced to give up'. But Brian returned home with a lighter step and renewed determination, as he told Ronnie Mason. 'Now to get back to work and try to make some money before going off to Dublin (some time in the first half of September)' for the Festival. He gathered notes for another play, a sombre coda to *Philadelphia*, about a returned emigrant and her failure to reconnect with her newly prosperous brother. It would eventually become *The loves of Cass McGuire*. For now, Brian dug up one of his newspaper columns about Donegal, first titled 'Down to the sea' for the *Irish Times* and later 'The demon fisherman' for the *Irish Press*, and added his shipwreck motif and a new title, 'The gold in the sea', as he reshaped it into a *New Yorker* submission. Angell and his colleagues were 'charmed and interested by the background, the dialogue, and the general tone of the story', and were 'delighted to have another solid piece of work from you'. The income meant Brian could breathe easier while *Philadelphia* prepared to launch. (He had already confided in Angell that 'money is not all that plentiful'.) Meanwhile, Ronnie Mason planned to direct *The blind mice* at the Lyric Theatre in October, so Brian sent his last copy of that script and wished him 'Good luck with it' – he had moved on from Mary O'Malley's garage.

As plans for *Philadelphia* progressed, Brian continued to revise. Edwards preferred to work collaboratively with playwrights as he was 'getting up steam' to direct; he explained to Brian that 'By this stage in a production I have usually convinced myself that I have written the play and it becomes more than ever necessary that I should discipline myself by contact with the author.' Despite his status as a doyen of Irish theatre, Edwards' openness to the younger playwright's still-evolving ideas and contributions proved so productive that after *Philadelphia*, Brian enlisted him to direct his next three plays. Brian's first revision for Edwards saw the inclusion of Private Gar's mantra, the opening of Edmund Burke's pamphlet about the French Revolution ('It is now sixteen or seventeen years since I first saw the Queen of France, then the Dauphiness, at Versailles … ') which signals Gar's internal crises throughout the play. Edwards lent his expertise to questions of publicity – 'I agree that the light note must be stressed in contrast to the prevailing Festival Gloom' – and overall length. 'It is far better that we should get the play tight than have a ghastly pruning session after the first night and send the cast on shaky on the second night as is usually the case.' Brian heeded Edwards' advice and cut passages that he 'could dispense with, with the least heart-break' to get the play below two-and-a-half hours. Without a prologue, Edwards worked with Brian on introducing Gar's dual personae, and landed on the solution of keeping Private Gar offstage until three pages into the script, when Private emerges from a hidden door to begin speaking Gar's interior monologue while Public, alone in his bedroom, sings the play's title song.

There remained the question of casting, which had been a primary focus of production from the start. Lewenstein's interest in the play began with a promise to cast it at a level on par with the West End; Guthrie declined to direct due to his insufficient knowledge of Irish actors. Now, with seven weeks to opening night, Edwards had confirmed only his two leads, Patrick Bedford and Donal Donnelly as Public and Private Gar. He told Brian he was proceeding carefully because 'I don't want to be rushed'. At last, at the end of August, with the Festival due to open in September, he was able to report, 'I have, with the utmost difficulty, got a cast together. It is not all I could wish – but then, no cast ever is. It has been particularly difficult getting a Madge.' He had just signed Eileen Crowe, who had played a nosey neighbour in *The quiet man*. 'One would think that this would be the easiest character to cast in Dublin', Edwards complained, but in the run-up to the Festival, 'every company is cutting every other company's throat in the rush for actors. I have spared no effort and I have waited until the last moment to cast so as to leave no source untapped.' A few days later, Crowe 'changed her mind' and was replaced with Máirín O'Sullivan, a member of the Radio Éireann players and former pupil of the Gate school of acting. Edwards sent Brian a hopeful note, with just three weeks until curtain, that 'This completes the cast'.

On a Sunday afternoon in mid-September, Brian drove to Dublin to meet Edwards and the cast for rehearsals – no longer an observer, as in Minneapolis, but a creator and fellow artist. The director requested 'a few days to get things roughed out' with the actors but encouraged the playwright to join them 'any time from 14th September', and Brian took him at his word. At Lewenstein's expense, he rented a semi-detached house in Clontarf, just north of the city centre, to accommodate Anne and the children, who arrived a week before the first performance and stayed through the end of the Festival. Ronnie Mason brought Richard Imison of BBC London to observe rehearsals one afternoon. As opening night approached (and afterward), Brian continued to make changes to the script. The ending still needed work, as many early readers of the play had told him. Guthrie had advised giving Madge the last word in a soliloquy to the audience, allowing 'a bit more of a "dying fall."' Brian had excised the airplane scene and wrote Madge a new monologue, so that the Festival premiere closed with her quiet gift of two pounds tucked into the pocket of Gar's coat as it lies draped over his packed suitcase. 'That'll get him a cup of tea on the plane ... When the boss was his age, he was the very same as him: leppin', and eejitin' about and actin' the clown; as like as two peas. And when he's the age the boss is now he'll turn out just the same.' Later, in the second week of performances, Edwards would move these lines two pages forward, and end instead with Private Gar's question, 'God, boy, why do you have to leave? Why? Why?' and Public's response, 'I don't know. I – I – I don't know'. When he reported the change to Lewenstein, Brian explained, 'My original objection to this was that the play could end on a negative, nihilistic note, but this is not what comes across. What comes across is a young man's confusion + bafflement + his necessity to respond to an age old urge (to leave home) that he doesn't understand.'

Festival audiences understood it, and loved it. When the play opened at the Gaiety on 28 September, Oscar Lewenstein was in the audience to witness its immediate acclaim. Catapulted into celebrity, Brian made a memorably terse curtain speech after the performance, peering into the audience and offering only one sentence – 'I want to thank everyone very much' – before retreating backstage. One reporter described his 'touching impersonation of an opossum playing dead at the approach of danger'. But his family and friends were ecstatic, and showered him and Anne with congratulations after the show. Brian saved notes he received from 'Derry wans' written at '11:15 pm Outside G.P.O. – your first night' that '"Philadelphia" was wonderful – so say us, the people behind us, and everyone in the bar.' His sister Nanette wrote, 'you must be walking on air'. The next morning, headlines proclaimed, 'At last – it's the best new Irish play of year' and 'Friel gives new twist to an "American wake"'. Its run was extended for a second week, beyond the end of the Festival, and Tyrone Guthrie, at home in Annaghmakerrig between the end of his Minneapolis season and the start of student rehearsals, drove down to see it with Lady Judith, wading into 'the SURGE at the box office' among 'a right good and eager and <u>bright</u> crowd in on a Monday night'.

Guthrie sent Brian a detailed critique of every aspect of the show: lighting, set, blocking (which he called 'choreography'), costumes, music and casting. He commented that Patrick Bedford as Public Gar 'wasn't nearly so queeny as I'd feared – indeed really not queeny at all' but that in his final scene with lost love Katie Doogan he seemed 'peevish instead of powerful', a flaw Guthrie believed was 'easily remediable' with more attention to 'speed and breathing and long phrasing'. Most importantly, Guthrie validated the key risk that Brian had taken and congratulated him on its success: 'The device of the inner and the outer Gareth comes off quite splendidly'. Though Guthrie went on to question whether suspense could be heightened with more conflict between Private and Public, or whether the order of scenes should be altered, his approval of Brian's experiment outweighed his previously hesitant assessment that 'I guess it ought to be tried'. His typed suggestions covered two-and-half single-spaced pages, and then, seemingly unable to stop himself, he added another full page in pencil, venturing so far as to write a completely new ending for the script, involving Gar's former teacher, Master Boyle, and Boyle's nephew, invented by Guthrie. The nephew, an Aer Lingus employee, was to book Gar's ticket, but somehow 'the master has fucked up the arrangements' for departure. 'Is there <u>anything</u> in this?' the director asked. The playwright ignored the question: a sign of his growing self-confidence.

Brian's profile was rising in Dublin, all the higher when he sparred with his *New Yorker* predecessor, Frank O'Connor, in the theatre pages of the *Irish*

Independent. O'Connor objected to Edwards' direction of *Philadelphia*, which he argued had turned Brian's 'gentle play' into a 'rip-roaring revue' laced with 'anti-clericalism' and 'jeers at the Church' – presumably in the character of Canon Mick O'Byrne, who visits Gar's home to play draughts with Screwballs. O'Connor vouched to 'Having read most of what Mr Friel has written', which must have pleased Brian, and he adjudged that 'Mr Friel is a very fine short story writer, and in outline "Philadelphia Here I Come" is a perfect short story'. But O'Connor disliked Gar's division into two selves he called 'Taciturn and Talkative' and complained that 'I lost Mr Friel completely in the first couple of minutes', especially 'by the time Talkative had recited from Burke's "Reflections on the French Revolution" for the tenth time'. It had been only four years since Brian's stories were eclipsed by O'Connor's as they crossed Roger Angell's desk, but success now emboldened the younger writer to step into the crossfire between two elder statesmen of Irish culture. In a letter to the editor the following week, Hilton Edwards accused the critic of hypocrisy, alluding to his own public and private personae as the author Frank O'Connor, 'as rich a piece of theatrical flamboyance as any in the history of comedy or melodrama', who fronted for the real-life Michael O'Donovan, as O'Connor was still known to family and friends.

Brian scored the final riposte, opening his letter with reverence that skewered the senior writer in a swift turn of phrase. 'Sir – It is beyond question that Frank O'Connor is the best short story writer in Ireland, perhaps the best in the world; and I have learned so much from him and admire him so unreservedly that I read his review of my play not as a critique but as the delightful fiction that it was.' Brian's loyalties lay with his director, who had collaborated with the playwright throughout rehearsals and was 'still endeavouring to extract from certain scenes a greater degree of comedy than we have so far achieved', as Edwards had explained. 'So I plead with Mr O'Connor', wrote Brian in closing, 'not to beat Mr Edwards to death with his programme' – as O'Connor had threatened – 'because I want Mr Edwards, alive and perceptive as he is, for my next play, and because Mr O'Connor's arrest and execution would be an irreparable loss to the world of letters.'

But had the director and playwright achieved their goal? The Festival production was attended by American reporters from the *Washington Post*, *New Republic* and *Time* magazine, and a reviewer for *Variety* called it 'a strong local b.o. [box office] click'. Eventually, Brian received £290 in royalties of five per cent of total ticket sales, which were £5,300 for *Philadelphia*'s two-week run, though he and his agent spent weeks after the Festival chasing the final payment of £24 18s. 8d. (agent Suzanne Finlay called the Gaiety's convoluted office procedures 'a comedy of the absurd'). Oscar Lewenstein, meanwhile, had decided after opening night that the play might earn a better reception in New York than in London, despite previous ideas about the West End. In December 1964, Lewenstein told Brian his plans were 'still in such a fluid state' that he could give no news, but said he was 'in touch with a number of American producers' as potential partners. Among these was Kermit Bloomgarden, producer of *Death of a salesman* among other critical successes, who was intrigued by Brian's script and sent it to *Psycho* film star Anthony Perkins, inviting him to consider the role of Private Gar. In the end, Bloomgarden was unwilling to meet Lewenstein's terms, which he felt had 'no basis in reality' since *Philadelphia* had not yet proved itself outside of Dublin. Lewenstein, meanwhile, was completing work on a new film, *The knack ... and how to get it*, adapted from Ann Jellicoe's hit play on the Royal Court stage and featuring Donal Donnelly as an Irish lodger in London and third wheel to the story's star couple. Lewenstein assured Brian that all would fall into place for *Philadelphia*. 'I hope your nerves will keep steady!'

Throughout November and December, Brian continued writing his next play, a bookend of sorts to Gar O'Donnell's departure story, the elegiac return of work-worn emigrant Cass McGuire. His agent sold publication rights for *Philadelphia* to Faber and Faber for an advance of £50 and negotiated contracts for the play to be translated into German, Finnish and Greek. While Brian waited for news from Lewenstein, amateur drama societies from all over Ireland wrote to request performance rights to *Philadelphia*, which Brian and his agent repeatedly refused. So many letters poured in from near and far – Donegal, Sligo, Meath, Waterford, even a Castleblaney football club boasting identical twins who could portray Private and Public Gar for their annual play – that Brian began sending pre-printed reply slips to explain that his contract with Lewenstein precluded selling amateur rights until after a West End run. Among handwritten notes clamouring to perform *Philadelphia* in parish halls and little theatres arrived a letter from Ernest Blythe, dated the last day of 1964, commiserating on the play's 'short run in the Gaiety' during the Festival and offering, on behalf of his board, to stage it at the Abbey 'if that were agreeable to you. But perhaps it is tied up.'

It may have been a tempting offer, but there is no record of Brian's response. A few days into the new year, Lewenstein broke his silence and invited the playwright back to London. Just after his thirty-sixth birthday, Brian again boarded a plane and flew to London for one day, enough time for an afternoon meeting at Lewenstein's Curzon Street office followed by a conversation with Spencer Curtis Brown at his office in Covent Garden. Lewenstein covered the travel expenses of £14 15s. and proposed a much more ambitious trip: he was sending Brian to New York to meet Gower Champion, director of *Hello, Dolly!* and *Bye bye Birdie*, who had expressed a 'keen interest' in *Philadelphia, here I come!* Tony Richardson, who had just won an Oscar for directing *Tom Jones*, agreed that 'Gower would be an absolutely wonderful idea'. In February 1965, Brian would travel to Manhattan and be met by Woodfall Films' American representative Neil Hartley, since Lewenstein was 'rather nervous of the idea of pitchforking you alone and unattended into the wilderness of New York'. Hartley had over a decade of experience as a stage manager and associate producer, primarily with the David Merrick Organization, whose shows included *Oliver!* and *Hello, Dolly!* Hartley would also arrange meetings with 'one or two other possible directors' in case discussions with Champion came to nothing.

Brian reported all of this to Tony Guthrie, who sounded a note of caution when it came to Broadway producers. In late January, Guthrie stayed overnight with Brian and Anne in their Marlborough Street terraced house, and he and Brian talked through 'the US trip and all the negotiations so far'. One name in particular triggered Guthrie's protective instincts. As Brian reported to his London agent, 'as soon as he heard Broadway mentioned – and more specifically David Merrick – he insisted I must have an agent over there who knows the play business backways'.

Merrick and Guthrie had tangled ten years earlier, when Merrick invested in Thornton Wilder's comedy *The Matchmaker* after seeing Guthrie direct it in London. Merrick brought the production to America, beginning with a pre-Broadway run in Philadelphia, where, as Guthrie recalled, 'business was good but the laughs were few and far between'. Merrick wheeled on Guthrie, 'declared with some heat that this was not the play he had bought in London', and he and Wilder lambasted the director 'as if I were a fraudulent dog-breeder who had sold them a mongrel with a forged pedigree'. What Guthrie described as 'Undignified scenes in hotel rooms' pale in comparison to Merrick's fights with other directors, when he threw things, screamed, and fired those who disagreed with his demands to cut scenes after preview performances. Speaking to *Time* magazine for a cover feature on Merrick, one actor compared him to Hitler. Merrick embraced his nickname as 'the Abominable Showman', according to *Time*, which described him as 'a bold, bad Broadway producer with a rubber leer, a big black Groucho Marx mustache and a tongue that can tirelessly slice baloney and burble ballyhoo' about his money-making productions. Between 1954 and 1965, he presented thirty-seven Broadway shows, of which almost all made a profit and eleven became smash hits. Over that decade he invested a total of $7 million and grossed $115 million, and at any given time, about twenty per cent of New York's theatre workforce were on his payroll. Merrick was equally renowned for his promotional stunts: he sent a monkey driving an ad-covered car up Broadway, paid a woman to jump onstage and slap a lead actor, and planted a nude female statue in Central Park to draw publicity for his various shows. Guthrie, for his part, decried Merrick's 'cynically, successfully, and vulgarly sensational' showmanship. Directing *The Matchmaker* won Guthrie a Tony award in 1956, but the experience left him with a sour opinion of the producer. No matter to Merrick: he repackaged *The Matchmaker* as a musical named for its title character, and in 1964 *Hello, Dolly!* took Broadway by storm.

Into the Merrick maelstrom arrived Brian Friel in February 1965. The Abbey Theatre had just named him to its newly expanded board along with twenty-four other writers, actors, directors and scholars, and the *New Yorker* had sent him 'a lovely pile of money' for his story 'The gold in the sea': $1,748 as well as a quantity bonus of $595, plus a cost of living adjustment and renewal of his first reading agreement, this time for $500. Brian opened a savings account at Chase Manhattan Bank and deposited one of the cheques for holding until his arrival. After landing at Idlewild, he booked into the Algonquin Hotel and called upon theatre agent Audrey Wood, as arranged by Lewenstein after Guthrie warned Brian he needed 'a competent person at my elbow' whose vigilance over Merrick's schemes would be even 'more important when the show goes into rehearsal'. Wood, 'a small woman, with a quiet, well-bred voice', grew up in the theatre as the daughter of a Broadway manager. An 'endearingly tough' agent, she compared her work with new playwrights to a 'birthing process' that she coached and guided with the watchfulness of a midwife. As a young woman, Wood married her collaborator, casting agent William Liebling, with whom she built a highly successful business. Most famously, she signed the young, unknown Tennessee Williams as her client in 1939, and nurtured his career for the next three decades.

When Brian ended his first day in Manhattan and took refuge in Roger Angell's apartment for dinner, the *New Yorker* editor was stunned to hear that Brian had landed both Wood and Merrick to produce *Philadelphia, here I come!* 'His career entirely turned over in one day. He had arrived', Angell recalled. 'But he was here and he pretended he didn't quite know what it meant. He came here for dinner, so that was the conversation. So then I knew what was probably going to happen. I was delighted. It was terrific. I didn't feel, Oh no, you're a short story writer – if you're a playwright, you're a playwright.'

On his last day in New York, at the behest of producer Kermit Bloomgarden, Brian met Yip Harburg, writer of 'Over the rainbow' and dozens of other songs for film and stage. Bloomgarden had just purchased the rights to Liam O'Flaherty's novel *The Informer*, set in Dublin during the Civil War, which John Ford had adapted into an Oscar-winning film. Bloomgarden wanted Brian's help to turn it into a Broadway musical. Harburg was already on board, as was Burton Lane, Harburg's collaborator on the musical *Finian's rainbow*, the story of an Irish emigrant carrying a stolen crock of gold, pursued by the leprechaun who wanted it back. Lane suggested *The Informer* could use a 'balletic approach' similar to *West Side story*, possibly choreographed by Jerome Robbins, himself a 'former informer' before the Un-American Activities Committee during Senator McCarthy's anti-Communist campaign. But Brian feared Lane and Harburg's angle might be too 'stage-Irish' and their lyrics 'so out of harmony with the sort of dialogue I would write that the whole thing would be a hash of discordant sounds.' His lived experience of Northern Ireland outweighed the composers' shelves of trophies. 'I know I could do the book to a T – there's brashness for you! – because I know these people and this situation fully.' Bloomgarden agreed, and offered a $500 advance, even if it meant losing Harburg and Lane. Over the next two years, Brian drafted an outline and an entire script for a musical version of *The Informer*, 'dealing with the events and characters with absolute simplicity' and anchored by a blind singer, 'a narrator and link-man' who lets 'the telling of the plot evolve from a folk-ballad'. Bloomgarden sought Stephen Sondheim's advice on Brian's proposal. Richard Harris volunteered to play the informer – though Brian wanted Ray McAnally for his 'animal, bullish quality' – and Guthrie signalled interest in directing. Although Bloomgarden eventually rejected the script and killed the project, Brian would salvage the balladeer as a character in his 1973 play *The freedom of the city*, singing the community's response to an unfolding standoff between troops and protesters in the Derry Guildhall.

As for *Philadelphia*, Merrick's interest and Wood's endorsement did not translate into instant success. Lewenstein wanted Brian to choose an American director, but Champion's interest cooled, and 'the other "hot" directors in N.Y. have turned the play down', Brian sadly reported to Angell after he returned home from his high-flying trip to Manhattan. Wood shopped the play to Ulu Grosbard, who had just made his Broadway début as director of *The subject was roses*; William Ball, who had just directed *Tartuffe* at Lincoln Center; and Elia Kazan, who had recently returned from Hollywood to direct Arthur Miller's *After the fall*. All were either unwilling or unavailable, and the future of *Philadelphia* was once again in doubt.

It must have been bittersweet for Brian to hear *Philadelphia* on the BBC's Third Programme in late February 1965, five months after the Dublin Festival premiere, and a week after he returned from New York empty-handed, with hopes of a major production in peril. Ronnie Mason directed the radio broadcast, and Harold Goldblatt, who had greenlighted *The Francophile* at the Group Theatre seven years earlier, played Senator Doogan, father of Gar

O'Donnell's lost love. Donal Donnelly voiced both Private and Public Gar, with one role pre-recorded and the other acoustically engineered to help listeners tell them apart. No one else from the original cast participated in the radio production. To open the broadcast, Private Gar narrated as Gar salts his last barrel of fish in his father's shop – 'Take note, America! Ireland's Champion Gutter and Salter of Pollock will soon descend on your shores!' – and then capitalized on the aural medium to describe scenery never to be constructed onstage: 'a last look round at the dear old shelves and the mahogany counter and the sacks of meal on the floor and – ha-ha! old S.B. O'Donnell Prop. himself! So long, Daddy-baby! Stick around! Be good!'

Listeners loved it – the play scored 71, well above average on the BBC's appreciation index – so Ronnie Mason, emboldened, lobbied for a local broadcast on the Northern Ireland Home Service. But that was another dead end. It was not that Public and Private Gar were too confusing, nor that anything in the script inflamed sectarian sensitivities: the problem was the expletives 'bugger' and 'bloody' uttered by Gar in almost every scene. H.W. McMullan, head of Northern Ireland programmes, shut down all hope for the play to be broadcast from Belfast, sternly declaring he was 'quite sure that a repeat on the Northern Ireland Home Service is not feasible. The continuous use of the word "bugger" and the "richness" of the dialogue would undoubtedly be offensive to our audience.' Meanwhile Mason found renewed success pitching a television version of *The enemy within*, with Scottish actor Tom Fleming as Columba and Harold Goldblatt among the elderly monks. Mason directed and filmed it at outdoor locations around the north Antrim coast, and it aired on BBC Northern Ireland in March 1965.

The question of audience continued to dominate discussions of *Philadelphia*'s future. Lewenstein extended his option on the script but again voiced reluctance to stage it in the West End, citing English theatregoers' resistance to Irish drama. He had co-produced Brendan Behan's *The Hostage* in 1959 and claimed it was the only 'new Irish play that has made a profit in London in the last ten years'. Even *Stephen D*, Hugh Leonard's updated take on James Joyce, had lagged at the British box office despite being a critical success and, later, a hit in America. Regarding *Philadelphia*, Lewenstein warned, 'I don't think this play is a sure thing for London'. Instead, he proposed re-staging it in Dublin, where he could 'invite certain Americans to come and see it' and decide how to bring it to New York. Brian, recovering from surgery for two impacted teeth, confessed misgivings about Lewenstein's proposal. Donal Donnelly had a film offer that summer, and his absence as Private Gar would be 'a <u>huge</u> loss' to the cast. Hilton Edwards, on the other hand, could likely return as director, and Brian was amenable to extending

Lewenstein's contract 'because we know one another and get on well and are able to talk frankly'. The fact remained that *Philadelphia* had played only two weeks in the Dublin Festival and once on BBC radio, and Brian stressed that 'I have got to earn money from this play, and – as important to me – I WANT TO GET IT ON. Now, if possible.'

Thankfully Donal Donnelly's calendar opened up, and Hilton Edwards agreed to direct a six-week revival of *Philadelphia* at his own theatre, the Gate, in August 1965. The news cheered Brian enough to finish his script about Cass McGuire and assemble a new short story anthology, *The gold in the sea*, for publication the following year in both the US and UK. He and Anne 'took a mad notion' and holidayed in Ibiza with their daughters, now aged nine, seven, and nearly two, and, as Brian told Roger Angell, 'we keep telling each other that we are all looking much better since'. He was upset about Bloomgarden's tepid response to *The Informer*, and uneasy about the future of *Philadelphia*. 'The theatre is absorbing me more and more,' Brian told Angell, 'and I'm not altogether happy about that. Apart from the fact that it is taking me away from stories (which keep us in bread and butter) it is involving me in a lot of devious people, and for the greater part of the time I am out of my depth and more than slightly confused and worried.' Angell replied with amusement that 'you complain to me about your involvement in the theatre, and then tell me you have just finished another play. You sound like the mother of a huge family who finds herself pregnant again' – echoing the plot of Brian's story 'The queen of Troy Close', which Angell had just rejected. Still, Angell applauded Brian's progress and the second anthology deal. 'You are at least twice the writer you were five or six years ago, and although I loved the stories in "The saucer of larks," I'm sure this will be a more impressive book in every way.'

Lewenstein, too, was juggling multiple projects. In May 1965, he flew to Cannes to launch *The knack ... and how to get it* at that year's film festival, where British pop culture reigned on the beaches of the Riviera. Sean Connery, promoting his military prison drama *The Hill* on a break between 007 movies, posed for photos with bikini-clad starlets, and John Lennon gave seaside interviews about the Beatle film *Help!* while twelve Daleks roamed the promenade, promoting the first *Dr Who* film. *The knack*, Lewenstein's first film as producer, won the Palme d'Or, the Grand Prix du Festival. Lewenstein was 'so busy with film affairs that he is not sure that he would have the full time to look after the play himself', so he delegated *Philadelphia* to a young Scottish-born producer, Michael White, with whom he had partnered on a season of 'esoteric literary plays' at the Theatre Royal, Stratford East. White, like Lewenstein, was descended from a Russian Jewish family, but his youth was spent in Swiss boarding schools and, later, in New York City. He had come to Lewenstein's attention after his first West End production, *The Connection*, provoked protests against its realistic portrayal of drug addiction. Not yet thirty years old, White would later produce many of the most outlandish, transgressive plays and films of the 1970s, including *Oh! Calcutta!*, *The Rocky Horror show* and *Monty Python and the Holy Grail*.

As the summer progressed, plans for reviving *Philadelphia* to catch American interest gathered momentum. Brian and Anne decamped with their daughters as usual to Donegal for most of July and August, but Brian instructed Hilton Edwards, Michael White and Spencer Curtis Brown to keep him updated by telegram, so he could reply by phone from the local callbox. Edwards once again had 'difficulty in mustering a cast', which delayed the revival's opening a full week, and he and Brian worried about the impact of a newspaper strike that halted all publications across Ireland for the entire month of July. By then, Lewenstein was on location in France with Jeanne Moreau and Tony Richardson for his next film, *Mademoiselle*, but he hoped for a break in production to come see *Philadelphia* open. Michael White arranged travel to Dublin to observe rehearsals, and again the Friels rented a house in the city so Brian could collaborate with Edwards and the cast as the performance took shape. David Merrick himself would be in the audience on opening night.

When the curtain rose at the Gate Theatre on 10 August 1965, Brian, Hilton Edwards and Michael White must have held their breath and hoped for the best. Dublin theatregoers who had missed the Festival the previous year filled the seats, and the returning actors – Patrick Bedford and Donal Donnelly as Public and Private Gar, Eamon Kelly as Screwballs, Máirín O'Sullivan as Madge – reprised their roles alongside newcomers: Gar's returned American aunt and uncle, the local canon, the schoolmaster, and Katie Doogan and her father. Amid the enthralled audience sat Ria Mooney, now retired from the Abbey, who deemed the production 'flawless in Casting, Direction, and Acting' and thanked Brian for restoring her faith in Irish theatre. But David Merrick was not convinced, and his lukewarm reaction left Brian 'more than slightly perplexed'. Merrick tentatively offered to bring the play to New York in early 1966, but not without conditions: he wanted to re-cast the lead roles, recruit stars if possible, and use American actors in minor parts to ward off trouble with Equity, the actors' union. Brian stood his ground. 'We all agree that the situation dealt with in this play is not peculiarly Irish; but the validity of the situation is weakened if we try to substitute Blueberry Hill for Ballybeg. In other words what I am trying to say is that the "Irishness" of this present production & company is its most valuable asset.'

To keep the Irish cast together, Brian argued, a London production was imperative. Michael White canvassed West End theatres with fewer than a thousand seats, as he and Lewenstein believed it would be 'madness' to aim for a larger audience with any Irish play – but all were fully booked until the end of 1965. More bad news arrived from the Lord Chamberlain's office, which denied *Philadelphia* a performance licence, citing twenty-eight instances of the word 'bugger' throughout the script, and a scene in which Gar O'Donnell's friend Tom 'grips his loins, doubles up, and rolls about in agony' as he recounts his flirtation with a local girl. 'With regard to this action the actor must double up with his hands somewhere in the region of his stomach', the Lord Chamberlain commanded. 'There must be no question of his placing his hands on his private parts.' If needed, White knew, he could circumvent the Lord Chamberlain by staging a 'club' performance of *Philadelphia* – he would employ this tactic to present the anti-war trilogy *America hurrah*, and he later skirted censorship of *Oh! Calcutta!* and *Rocky Horror* – but lack of available theatre space in the West End was a devastating blow. Brian, in Derry, was 'stunned' and 'disturbed' when he received the 'shattering news'. He wanted to trust Lewenstein that Merrick would confirm plans for Broadway, but lamented, 'I have had so many disappointments over this play ... that I just cannot face further tentative plans for January in New York'.

Philadelphia's Dublin revival risked closing yet again without firm plans for either a London or New York production. Guthrie telegraphed his friend Harry Saltzman, Lewenstein's sometime partner and a producer of the James Bond series, to 'SEND TRUSTWORTHY SPY' to see the play before its final curtain. 'POSSIBLY THIS PROPERTY AVAILABLE', Guthrie pleaded, 'THINK WELL WORTH YOUR WHILE FLY DUBLIN'. Spencer Curtis Brown, meanwhile, lobbied American heiress Irene Selznick, who was 'extremely intelligent with only the slightest tendency towards dipsomania', he reported to Brian. 'You would like her.' Selznick, the daughter of movie magnate Louis B. Mayer, had bankrolled *A streetcar named Desire* in 1947, and was known to have deep pockets and good taste. Curtis Brown personally escorted her from London to Dublin by plane. After seeing *Philadelphia*, she was 'enormously moved and impressed' and stood ready to invest in its American future if Lewenstein's option expired. Yet another plan was hatched by Audrey Wood, who remained in contact with Kermit Bloomgarden, and expressed confidence that 'we can still work out a deal between Kermit and Oscar failing Merrick'. At last, in late September, a full year after *Philadelphia*'s premiere in the Dublin Festival, Wood telegraphed Brian in Derry, confirming that Merrick was ready to sign a contract. The play would open, appropriately, in Philadelphia, then Toronto in mid-January 1966, and then proceed to Broadway. Merrick was

'AGREEABLE USING EDWARDS AS DIRECTOR BOTH LEADING MEN PLUS WOMAN PLAYING MADGE' but 'NOT KEEN TAKING ACTOR PLAYING FATHER'. Brian consented. Relieved, because 'I could do with the money', he collected his royalties of just under £221, five per cent of the Gate's box office take of £4,420 over *Philadelphia*'s six-week revival run. His agent kept £20 as commission.

Union rules and immigration laws limited the number of actors who could be imported from the Dublin production, so, in November 1965, Edwards flew to New York to hold auditions for the play's supporting roles. He found Mavis Villiers, an Australian who had perfected her American accent in Hollywood, to play Gar's returned aunt Lizzy, and he cast Americans as Lizzy's husband Con and their travelling companion Ben Burton. Experienced television actors played Gar's sweetheart Kate Doogan and her father the senator, while Irish actors resident in New York leapt at the chance to fill other roles: Gar's friends Ned, Tom and Joe, his teacher Master Boyle and Canon Mick O'Byrne. In the end, Edwards brought back Eamon Kelly, who had originated the role of S.B. 'Screwballs' O'Donnell, despite Merrick's initial inclination to drop him from the Broadway cast. Like Máirín O'Sullivan, who played Madge, Kelly was a veteran of the Radio Éireann Players, and both were natives of County Kerry. During the Dublin Festival, Guthrie had singled out Kelly's veracity as 'The one piece of casting which seemed absolutely bullseye'. His wordless simplicity shone, and his 'Every single move, every turn of the head, every pause, every inflection were loaded with meaning and imagination'. In Guthrie's estimation, 'he was of <u>enormous</u> assistance to the poetry and meaning of the play'.

Two days after Christmas 1965, Kelly and O'Sullivan, with Donal Donnelly, Patrick Bedford and Hilton Edwards, climbed an Aer Lingus gangway in early morning darkness. Brian joined them and posed, hat in hand, for a press release photo as together they boarded their flight for New York. When they landed, they were welcomed with open arms by Irish Americans, who themselves had at last arrived into positions of power and privilege. Irish culture was in vogue in the United States, as attested by the popularity of *The quiet man*, the Clancy Brothers, and Irish lace and Aran sweaters worn by fashionable celebrities like Philadelphia's own Grace Kelly. Merrick ditched Toronto and adjusted the play's preview tour to follow its Philadelphia opening with a move to the Wilbur Theatre in Boston. In both cities, the playwright, director and actors were fêted by Irish American professionals and business societies, riding a wave of post-JFK enthusiasm for the Irish and Irish American Catholic politicians. 'We were invited to luncheon parties, dinner parties, and after-theatre parties', Brian later recounted. 'Even the taciturn Mr

7.1 Brian Friel, Hilton Edwards, and cast of *Philadelphia, here I come!* boarding plane to New York. *Clockwise from top left*: Donal Donnelly, Eamon Kelly, Patrick Bedford, Máirín O'Sullivan.

Merrick threw a party on opening night and on his lapel sported a green flag that bore the legend 'Erin Go Brath.' Bobby Kennedy attended, along with his wife Ethel and his sister Jean. Brian, Edwards and the cast were invited to Philadelphia City Hall and posed for photographs with the city's first Catholic

7.2 Brian Friel, Hilton Edwards, and cast of *Philadelphia, here I come!* with Mayor James Tate in Philadelphia; Friel and Edwards hold Liberty Bell replicas. *Back row, left to right*: Patrick Bedford, Donal Donnelly, Friel, Edwards, Eamon Kelly. *Front row, left to right*: Mavis Villiers, Tate, Máirín O'Sullivan.

mayor, James Tate. Actress Máirín O'Sullivan wore an Aran cardigan to that event, where Brian and Edwards received miniature Liberty Bell replicas as keepsakes. In Boston, Hilton Edwards gave a lecture to the Éire Society followed by a reception for the entire theatre company at the Harvard Club.

Brian spent his thirty-seventh birthday in New York, where Edwards and the cast rehearsed for their American début at Philadelphia's Walnut Street Theatre on 17 January 1966. On opening night, Michael White's wife gave birth to a daughter, their second child, named Liberty ('for the statue not the store', White explained). Merrick called him to a meeting the next morning and threatened to fire Edwards, to 'do something to liven this play up', but White resisted, and the matter was dropped. Reviews in Philadelphia were good, and so were box office returns. *Variety* called it 'a sort of Irish "Death of a Salesman"' with a 'flavorful' turn of phrase. It grossed $27,428 in its first week, and $35,557 in its second before making the move to Boston. There, despite the *Globe*'s withering review of the play's 'hackneyed' theme, its 'blathering bathos' and its author's 'terribly sober state of mind for an

Irishman', the Wilbur Theatre reaped $25,650 in ticket sales in its first week and $30,161 in its second.

Prospects grew for a profitable Broadway opening, but David Merrick wanted to leave nothing to chance. Brian and the cast felt 'a tightening of the nerves' as they drove back to New York 'in a deluge of rain, and scattered to our various hotels and rooming-houses. I don't think any of us had the heart to unpack.' For weeks, Merrick and other producers had been warring with newly appointed *New York Times* critic Stanley Kauffmann, complaining about Kauffmann's practice of attending plays on their last night of previews, rather than opening night, so that he could take time to craft his reviews. New York papers were fiercer than their Dublin counterparts, in whose pages Frank O'Connor had protested Gar's irreverence. American critics held the power to kill productions, and reviews could mean 'either bonanza time or sudden death on Broadway'. For *Philadelphia*'s second and final preview night at the Helen Hayes Theatre on 15 February 1966, Merrick sent the *New York Times* two tickets and a note with three words: 'At your peril'. When Kauffmann arrived at the theatre, amid hundreds of paying ticket holders, Merrick abruptly cancelled the performance, citing only 'technical difficulties' that were never explained. The sold-out crowd of 1,100 spilled into Broadway restaurants, buzzing about the turn of events. Rain checks would cost Merrick $4,000, but the gossip he generated was priceless. The *New York Times* carried the story on its front page, complete with a photo of the producer's ominous three-word note, and the *New Yorker* and *Time* were agog. Merrick appeared on the popular *Merv Griffin* TV show, where he criticized the *Times* drama desk roundly. Audrey Wood's husband, William Liebling, praised the stunt for buying 'a million dollars worth of publicity'. By the time Kauffmann's review was published, its barbs had no sting. For the critic, Gar too closely resembled other 'Billy-Liar youths dreaming fantasies in drab bedrooms'. Though Kauffmann faulted the play's 'not-quite-novel novelty of view', faintly praising its 'considerable pleasantness' while damning its 'little poetry and insufficient power', audiences did not care that he found it 'amiable and appealing enough but unexciting'. Instead, they queued at the ticket windows, propelling *Philadelphia* to 'a promising box office start', with proceeds of $22,226 in its shortened first week.

Brian returned home and described the peculiarities of his first American theatre tour in an essay titled 'Philadelphia, here the author comes!' which he read for radio broadcast on the Northern Ireland Home Service, despite that channel's banning of the play itself. To Northern Ireland listeners, he confided that during the pre-Broadway run at the Walnut Street Theatre, he had prowled the aisles to eavesdrop during intermission. As he reported, 'One corpulent, silver-haired lady exploded into her husband's face, "So he's coming to Philadelphia! So what the hell's he crying about!"' After the convoluted path the play had taken to break through, Brian returned to Derry sobered by the vicissitudes of show business. 'The fact that a play is successful on Broadway doesn't mean that the play is a good play; nor does it mean that the play is a bad play. All it means is that on a particular night the majority of the critics liked what they saw on stage, and told their readers; and the readers in turn said to themselves: "Ah! Howard Blinks says this is a good play, honey. We must go and see it because this is a good play." And success breeds success.'

Success, for *Philadelphia*, meant box office returns that dwarfed all previous income Brian had earned by writing or teaching. The play's second week brought in $34,427, and it soon settled into weekly receipts topping $35,000, a 'steady climb' noted by *Variety* as word of mouth drew growing audiences. Brian's contracts with Lewenstein and Merrick assured him ten per cent of gross proceeds, over $3,000 per week. At the 1966 exchange rate of $2.79 to the pound sterling, his weekly royalties from *Philadelphia* were over £1,000, almost double his annual teacher's salary and more than enough to pay his mortgage in Marlborough Street many times over. *Variety* highlighted the disparity in a front page headline, 'Ex-teacher Friel hits cash mark', proclaiming that Brian had 'struck gold' on Broadway while, in contrast, 'his freelance writing income last year averaged about $50 a week', just 'enough for a modest livelihood in Ireland'. And *Philadelphia*'s success continued to grow: it ran for forty-one weeks on Broadway and grossed over one million dollars before a six-month tour across America. In Chicago, its run was extended after it 'took a mighty leap' with weekly ticket sales over $40,000. Brendan Smith's royalty agreement for the Dublin Theatre Festival continued to pay dividends of 1½ per cent on the play's gross returns throughout its first two years. Patrick Bedford negotiated a salary raise to $1,000 per week and did a star turn in the *Chicago Sun-Times*, smiling for press photos as he cooked dinner in his temporary apartment, where he demonstrated an Irish recipe for lamb with herbs and potatoes. *Philadelphia* struck such a chord with US audiences and critics that it was one of four Tony nominees for Best Play of 1966 and became the longest-running Irish play in Broadway history. Brian's royalties from Broadway alone were over £35,000, a staggering sum for a playwright who, two years earlier, had to pester Gaiety management for his last £24 after *Philadelphia*'s Festival premiere.

EPILOGUE

Curtain call

IN 1996, MARKING THE thirtieth anniversary of *Philadelphia*'s Broadway début, Patrick Bedford wrote to Brian in spidery script to thank him for 'the role of my life'. He remembered their flight together from Dublin that wintry morning, when, as in the play's jettisoned epilogue, the young actor was overcome with emotion. In real life, Madge sat beside him on the plane, in the person of Máirín O'Sullivan, and below them, Ireland's snow-covered fields lay serenely, 'looking like a Japanese print'. Anxious, Bedford could not hide his tears, and when O'Sullivan asked, 'Why are you crying?' he replied, 'O Máirín, if we are a flop it will be disgraceful. If we are a hit it will change us forever.'

As he recalled gratefully from a distance of three decades, 'It was and it did!' Bedford lived out Gar O'Donnell's destiny as a permanent transplant to America, where he acted Gar's emigration night after night for a year-and-a-half. The play transferred from the US to London in September 1967 – the Lord Chamberlain's authority over censorship had at last been abolished – but its West End box office returns were disappointing, as Lewenstein had predicted. When Hilton Edwards died in 1982, Bedford inherited half his estate as well as his piano, car and shares of the Gate. It was Bedford who arranged Edwards' wake in the Harcourt Terrace house he had shared with Micheál MacLiammóir, and in 1988 Bedford became a Gate trustee, visiting Dublin often for opening nights and board meetings. Like so many immigrants, he felt at home neither in his new country nor his old one, and was trapped in the borderland between. He had been so homesick during *Philadelphia*'s initial run, he told Brian, that he threatened to leave before its national tour, but 'it was in Chicago when they told me they dye the river green on Patrick's Day that I gave up my homesickness and decided America was so outrageous one has to love it. I still don't! but I don't love Ireland either. Where the hell am I. Is this Limbo?'

Philadelphia changed Brian's life, too. In 1967 he and Anne built a house near Muff and moved into 'the Royalty Arms', as Roger Angell christened it

– 'your new tax haven' just over the Donegal border from Derry. Brian replied that they still shared it 'with a squad of builders who spend the day sprinkling us with cement dust', but there was space enough for a tennis court, where, playing one day with his daughters, 'in a wild effort to show how enjoyable and exhilarating the game can be', he fell backward and broke his hand, an accident that caused him to miss Ray McAnally's revival of *The enemy within* at the Olympia Theatre in Dublin. Brian and Anne later had two more children, a daughter, Sally, and son, David. Beside their cottage in Kincasslagh they eventually built a more modern summer house, Teach Annie, whose roofline mimics the sweep of Mount Errigal above it.

After 'The gold in the sea', Brian published no more stories in the *New Yorker*, nor anywhere else. Angell teased that he was 'just too good for your old friends', too busy with 'your new toff friends and fellow-celebrities', and 'Too rich to remember those who used to take you in off the street and give you a crust of bread and a clean collar. Sad.' Brian claimed not to have abandoned fiction as a genre. 'I did make several attempts at stories recently. All failures. Maybe a facility will come in 1968. I hope it does because I much prefer story writing to plays.' But even as Angell renewed the *New Yorker*'s first reading agreement – for a reduced premium of $100 – he admitted 'severe doubts that Brian Friel will ever write another short story, now that he is on his way to becoming the Edward Albee of North Ireland'.

Brian's stature far surpassed Albee's – or Guthrie's, or O'Connor's – in the years to follow. In a brazen attempt to capitalize on the playwright's growing fame, David Merrick launched *The loves of Cass McGuire* while *Philadelphia* was still on Broadway. Hilton Edwards directed, and Ruth Gordon, who had starred in Guthrie's Tony-winning *Matchmaker* a decade earlier, played Cass, the broken emigrant, returned to her homeland only to be spurned by her upstart bourgeois brother. Early reviews praised Gordon's 'glorious performance' and the play's 'excellent blend of lusty comedy and affecting drama' but warned that its box office appeal might falter 'because of its emphasis on such traditionally unpopular theatrical subjects as old age and confinement in nursing homes'. The play ran for only twenty nights on Broadway, averaging $13,000 in weekly ticket sales, before Merrick shut it down at a loss of $75,000. Brian faulted Merrick – not the play, not the director. A few weeks after *Cass*'s final curtain, he absolved Edwards of any '"blame" for what happened in America. I don't think either of us should hastily assume any great responsibility. Miss Gordon was never right. Merrick broke my heart. You worked yourself to the bone.' Since *Cass* ran for fewer than fifty performances, Brian was released from his contract with Merrick the 'Abominable Showman'. He quickly submitted the play to the Abbey, where

Ernest Blythe accepted it and handed it to Tomás Mac Anna to direct. It opened in Dublin six months after closing on Broadway and enjoyed a warmer reception than from American audiences. Soured by the experience, Brian told an interviewer a few years later that 'I don't like America at all. It still has some virtues and it's a very generous country. I loved it when I first went there and I was very enamoured of it, but this left me very rapidly. Now I dislike it very much.'

Oscar Lewenstein's efforts to transfer *Philadelphia* to film stalled at the distribution stage. It was shot at Ardmore Studios in Wicklow in late 1970 – Siobhán McKenna headlined as Madge, and Eamon Kelly and Mavis Villiers reprised their stage roles as Screwballs and Aunt Lizzy – but was not released until 1975 due to copyright negotiations. Meanwhile, Lewenstein produced Brian's 1973 play *The freedom of the city* at the Royal Court, London, with Albert Finney as director and Stephen Rea in the cast, his first encounter with Brian – while the Abbey staged a simultaneous production, with Micheál Ó hAongusa, who had been the deaf cook Dochonna in *The enemy within*, as the balladeer who elegizes unarmed Derry civil rights protesters shot by British troops in Brian's most controversial play. Premiering just after the first anniversary of Bloody Sunday, *The freedom of the city* received a chilly reception from London critics, and Lewenstein sang the Internationale to rally Brian's resolve in the wake of 'hostile reviews'.

After *Philadelphia*, Brian worked with Edwards on two more plays, *Lovers* and *Crystal and Fox*, but he was never again as pliant with future directors. Having compared himself to 'a bit of a dog's tail in this revision business' when following Roger Angell's advice, Brian explained, 'There's a Gaelic expression, ruball a' mhadaidh (it means literally "a dog's tail"), which is used to describe a person who is so lacking in determination that he agrees with everybody – the stray dog who goes a bit of the road with every stranger he meets'. After *Cass*, he would no longer be so trusting. In his 'Self-portrait' for BBC Northern Ireland radio in 1971, Brian lamented directors who 'expect writers to approach them with awe' and 'surrender the entire interpretation of a play into their artistic hands'. Having suffered the vicissitudes of Broadway, he now compared his scripts to 'an orchestral score' and tasked 'the director and the actors to interpret that score exactly as it is written'.

But the spirit of collaboration that graced Brian's work with Edwards, Angell and Mason carried into his co-founding of the Field Day Theatre Company in 1980, as did his observation of Guthrie at work in Minneapolis. Like Guthrie in the Twin Cities, Brian and his collaborator Stephen Rea brought world class theatre to a provincial capital when they premiered Brian's play *Translations* at the Guildhall, home of the Londonderry Corporation, during the height of the Troubles. The company improvised a thrust stage that recalled Guthrie's ideal of theatre in the round, built as an extension to the Guildhall's permanent platform beneath its historic pipe organ. Outdoors, a banner announcing ticket sales stretched across scaffolding that masked recent bomb damage to the stained glass windows, and audience members took their seats after being frisked at the door, while an RAF helicopter hovered overhead. The evening news reported increasingly intractable blanket and dirty protests at the Maze prison, which would soon evolve into harrowing hunger strikes. Over the next decade, Field Day launched annual plays in the Guildhall, including Brian's adaptation of *Three sisters* in 1981 and his comedy *The communication cord* in 1982. All Field Day productions toured the island of Ireland, playing in market towns north and south of the border – Magherafelt, Dungannon, Ballyshannon, Tralee – crossing checkpoints that grew more and more militarized as the Troubles wore on.

Northern Ireland had changed, changed utterly. But decades later, Brian Friel's plays still resonate. *Translations* played to sold-out crowds at the National Theatre, London, in 2018 and 2019, as debates over Brexit and borders took centre stage in the political arena. In a cross-border collaboration between the Abbey and the Lyric, *Translations* played in Belfast and Dublin in the spring and summer of 2022. A Ukrainian production of *Translations* played at the Abbey in 2023 as Kyiv remained under siege. In northwest Ireland, the Arts Over Borders Festival has staged dozens of site-specific Friel plays since 2015, including Kabosh's readings of *The enemy within* in Catholic and Presbyterian churches across Donegal, Omagh, Belfast and Derry. An Grianán Theatre, Letterkenny, staged a full production of *The enemy within* in the autumn of 2021. The Abbey's production of *Faith healer* was postponed in 2020 as the pandemic forced a wave of lockdowns and shuttered theatres, but the Old Vic – where Guthrie and Edwards had their beginnings – staged *Faith healer* 'in camera' before empty seats during the first year of worldwide quarantine. Like the radio signals that bore Brian's first dramas across the Irish Sea to listeners in England, Scotland and Wales, the Internet livestreamed the image of itinerant healer Frank Hardy, his wife, and their manager as they wove their intersecting truths, lies and memories before the Old Vic's silent gallery of red velvet seats and gilded balconies. Housebound audiences in seventy-one countries watched, enrapt.

Cinematic success would elude Brian until 1998, when *Dancing at Lughnasa* brought the story of the Mundy sisters and their 'returned missioner' brother to the silver screen. Brian's two anthologies, *A saucer of larks* and *The gold in the sea*, fell out of print, but Gallery Press rescued some of his short fiction from oblivion when it published *Selected stories* in 2016. Other work still lies forgotten: Brian took *The blind mice* out of circulation in 1965, in response to a German translator who requested its rights, as well as rights to *The Francophile*, which Brian withheld, calling the script 'so poor that I still have bad dreams about it'.

And yet in Brian Friel's beginnings lay the seeds of his prodigious career: his preoccupations with memory, truth, duality in public and private life, the balance of humour and pathos, belly laughter and tears, the strain of comedy amid temptations toward bitterness. His prolific work during his early years leapt among genres as his voice grew stronger and more confident, and his mentors, editors and directors became true friends and role models. His experimentation with narration, chronology and language continued throughout his career, as witnessed in landmark plays like *Faith healer*, *The freedom of the city*, *Translations* and *Dancing at Lughnasa*. Economy of language, first learned through Ronnie Mason's 'ruthless use of a blue pencil', became a standard.

Roger Angell and his wife Peggy Moorman welcomed me into their apartment on an autumn afternoon in 2018 to reminisce about Roger's friendship with Brian. Carol Rogge Angell had died of breast cancer six years earlier, after instructing her husband to abjure 'memorial fidelity'. We had rescheduled our meeting date around the Harvard–Yale football game, which Angell, a Harvard alum, watched on television every November. Roger, Peggy and I drank mimosas and ate bagels with salmon and cream cheese while their fox terrier Andy (the nickname of Angell's stepfather E.B. White) begged for a game of fetch with a well-chewed tennis ball (Angell told me, 'Don't play. Pay no attention'). On the luncheon table were three large Harvard football badges Angell had worn to stadium games in years past.

'Brian had a wonderful voice, which is why he became such a great playwright', Angell mused, recalling Brian's early submissions to the *New Yorker*. 'And the fact that we are responding in this way, in this personal way, means that he is better than hundreds of other people who were doing the same thing. It's no great work of genius on my part to see that he is better, and writing stuff that will go on.' Guthrie once remarked that the theatre drew many who saw the stage as 'a hiding place', but for Brian Friel, the stage became a site of invention, a place to make physical the psychological and philosophical questions that underlay his writing in other genres. Through his recurring characters – teachers, fathers, exiles, conflicted constables, returned missionaries, carnival performers, bourgeois families, bitter families, broken families – he renewed his explorations with each new project, like Columba, inscribing eternal rituals through the eyes and ears of a novice, always ready to begin again.

Notes

Abbreviations to these notes

BBC – Plays   BBC WAC – NI 20/2/1 Plays – Contributors – Brian Friel – March 1957– October 1971
BBC – S/Writer   BBC WAC – FRIEL, BRIAN – RCONT 1 – File I – S/Writer
KB papers   Wisconsin Center for Film and Theater Research, Kermit Bloomgarden papers, box 46, folder 32
NLI, BFP   Brian Friel papers, National Library of Ireland
NY   *New Yorker* archives

In correspondence:

BF to RA   Brian Friel, letter to Roger Angell
BF to RM   Brian Friel, letter to Ronald Mason
EH to RA   Edith Haggard, letter to Roger Angell
RA to BF   Roger Angell, letter to Brian Friel
RA to EH   Roger Angell, letter to Edith Haggard
RM to BF   Ronald Mason, letter to Brian Friel

PROLOGUE: **Border Crossings, February 1965**
[**Page 13**] 'up in that big bugger of a jet': Brian Friel, *Philadelphia, here I come!* in *Collected plays*, vol. 1 (Loughcrew: Gallery Press, 2016), I.i.55.
'seized by a quiet panic': Brian Friel, 'Adrift in London', *Irish Times*, 21 October 1961.
[**Page 14**] 'superstitious': BF to RA, 7 November 1964, *NY*.
'This theatrical world': RA to BF, 23 February 1965, *NY*.
'I don't know anyone': RA to BF, 6 April 1965, *NY*.
[**Page 15**] 'whatever work I have on hands': BBC – Plays – BF to RM, 24 September 1957.
'equally horrified': Roger Angell, email communication, 22 October 2018.
'cosy security': BBC – Plays – RM to BF, 19 October 1960.

CHAPTER 1: **Rehearsals, 1952–9**
[**Page 17**] Brian Friel was born on 9 January 1929: Brian had two birth certificates, one for 9 January 1929 and another for 10 January 1929, as he disclosed to *Irish Press* readers, along with his baptismal name, Bernard Patrick, and his confirmation name, Casimir, in his first column for that newspaper, 'Meet Brian Friel', on 28 April 1962. In a letter dated 10 January 1964, Brian remarked to Roger Angell that he was celebrating his thirty-fifth birthday. When Richard Pine asked about the two birthdates, Brian replied, 'Perhaps I'm twins', according to the obituary Pine wrote for him, published 2 October 2015 in *The Guardian*.

'three-classroom building': Brian Friel, 'Self-portrait', *Aquarius*, 5 (1972), 17–22.

'a soft-spoken, courteous man': 'Beloved teacher', *Irish Press*, 4 March 1960. Patrick Friel taught at Culmore Primary School for sixteen years, 1923–39.

'I can see him now': Brian Friel, 'Lurchers and letters', *Irish Times*, 11 December 1961.

[**Page 18**] 'vivid memories of complete despair': Brian Friel, 'Meet Brian Friel', *Irish Press*, 28 April 1962.

'Sunday singing episodes': BBC WAC – 'Some people and places' script, Brian Friel, broadcast 7 November 1962, Northern Ireland Home Service, p. 3.

'troubled by an ambition': Brian Friel, 'My father and the sergeant', *The saucer of larks*, p. 183.

'Brian's sister Nanette': 'Omagh notes', *Ulster Herald*, 25 August 1956.

'The war supplied work': Brian Barton, *Northern Ireland in the Second World War* (Belfast: Ulster Historical Foundation, 1995), pp 78–83.

'Up to 149 ships': Barton, p. 101.

'the city's entire pre-war population': Northern Ireland Statistics and Research Agency, 1937 census, http://www.histpop.org/ohpr/servlet/PageBrowser?path=Browse/Census%20(by%20date)/1937&active=yes&mno=341&tocstate=expandnew&tocseq=4100&display=sections&display=tables&display=pagetitles&pageseq=first-nonblank and https://www.nisra.gov.uk/statistics/2001-and-earlier-censuses/1937-census

'American soldiers': Barton, pp 106–7.

'Brian's family lived at 5 St Joseph's Avenue': Marriage announcement, Brian and Anne Friel, 28 December 1954, NLI, BFP, MS 37,451.

'the whole drama of military life': BBC WAC – 'The green years' script, Brian Friel, broadcast 30 April 1964, Northern Ireland Home Service, p. 2.

[**Page 19**] 'He gathered with other boys': BBC WAC – 'Some people and places' script, Brian Friel, broadcast 7 November 1962, Northern Ireland Home Service, p. 7.

'he roller skated': Friel, BBC WAC – 'The green years', Brian Friel, pp 4–5.

'I don't remember the details of those private lessons': BBC WAC – 'The green years', Brian Friel, p. 2.

'special and sacred' ... 'I remember in detail': Brian Friel, 'Self-portrait', *Aquarius* 5 (1972), 17–22, p. 18.

'requiem high Mass': 'The "Wee Donegal Priest" is no more: the late Father MacLoone, Glenties', *Ulster Herald*, 15 July 1950, p. 3.

'Omagh Technical School': 'Omagh Notes', *Ulster Herald*, 29 July 1950, p. 8.

[**Page 20**] 'there is no publishing house in Ulster', John Hewitt, 'Writing in Ulster', *The Bell*, 18:4 (July, 1952), 197–202, p. 198.

'Dear God …': Friel, 'The Child', *The Bell*, 18:4 (July 1952), 232–3, p. 233. These lines resemble the final words in James Joyce's story 'Counterparts' in *Dubliners*: "'O, pa!' he cried. 'Don't beat me, pa! And I'll … I'll say a Hail Mary for you … I'll say a Hail Mary for you, pa, if you don't beat me … I'll say a Hail Mary …'"

'Pleasant memories' and 'blinded with tears': Friel, 'The Child', p. 233.

'teaching posts in Derry': 'Omagh notes', *Ulster Herald*, 25 August 1956, p. 8, describes the Friel family's 'fishing holiday at the home of Mrs Friel's sister, Miss MacLoone, The Laurels, Glenties' and notes that 'They had considerable success on Lough Eagh for sea trout and Lough Anna for brown trout.' Brian Friel, B.A., is listed as a teacher at the Christian Brothers' School, Derry; his sister Nanette and her husband, a commissioned officer in the RAF, were visiting from Yorkshire, and Brian's sister Mary is listed as a teacher at St Columba's School, Derry, where her father was headmaster.

'Anne's photo': 'Degree day at U.C.D.', *Evening Herald*, 6 November 1953, p. 1.

'She and Brian met as teenagers': Mel Gussow, 'From Ballybeg to Broadway', *New York Times magazine*, 29 September 1991, p. 56.

'sharp Waterside tongue': BBC – Plays – BF to RM, 11 August 1964.
'Anne became Brian's first reader': Mel Gussow, 'From Ballybeg to Broadway', *New York Times magazine*, 29 September 1991, p. 60.
'the couple moved into 13 Marlborough Street': Marriage announcement, Brian and Anne Friel, 28 December 1954, NLI, BFP, MS 37,451.
'checked cap' and 'brown shoes': Brian Friel, 'Projecting with dogs', *Irish Times*, 20 December 1961, p. 8.
[**Page 22**] *'The Bell*'s rate of one guinea per thousand words': Kelly Matthews, *The Bell magazine and the representation of Irish identity* (Dublin: Four Courts Press, 2012), p. 13.
'Brian received twelve guineas': Contract between Brian Friel and BBC Northern Ireland Home Service, 6 April 1956, BBC Written Archives Centre, for broadcast of 'The good old days' on the 'Ariel' programme, 2 May 1956.
'Dear Editor': BBC – S/Writer – Brian Friel, letter to the BBC, 18 June 1956.
'The mental rehabilitation of an architect': BBC – S/Writer – Mollie Greenhalgh, memo to assistant script editor, drama (sound), 11 July 1956.
'polite rejection slip': BBC – S/Writer – Cynthia Pughe, letter to Brian Friel, 18 July 1956.
'I am not at all sure': Mrs Edith Sewell Haggard, letter to Mrs K.S. White, 5 February 1957. *NY*, New York Public Library.
'We can't use Brian Friel's "The nest"': K.S. White, letter to Edith Sewell Haggard, 11 February 1957. *NY*, New York Public Library.
'Katharine White had joined the *New Yorker*': Nancy Franklin, 'Lady with a pencil', *The New Yorker*, 26 February 1996. See also Brendan Gill, *Here at the New Yorker* (New York: Random House, 1975): 'At the time that she resigned her full-time position, she was in charge of fiction at the magazine, but her influence extended far beyond that department; she had helped to invent the magazine as a whole …' (p. 291).
[**Page 23**] Brian Friel, 'For export only', *The Commonweal*, 15 February 1957, 509–10.
'I am enclosing the opening pages of a script': BBC – Plays – BF to RM, 28 March 1957.
[**Page 24**] 'I have no experience of radio drama': BBC – Plays – BF to RM, 28 March 1957.
'both poet and politician': John Tydeman, 'Obituary: Ronald Mason', *The Independent*, 19 January 1997.
'Trust you are not missing London': BBC – Plays – John Tydeman, letter to Ronald Mason, 6 May 1964.
'many who knew Mason suspected he was homosexual': Paul Muldoon, in conversation, 3 March 2018; Michael Longley, in conversation, 18 March 2019.
'The dialogue is really v. good': BBC – Plays – Ronald Mason, memo to H.W. McMullan, 10 April 1957.
'looks very promising indeed': BBC – Plays – RM to BF, 30 April 1957.
[**Page 25**] 'BBC's policies throughout the United Kingdom': Asa Briggs, *The history of broadcasting in the United Kingdom*, rev. ed. vol. 4 (Oxford: Oxford UP, 1995), p. 637.
'a typical afternoon play on the Home Service': Asa Briggs, *The BBC: the first fifty years* (Oxford: Oxford UP, 1985), p. 335.
'The BBC's national and regional stations aired 600 new plays per year': Briggs, *The BBC: the first fifty years* (Oxford: Oxford UP, 1985), p. 335.
[**Page 26**] 'Could you let me know': BBC – Plays – BF to RM, 13 May 1957.
'Grief for what?': BBC WAC – *A sort of freedom*, Brian Friel, broadcast 16 January 1958, Northern Ireland Home Service, p. 42.
Look back in anger … aired on BBC television: John Wyver, 30 June 2013, https://screenplaystv.wordpress.com/2013/06/30/from-the-50s-look-back-in-anger-bbc-and-itv-1956/

'I can't fill my belly on your pride': BBC WAC – *A sort of freedom*, Brian Friel, broadcast 16 January 1958, Northern Ireland Home Service, p. 40.
'If the play has any moral purpose': BBC – Plays – Brian Friel, synopsis of *A sort of freedom*, 28 March 1957.
'Apart from a few obvious constructional flaws': BBC – Plays – Ronald Mason, drama producer, script report to H.W. McMullan, head of programmes, 31 May 1957.
'He has something here': BBC – Plays – H.W. McMullan, 4 June 1957, handwritten response to Mason memo of 31 May 1957.
[Page 27] 'vet the Trade Unionism': BBC – Plays – John Boyd, letter to David Bleakley, 9 August 1957.
'I have been very careful': BBC – Plays – BF to RM, 28 March 1957.
'Dear Brian Friel … I am sure you have a play here': BBC – Plays – RM to BF, 7 June 1957.
'clear, precise, and clean-cut dialogue': BBC WAC – NI Plays – RM to BF, 7 June 1957.
'I am not sure that the play says quite what you intended': BBC – Plays – RM to BF, 7 June 1957.
'He invited Brian to Broadcasting House': BBC – Plays – Brian Friel, letters to Ronald Mason, 10 June and 17 June 1957; RM to BF, 17 June 1957; Brian Friel, receipt for 3rd-class return rail fare of £1 6s. 10d. 'in connection with script discussion', 21 June 1957.
'Dear Ronald Mason … I enjoyed our talk immensely': BBC WAC – NI Plays – BF to RM, 28 June 1957. 'Fowler' may refer to *A dictionary of modern English usage* by Henry Watson Fowler (Oxford: Oxford UP, 1926).
'To be quite honest, I have battled with it for so long': BBC – Plays – BF to RM, 28 June 1957.
[Page 28] 'you have cleared up a good many of the points': BBC WAC – NI Plays – RM to BF, 2 July 1957.
'Dear Brian, Enough of this "Brian Friel" nonsense!': BBC – Plays – RM to BF, 15 August 1957.
'the post office': BBC – Plays – BF to RM, 14 August 1957.
'Brian invited Mason to his Marlborough Street home': BBC – Plays – RM to BF, 18 September 1957.
'The MS is in a horrible state': BBC – Plays – BF to RM, 29 August 1957.
[Page 29] 'What remains to be done': BBC – Plays – RM to BF, 18 September 1957.
'trade union plot': BBC – Plays – David Bleakley, 'Observations on trade union aspect of play: *A sort of freedom*', 21 August 1957.
'I hope you won't sit back and wait': BBC – Plays – RM to BF, 18 September 1957.
'discover all sorts of unlikely facial resemblances': Friel, 'Gunning for Sheriff', *Irish Times*, 21 September 1957.
'My only hope': Friel, 'Gunning for Sheriff', *Irish Times*, 21 September 1957.
'he received fifteen guineas': BBC – Plays – Contract for 'My true kinsman', 10 September 1957. The story was published in the *New Yorker*, 27 June 1960.
'This 50 guineas is to take Anne and myself to Verona': BBC – Plays – BF to RM, 24 September 1957.
[Page 30] 'Annual teacher salaries for married men': 'I.N.T.O. says Arbitration Board award is "insulting"', *Derry Journal*, 10 October 1955.
'Never has fifty guineas': BBC – Plays – RM to BF, 26 September 1957.
'I'm not idling': BBC – Plays – BF to RM, 24 September 1957.
'every possible facility': BBC WAC – *To this hard house*, Brian Friel, broadcast 24 April 1958, Northern Ireland Home Service, p. 5.
'poaching': BBC WAC – *To this hard house*, Brian Friel, broadcast 24 April 1958, Northern Ireland Home Service, p. 25.
'clings tenaciously': Friel, notes for *To this hard house*, p. 2, NLI, BFP, MS 37,140/1.

'The theme is good, I think': BBC – Plays – BF to RM, 24 September 1957.
'I was looking over some older stories': BBC – Plays – BF to RM, 24 September 1957.
[**Page 31**] 'one of those get-rich-quick families': BBC WAC – *To this hard house*, Brian Friel, broadcast 24 April 1958, Northern Ireland Home Service, p. 15.
'Take your hand off my shoulder': BBC WAC – *To this hard house*, Brian Friel, broadcast 24 April 1958, Northern Ireland Home Service, p. 36.
'Very probably I will take you up on that offer': BBC – Plays – BF to RM, 24 September 1957.
'How is the reading going?': BBC – Plays – RM to BF, 26 September 1957.
'more and more manuals for would-be playwrights': Jacob Stulberg, 'How (not) to write broadcast plays: Pinter and the BBC', *Modern Drama*, 58 (2015), 502–23 (pp 502–3).
'You suggested to me once': BBC – Plays – BF to RM, 7 October 1957.
[**Page 32**] 'to have made little use': BBC – Plays – BF to RM, 7 October 1957.
'I am dying to know what you think of it': BBC – Plays – BF to RM, 7 October 1957.
'My personal opinion': BBC – Plays – RM to BF, 11 October 1957.
'The play needs heavy cutting': BBC – Plays – Ronald Mason, 'Report on script submitted' to H.W. McMullan, 11 October 1957.
'agree': BBC – Plays – H.W. McMullan, response to 'Report on script submitted', 16 October 1957.
'I like it': BBC – Plays – RM to BF, 30 October 1957.
'invite him to view the rehearsals': BBC – Plays – RM to BF, 9 December 1957.
'unlimited freedom': BBC – Plays – BF to RM, 6 January 1958.
'not that I have anything to hide': Friel, 'Money for putty', *Irish Times*, 2 November 1957.
[**Page 33**] 'complicated theories of economics': Friel, 'Roundabouts and swings', *Irish Times*, 2 December 1957.
'irregular schedule': BF to RA, 27 July 1960, *NY*.
'Mason again travelled to Derry in January 1958': BBC – Plays – RM to BF, 7 January 1958.
'Be sure to call in the next time': BBC – Plays – BF to RM, 8 February 1958.
'I hope I have cut out': BBC – Plays – BF to RM, 8 February 1958.
'Northern secretary of I.N.T.O.': BBC – Plays – E.G. Quigley, letter to Brian Friel, 12 February 1958; Brian Friel, letter to Doris Johnston, 13 February 1958.
'It is a better play than his first': BBC – Plays – Ronald Mason, memo to head of Northern Ireland programmes, 10 March 1958.
'increased fee of £75': BBC – Plays – Brian Friel, contract for *Make vile things precious*, 17 March 1958; memo from BBC copyright department to Northern Ireland programme executive, 21 March 1958.
'final amendments and polishing': BBC – Plays – RM to BF, 25 March 1958.
'The play is too long': BBC – Plays – RM to BF, 25 March 1958.
[**Page 34**] 'unnecessary complication': BBC – Plays – Ronald Mason, script report to H.W. McMullan, 11 October 1957.
'Carlisle and Blake Premium': Friel, script summary for *Make vile things precious*, p. 3, NLI, BFP, MS 37,140/1–2..
'The last point is that we are none of us quite happy': BBC – Plays – Ronald Mason, script report to H.W. McMullan, 11 October 1957.
'Brian received the cheque': BBC – Plays – BF to RM, 20 March 1958.
'Here it is again, more grubbier and more grubbier': BBC – Plays – BF to RM, 30 March 1958.
'When I got down to the job of cutting': BBC – Plays – BF to RM, 30 March 1958.
'A further 120 lines were crossed out': BBC WAC – *To this hard house*, Brian Friel, broadcast 24 April 1958, Northern Ireland Home Service.

'One additional change': 'Seven villages become a unit', *Newtownabbey: 50 years of progress, 1958–2008* (Newtownabbey: *Newtownabbey Times* and *East Antrim Times*), p.4.
'In last Friday's *Telegraph*': BBC – Plays – BF to RM, 30 March 1958.
'1. Daniel Stone, Principal': Brian Friel, covering page for revised script of *Make vile things precious*, National Library of Ireland, BFP, MS 37,140 /1–2.
[**Page 35**] 'Of the three I prefer "The End of a Teacher"': Brian Friel, covering page for revised script of *Make vile things precious*, National Library of Ireland, BFP, MS 37,140 /1–2.
'*Death of a salesman* on British television': 'Independent television: *Death of a salesman* by Arthur Miller.' *The Times*, 28 November 1957, p. 3, cited in 'Production history of *Death of a salesman*' by Susan C. W. Abbotson, Rhode Island College, https://www.ibiblio.org/miller/Production%20History%20of%20SalesmanearlyFinal
'He was eager for the opportunity to observe rehearsals': BBC – Plays – Ronald Mason, telegram to Brian Friel, 1 April 1958.
'look on some day when you are working on it': BBC – Plays – BF to RM, 20 March 1958.
'If I can manage to get away from the wanes': BBC – Plays – BF to RM, 30 March 1958.
'You set it going at a good rattlin' pace': BBC – Plays – BF to RM, 26 April 1958.
'I consider it, pared as it was in production': BBC – Plays – RM to BF, 29 April 1958.
'a young Irish writer whose work interests me': EH to RA, 17 February 1958, *NY*. She had previously sent Friel's story 'Sister Bridget's miracle' to editor C.M. Newman in October 1957.
'the manuscript certainly contains enough promise': RA to EH, 26 February 1958, *NY*.
[**Page 36**] 'I kept having the feeling that he was trying very hard to write like Frank O'Connor': RA to EH, 26 February 1958, *NY*.

CHAPTER 2: Understudy, 1959–60

[**Page 37**] 'I would like to have him explain': RA to EH, 20 March 1958, *NY*.
'we gather by indirection': RA to BF, 26 June 1958, *NY*.
'a schoolboy at hometime': 'The Skelper', original copy for *The New Yorker*, 1 August 1959, in *NY*.
'which was then publishing two or three pieces of fiction in each of its weekly issues': Fiction run in *TNY*, 1950–1959, listed by issue, Editorial correspondence, *NY*, Box 777.
'a national cultural heavyweight': William Stingone, *The New Yorker: Records*, New York Public Library humanities and social sciences library manuscripts and archives division (1996), p. iv.
[**Page 39**] 'the *New Yorker* story': Jonathan Franzen, 'The birth of "*The New Yorker* story"', *The New Yorker*, 27 October 2015, www.newyorker.com; Brendan Gill, *Here at The New Yorker* (New York: Random House, 1975), pp 264–5. When I interviewed Angell in 2018, he expressed dismay at 'the idea of the *New Yorker* story, which goes back to the 1930s, sort of a suburban story with no ending; it sort of imposed itself in the public mind.'
'Most people misunderstand editing': Roger Angell, interview, 18 November 2018.
'I was new at this, too': Roger Angell, interview, 18 November 2018.
'In the relationship of a fiction editor and a fiction writer': Roger Angell, interview, 18 November 2018.
'a very nice little story': RA to EH, 20 March 1958, *NY*.
[**Page 40**] 'decided that it was time he took root somewhere': Friel, 'The Skelper', original copy for *The New Yorker*, 1 August 1959, *NY*.
'how a man of my caliber' and 'a ragged roar of voices': Friel, 'The Skelper', original copy for *The New Yorker*, 1 August 1959, *NY*.
'THE GREAT IRISH PLAY!': BBC – Plays – BF to RM, 9 May 1958.
'Goldblatt was a founding member': Richard Froggatt, 'Harold Goldblatt (1899–1982)', *New Ulster biography*, www.newulsterbiography.co.uk.

'I think myself it is in ways better than the two you did': BBC – Plays – BF to RM, 9 May 1958.
[**Page 41**] 'a good Ulster comedy': BBC – Plays – RM to BF, 5 June 1958.
'I have Harold Goldblatt in the cast tomorrow': BBC – Plays – RM to BF, 5 June 1958.
'I have had James Ellis of the Group (a director) read it': BBC – Plays – RM to BF, 5 June 1958.
'Ellis, then 27 years old': James Ellis, *Troubles over the bridge* (Derry-Londonderry: Lagan, 2015).
'He won Northern Ireland's first Tyrone Guthrie Scholarship': Ellis, pp 27–9.
'In August 1958, Ellis and Goldblatt officially accepted *The Francophile*': Ellen Andrews, Group Theatre secretary/manageress, letter to Brian Friel, 26 August 1958, NLI, BFP, MS 37,043/1.
'Mildly eccentric family': Advertisement, *Irish Times*, 12 February 1958. See also Scott Boltwood, '"Mildly eccentric": Brian Friel's writings for the *Irish Times* and the *New Yorker*', *Irish University Review*, 4:2 (Autumn–Winter 2014).
'for the interest you showed in this play': BBC – Plays – BF to RM, 2 August 1958.
[**Page 42**] 'pretty contrived and melodramatic': RA to EH, 26 May 1958, *NY*.
'a terribly familiar theme': RA to EH, 17 July 1958, *NY*.
'Brian's agent pitched': Edith Haggard, letter to Robert Henderson, 8 August 1958, *NY*.
'the strength or conviction of THE SKELPER': C.M. Newman, letter to Edith Haggard, 28 August 1958, *NY*.
'I'm afraid it falls between two categories': RA to EH, 4 September 1958, *NY*.
'He published humour pieces in the *Irish Times*': Brian Friel, 'A tank to fill', *Irish Times*, 19 July 1958; 'Purple Coat', *Irish Times*, 15 December 1958.
'He sent *The Francophile* to the Abbey Theatre': 2 October 1958, '*The country boy*, 3 act, submitted by John Murphy' and 22 October 1958, '*The Francophile*, 3 act, submitted by Brian Friel', *Plays received, April 1955–April 1964*, ATC/LIT/SL/05, p. 46, Abbey Theatre archives.
'Murphy's play was accepted': 2 October 1958, '*The country boy*, 3 act, submitted by John Murphy' and 22 October 1958, '*The Francophile*, 3 act, submitted by Brian Friel', *Plays received, April 1955–April 1964*, ATC/LIT/SL/05, p. 46, Abbey Theatre archives.
'Dear Brian, You can't have retired': BBC – Plays – RM to BF, 18 November 1958.
'Brian's family, too, owned greyhounds': Brian Friel, 'Memories and vagaries', *Irish Times*, 29 March 1960, p. 8.
[**Page 43**] 'the whole field': Brian Friel, 'The fawn pup', *The New Yorker*, 2 April 1960, 42–6, p. 46.
'Most of it is very pleasant and convincing': RA to EH, 21 January 1959, *New Yorker* archives.
'The pup, exulting in his freedom from the box': Friel, 'The fawn pup', pp 45–6.
'"He's going to go far, that fellow!"' and 'His voice as strong and confident': Friel, 'The fawn pup', p. 46.
[**Page 44**] 'seemed forced': RA to EH, 21 May 1959, *NY*.
'a little scattered': RA to EH, 21 January 1959, *NY*.
'we really don't understand the ending': RA to EH, 8 June 1959, *NY*.
'This was a close thing': RA to EH, 8 June 1959, *NY*.
'Dear Brian, It is a very long time since I have heard of you': BBC – Plays – RM to BF, 7 July 1959.
'Opera House Finals': The final performances of the annual Ulster Drama Festival were held at the Grand Opera House, Belfast.
'in grand indolence': BBC – Plays – BF to RM, 6 August 1959.
'comfortable bungalow': Brian Friel, advertisement in *Donegal Democrat*, 9 January 1959, p. 5.
'The stage play he was writing': 6 September 1960, '*The making of Mark*, 3 act, submitted by Brian Friel', *Plays received, April 1955–April 1964*, ATC/LIT/SL/05, p. 76, Abbey Theatre archives.

[**Page 45**] 'I hope you like it': BF to RA, 21 September 1959, *NY*.

'an error of technique': Roger Angell, letter to Emilie Jacobson of Curtis Brown, Ltd, 29 October 1959, *NY*.

'has some freshness and real laughs' and 'it would make a wonderful script': RA to EH, 17 November 1959, *NY*.

'His revisions to "The fawn pup"': RA to EH, 12 January 1960, *NY*.

'just seems too wild to us': RA to EH, 1 February 1960, *NY*.

'The Blind Boy', a recording admired by Brian's parents: Brian Friel, 'Memories and vagaries', *Irish Times*, 29 March 1960.

'first and only publicity agent': Friel, 'Friel and Boswell', *Irish Times*, 6 August 1958.

[**Page 46**] '"Rose will always be Rose"' and 'a black rabbit in the warren': Brian Friel, 'A man's world', *The saucer of larks*, New York (Doubleday), 1962, pp 108–9.

'I wish you would drop Mr Friel a note': RA to EH, 29 March 1960, *NY*.

[**Page 47**] 'trunkful of mysteries sent home from Kenya': Brian Friel, 'A man's world', *The saucer of larks*, New York (Doubleday), 1962, p. 109.

'a brother in Dublin': 'Funerals: Rev. B.J. MacLoone', *Irish Independent*, 11 July 1950, p. 8; 'The "wee Donegal priest" is no more', *Ulster Herald*, 15 July 1950, p. 3.

'Now, at the very outset, let me apologise for writing' and 'I am not looking for a gimmick': BF to RA, 6 April 1960, *NY*.

'the best way of explaining to you': and 'seems excellent up to page 8': RA to BF, 27 April 1960, *NY*.

[**Page 48**] 'official cemetery beside Glencree': 'Glencree German war cemetery', *Atlas Obscura*, https://www.atlasobscura.com/places/glencree-german-war-cemetery.

'in time – if they are left in peace there': Brian Friel, 'De mortuis', *Irish Times*, 7 September 1959, p. 6.

'the real strength of this story', 'a tendency to exaggerate' and 'you must be aware of the dangers': RA to BF, 27 April 1960, *NY*.

'The king of Knock Island' was rejected by RA to EH, 17 November 1959, *NY*.

'You and I know that you imitate no one': RA to BF, 27 April 1960, *NY*.

'Frank O'Connor, whose given name was Michael O'Donovan': James Matthews, *Voices: a life of Frank O'Connor* (New York: Atheneum, 1987), pp 216–17; Brendan Gill, *Here at the New Yorker* (New York: Random House, 1975) p. 93.

[**Page 49**] 'knew little about Catholics': Brendan Gill, *Here at the New Yorker* (New York: Random House, 1975), p. 93.

'many in the diaspora who were eager to reconnect': see Mary Burke, 'The cottage, the castle, and the couture cloak: "traditional" Irish fabrics and "modern" Irish fashions in America, *c.* 1952–1969', *Journal of Design History*, 31:3, September 2018.

'*The New Yorker* bought a total of 45 stories from him': James D. Alexander, 'Frank O'Connor in *The New Yorker*, 1945–1967', *Éire-Ireland*, 30:1, Spring 1995, 130–44, pp 130–1.

'wine-colored': Frank O'Connor, 'News for the church', *The New Yorker*, 22 September 1945, 24–7, p. 25.

'Tisn't much of a welcome': Frank O'Connor, 'The Mass island', *The New Yorker*, 10 January 1959, 26–31, p. 26.

'predictably Irish': BF to RA, 30 April 1960, *NY*.

'This – from editors': BF to RA, 30 April 1960, *NY*.

'I know that I am the last person in the world to judge': BF to RA, 30 April 1960, *NY*.

[**Page 50**] 'Angell wrote to accept "The saucer of larks"': RA to BF, 17 May 1960, *NY*.

'They're the glory of the world': Brian Friel, working proof of 'The saucer of larks', page 16 addition, *NY*.

'I feel that anger is justified all right': BF to RA, 27 June 1960, *NY*.

'Them and their notebooks': Brian Friel, 'The saucer of larks', *The New Yorker*, 24 September 1960, 109–19, p. 116.

'Angell and his *New Yorker* colleagues had balked at the word': RA to BF, 22 July 1960; BF to RA, 27 July 1960, *NY*.

'small rounded couples with foreign accents': Brian Friel, 'De mortuis', *Irish Times*, 7 September 1959, p. 6.

[**Page 51**] 'It is strange to think': Brian Friel, 'De mortuis', *Irish Times*, 7 September 1959, p. 6.

'fiction bonus': Roger Angell, letters to Brian Friel, 24 May 1960, 26 May 1960, 7 June 1960, *NY*.

'seems to trail off so quietly': RA to BF, 24 May 1960, *NY*.

'a hammering': Brian Friel, 'The potato gatherers', *The New Yorker*, 19 November 1960, 172–80, p. 179.

'his first opportunity': Brian Friel, 'The potato gatherers', *The New Yorker*, 19 November 1960, 172–80, p. 172.

'Where *is* this potato territory, Mistah?': Brian Friel, 'The potato gatherers', *The New Yorker*, 19 November 1960, 172–80, p. 174.

'The sun was a failure': Brian Friel, 'The potato gatherers', *The New Yorker*, 19 November 1960, 172–80, p. 179.

'a very small bit of dialogue': RA to BF, 24 May 1960, *NY*.

'"I think you're daft"': Brian Friel, 'The potato gatherers', working proof edited by Roger Angell, addendum to page 20, 28 June 1960, *NY*, original copy file for Nov. 19, 1960, Box 1954.

'your little paragraph': BF to RA, 20 July 1960, *NY*.

'in an excellent position': RA to BF, 7 June 1960, *NY*. Angell seems to have forgotten about 'The fawn pup' when he was counting Friel's accepted stories, and his rules about a starting date for the twelve-month period shifted from publication to acceptance in his letters to Friel. This chimes with archivists' observations that *The New Yorker*'s payment system may have been deliberately opaque so that writers would not know one another's earnings (Stingone, p. vi).

[**Page 52**] 'I think you are in an excellent position': RA to BF, 7 June 1960, *NY*.

'do my damdest': BF to RA, 27 June 1960, *NY*.

one that had been broadcast on the Northern Ireland Home Service: BBC – Plays – Contract for 15 guineas to broadcast a 15-minute story, 'My true kinsman', 10 September 1957.

'"Barry" is my main hope': BF to RA, 27 June 1960, *NY*.

'two main flaws': RA to BF, 6 July 1950, *NY*.

'Panic was rising in him': Brian Friel, 'Stories on the verandah', *The saucer of larks* (New York: Doubleday, 1962), 201–15, p. 212.

'Did you have a good holiday': BBC – Plays – BF to RM, 2 August 1958.

'Are you engaged or married': BBC – Plays – BF to RM, 28 September 1960.

'homosexual scene': RA to BF, 25 May 1961, *NY*.

'it is too easy to see' and 'this has the chance of being a good story some day': RA to BF, 6 July 1960, *NY*.

'This is in no way a criticism': RA to BF, 11 July 1960, *NY*.

[**Page 53**] 'and at this stage': BF to RA, 27 June 1960, *NY*.

'slightly stunned': BF to RA, 20 July 1960, *NY*.

'The man of the house', Frank O'Connor, *The New Yorker*, 3 December 1949, 32–6.

'The smell was through me': Brian Friel, 'My true kinsman', *The New Yorker*, 2 December 1961, p. 205.

'an expression of our confidence in you': RA to BF, 12 July 1960, *NY*.

'give us first look': RA to BF, 12 July 1960, *NY*.

'his pay rate per story': First Reading Agreement contract, attachment to RA to BF, 12 July 1960, NLI, BFP, MS 37,041/4.
'they are very pleased': RA to BF, 12 July 1960, *NY*.
'short, humorous feature': BF to RA, 27 July 1960, *NY*.
'listing his name on the paper's front page:' 'In to-day's issue', *Irish Times*, 25 August 1960, p. 1.
'percentage point ratings': See *Radharc* programme 2, broadcast 1962, available via IFI and YouTube courtesy of Donegal Today, https://www.youtube.com/watch?v=hQqekPeNPWY
[**Page 54**] 'My mother's people were MacLoones': Brian Friel, 'A tidy inheritance', *Irish Times*, 30 October 1959, p. 8.
'They know how well I would look': Brian Friel, 'I'm all theirs', *Irish Times*, 8 May 1959, p. 8.
'in their Sunday clothes': Brian Friel, 'Lunchtime interlude', *Irish Times*, 23 September 1959, p. 10.
'the beginning of a long and profitable association': RA to BF, 26 July 1960, *NY*.
'McKee's opposition': Ritchie McKee also chaired C.E.M.A., the Council for the Encouragement of Music and the Arts (predecessor to the Arts Council). For more detail, see Lionel Pilkington, 'Theatre and cultural politics in Northern Ireland: the *Over the bridge* controversy, 1959', *Éire-Ireland*, 30:4 (1996), 76–93.
[**Page 55**] 'Goldblatt's resignation': 'Ulster Group Theatre loses three directors after row with board', *Variety*, 20 May 1959, p. 11.
'With Thompson in tow': James Ellis wrote a detailed and colourful history of the entire controversy, including its effect on *The Francophile*, in his memoir *Troubles over the bridge* (Derry–Londonderry: Lagan), 2015.
'That is': Jonathan Goodman, letter to Brian Friel, 23 March 1960, NLI, BFP, MS 37,043/2.
'too keen-featured': BBC – Plays – BF to RM, 6 January 1962.
'just avoids bathos' and 'The author, an Ulsterman': New Ulster play at Group just avoids bathos', *News Letter*, 24 August 1960, NLI archives, BFP, MS 37,043/2.
'crime writer': Obituary for Jonathan Goodman, *The Telegraph*, 14 January 2008. His first crime book was *The killing of Julia Wallace*, published in 1969.
[**Page 56**] 'I have been at no rehearsals': BBC – Plays – BF to RM, 20 August 1960.
'Sometime too, perhaps we could have a chat': BBC – Plays – BF to RM, 20 August 1960.

CHAPTER 3: **Off book, 1960–1**
[**Page 57**] 'I sincerely hope': BF to RA, 22 December 1959, *NY*.
'He also hoped': BF to RA, 25 October 1960, *NY*.
'For better or for worse': BBC – Plays – BF to RM, 28 September 1960.
'The world is full of counsellors': BBC – Plays – RM to BF, 19 October 1960.
[**Page 58**] 'Thank you for siding with me': BBC – Plays – BF to RM, 22 October 1960.
'The *New Yorker* declined his story "Mr Sing my heart's delight"': RA to BF, 8 September 1960, *NY*.
'to illustrate the life of a child': BBC – Plays – Brian Friel, synopsis of *The world of Johnny del Pinto*, radio play submitted to Ronald Mason, 28 September 1960.
'flashes of brilliance in the writing': BBC – Plays – RM to BF, 13 December 1960.
'This is not the usual product of an Ulster writer': BBC – Plays – Ronald Mason, Report on script submitted by Brian Friel (*The world of Johnny del Pinto*), 22 November 1960.
'Just now at the end of all this': BBC – Plays – RM to BF, 13 December 1960.
'a Londonderry man, a professional playwright': BBC – S/Writer – Ronald Mason, memo to Michael Bakewell, 19 December 1960.
'this is a writer well worth encouraging': BBC – S/Writer – Michael Bakewell, memo to Drama Producer, Belfast, 19 January 1961.

'I sincerely hope': BBC – Plays – RM to BF, 23 January 1961, BBC Written Archives Centre.
'The play eventually found a home on Radio Éireann': 'Radio Eireann highlights', *Irish Press* 10 June 1961, p. 8.
[**Page 59**] 'difficult to follow': Donal O Conaill, 'Sound and Sight', *Irish Press*, 17 June 1961, p. 14.
'your criticism of past stories has been very astute': BF to RA, 11 October 1960, *NY*.
'But they do not fool me': Brian Friel, 'NATO at night', *The New Yorker*, 1 April 1961, 105–9, p. 109.
'fresh and amusing': RA to BF, 21 October 1960, *NY*.
'I am delighted to find': RA to BF, 21 October 1960, *NY*.
'What I have dreaded': RA to EH, 18 November 1960, *NY*.
'I hope you will not dwell on this disappointment': RA to BF, 25 November 1960, *NY*.
[**Page 60**] 'If we purchase two more pieces from him': RA to EH, 12 December 1960, *NY*.
'Needless to say I will try my damnedest!': BF to RA, 30 December 1960, *NY*.
'Anne, my wife, was sick': BF to RA, 30 December 1960, *NY*.
'The night the bomb fell': Brian Friel, 'When the bomb fell on Derry', *Irish Press*, 2 June 1962, p. 10.
'Now I am really getting worried': RA to EH, 4 January 1961, *NY*.
'appear to be a good deal more difficult' and 'we couldn't agree to your comparison': RA to BF, 4 January 1961, *NY*.
'keeping my fingers crossed': RA to EH, 26 January 1961, *NY*.
[**Page 61**] 'This is one of those stories we must turn down': RA to EH, 7 February 1961, *NY*.
'grass-covered track': Brian Friel, 'Among the ruins', *The New Yorker*, 19 May 1962, 118–28, pp 120–3.
'The garden, the path, the gooseberry tree': Brian Friel, 'Among the ruins', *The New Yorker*, 19 May 1962, 118–28, pp 120–3.
'genuine': RA to BF, 2 March 1961, *NY*.
'I go quite stupid': BF to RA, 6 March 1961, *NY*.
'a completely new ending': BF to RA, 7 March 1961, *NY*.
'he did this rewrite very quickly': RA to EH, 13 March 1961, *NY*.
[**Page 62**] 'presumptuous hope', 'now clear but strikes us' and 'some more complex conclusion': RA to BF, 13 March 1961, *NY*.
'as far as I remember': BBC – Plays – BF to RM, 14 March 1961.
'a well-drawn character': BBC – Plays – Ronald Mason, 'Report on script submitted by Brian Friel', 25 April 1961.
'cut great chunks' and 'You are going to lose money': BBC – Plays – RM to BF, 19 May 1961.
'The writing business has its off and on days': BBC – Plays – BF to RM, 30 May 1961.
'seventy-five guineas': BBC – Plays – Brian Friel, contract for *A doubtful paradise*, 4 August 1961.
'thoroughly boned': BBC – Plays – Ronald Mason, memo to H.W. McMullan, 5 June 1961.
Brian Friel, 'Down to the sea', *Irish Times*, 16 September 1960, p. 9.
'Dan Doalty': Brian Friel, 'Two men and a dog', *Irish Times*, 25 August 1960, p. 8.
'Good on you, my aul delight and joy': Brian Friel, 'Glenties Abu!', *Irish Times*, 25 November 1960, p. 8.
[**Page 63**] 'you can't imagine our blessed Lady': *Radharc* Programme 2, broadcast 1962, available via Irish Film Institute courtesy of *Donegal Today*, https://www.youtube.com/watch?v=hQqek PeNPWY
'The plain fact is': Brian Friel, 'Taking one's oil', *Irish Times*, 4 November 1960, p. 8.
'Irish censorship': Brian Friel, 'The game bookseller', *Irish Times*, 8 December 1960, p. 8.
'laughs more at himself': Brian Friel, 'Books for Christmas', *Irish Times*, 26 November 1960, p. 7.
'obvious and forced': RA to BF, 17 March 1961, *NY*.

'this picture of an American': RA to EH, 17 March 1961, *NY*.
'too close to draw him accurately': BF to RA, 20 July 1960, *NY*.
[**Page 64**] 'A good many writers', 'I am going to make so bold as to make a suggestion to you' and 'that final last touch': RA to BF, 16 March 1961, *NY*.
'all the more thankful' and 'I am inclined to over-produce': BF to RA, 18 March 1961, *NY*.
[**Page 65**] 'a grand six-footer': Brian Friel, 'Segova, the savage Turk', *The saucer of larks* (New York: Doubleday, 1962), pp 116–21, p. 116.
'grew close and thick': Friel, 'Segova, the savage Turk', p. 116.
'fine, white down': Friel, 'Segova, the savage Turk', p. 118.
'well written, neatly done' and 'I feel sympathy': RA to BF, 22 March 1961, *NY*.
[**Page 66**] 'In a blue maths exercise book': Brian Friel, notes for *The enemy within*, NLI, BFP MS 37,044/1.
'On his typewriter': Brian Friel, notes for *The enemy within*, NLI, BFP MS 37,044/1.
'He titled the script': Abbey Theatre, receipt of script addressed to Brian Friel, 11 April 1961, NLI, BFP MS 37,044/1.
'another story': RA to BF, 28 March 1961, *NY*.
'the best work you have given us in a long time': RA to BF, 7 April 1961, *NY*.
[**Page 67**] 'Many of its details would resurface': Brian Friel, 'Foundry House', *The New Yorker*, 18 November 1961, 50–7.
'almost right as it is', 'The social situation', 'The idea we have for an ending', 'frightened', 'lie to her' and 'more effective': RA to BF, 7 April 1961, *NY*.
'Almost two decades later': Brian Friel, *Aristocrats*, in *Collected plays*, vol. 2 (Loughcrew: Gallery, 2016), Act II.
'PURCHASING FOUNDRY HOUSE': Roger Angell, telegram to Brian Friel, 17 April 1961, *NY*.
'There were still cuts to be made': RA to BF, 16 May 1961, *NY*.
[**Page 68**] 'an unusual request', 'the last four or five pages' and 'retroactive bonuses': RA to BF, 3 May 1961, *NY*.
'notoriously Byzantine': William Stingone, *The New Yorker: Records*, New York Public Library humanities and social sciences library manuscripts and archives division (1996), p. vi.
'esoteric and bendable': Roger Angell, interview, 18 November 2018.
'far from sure': RA to EH, 19 June 1961, *NY*.
'That makes two of us': EH to RA, 20 June 1961, *NY*.
'well aware of the financial side': BF to RA, 6 May 1961, *NY*.
'no mod. cons.': BBC – Plays – BF to RM, 12 May 1961.
'not working on a story': BF to RA, 6 May 1961, *NY*.
'difficult to stay indoors and work': BF to RA, 30 May 1961, *NY*.
'go native': BBC – Plays – BF to RM, 12 May 1961.
'congratulations on your aeronaut': BF to RA, 6 May 1961, *NY*.
[**Page 69**] 'rashly': RA to BF, 16 May 1961, *NY*.
'submitted it to William Shawn': RA to EH, 16 May 1961, *NY*.
'impulsiveness': RA to BF, 16 May 1961, *NY*.
'just simplifications': RA to EH, 16 May 1961, *NY*.
'PURCHASING AMONG THE RUINS': Roger Angell, telegram to Brian Friel, 16 May 1961, *NY*.
'thrilled': BF to RA, 17 May 1961, *NY*.
'The fact that Peter would never remember it': Brian Friel, 'Among the ruins', *The New Yorker*, 19 May 1962, 118–28, p. 128.

'Doubleday offered a contract': Perry Knowlton, letter to Brian Friel, 28 August 1961, NLI, BFP, MS 37,042/3.
'better suited to a general public' and 'John Synge mixed with Frank O'Connor's': John O'Connor, letter to Brian Friel, 13 September 1961, NLI, BFP, MS 37,042/3.
'the remaining $2.97 balance': Doubleday & Company, royalty statement to Brian Friel, 30 April 1967, NLI, BFP, MS 37,042/3.
'short stories are very difficult': Perry Knowlton, letter to Brian Friel, 28 August 1961, NLI, BFP, MS 37,042/3.
'Curtis Brown's representative hinted': James MacGibbon, letter to Brian Friel, 30 August 1961, NLI, BFP, MS 37,042/3.
[**Page 70**] 'fat quantity bonus': RA to EH, 3 May 1961, *NY*.
'$881.25 paid retroactively': RA to BF, 19 June 1961, *NY*.
'I have no doubt that Irish cars': BF to RA, 10 June 1961, *NY*.
'cheerful and original reminiscence': RA to BF, 19 June 1961, *NY*.
'limiter system': Brian Friel, 'Downstairs no upstairs', *The New Yorker*, 24 August 1963, 82–5, p. 82.
'This is such a light piece': RA to BF, 19 June 1961, *NY*.
'Angell arranged payment': RA to BF, 14 July 1961, *NY*.
'has left me almost wordless': BF to RA, 23 June 1961, *NY*.
'in the same way as I appeared': Brian Friel, 'My father and the sergeant', *The saucer of larks* (New York: Doubleday, 1962), pp 182–200, p. 183.
[**Page 71**] 'never for a moment': 'My father and the sergeant', p. 183.
'familiar', 'the narrator's attitude', 'This is not at all a matter of taste', 'some entirely different way' and 'put this story aside': RA to BF, 25 May 1961, *NY*.
'I have now come to accept': BF to RA, 30 May 1961, *NY*.
'A pause of a few weeks': RA to BF, 14 July 1961, *NY*.
'bulge in the raincoat pocket': Brian Friel, working proof of 'The Diviner', *NY*, Copy and Source file, 31 March 1962, Box 1984, Folder 4.
'finding those bottles' and 'the man who was asked': RA to BF, 8 January 1962, *NY*.
[**Page 72**] 'Brian followed Angell's outline': BF to RA, 11 January 1962, *NY*.
'An acceptance by you': BF to RA, 11 January 1962, *NY*.
'the champion cock of Ireland': Brian Friel, 'Ginger Hero', *The gold in the sea* (New York: Doubleday, 1966), pp 167–87, p. 174.
'convincing and exciting and horrible': RA to EH, 3 April 1962, *NY*.
'because of its violence and bloodiness': RA to BF, 3 April 1962, *NY*.
'human part of the story': RA to EH, 3 April 1962, *NY*.
'closing the story with a secret tryst': Brian Friel, 'Ginger Hero', *The gold in the sea* (New York: Doubleday, 1966), pp 167–87.
'I must confess to you' and 'While I am being so unpleasant and so free': RA to BF, 11 May 1962, *NY*.
[**Page 73**] 'harsh': RA to BF, 18 May 1962, *NY*.
'He's too good a writer': RA to EH, 11 May 1962, *NY*.
'You know all about this business yourself': BF to RA, 14 May 1962, *NY*.
'entirely baffled': RA to BF, 15 October 1962, *NY*.
'mixed notices': Roger Angell, letters to Brian Friel, 2 January 1963 through 18 February 1964, *NY*.
'It would be so much easier for you' and 'I probably mentioned to you before': BF to RA, 14 May 1962, *NY*.
[**Page 74**] 'You must not believe for one moment': RA to BF, 18 May 1962, *NY*.
'Ronald Mason made a special excursion': BBC – Plays – RM to BF, 24 August 1962.

CHAPTER 4: **Stage directions, 1961–2**

[**Page 75**] 'F.R. Higgins': See, for example, Seán O'Faoláin, 'F.R. Higgins, died, January 7th, 1941', *The Bell* 3:4 (January 1942), 251–3, and 'Frederick Robert Higgins (1897–1941)', *The Bell* 1:5 (February 1941), 53–5.

'a Buddha in grey plaster': Frank O'Connor, *My father's son*, p. 157.

'cantankerous personality': David Fitzpatrick, *Ernest Blythe in Ulster: the making of a double agent?* (Cork: Cork University Press, 2018), p. vii.

'befriended Seán O'Casey': David Fitzpatrick, *Ernest Blythe in Ulster*, pp 35–6.

'Scholarships for young actors from the Gaeltacht': Robert Welch, *The Abbey Theatre, 1899–1999: form and pressure* (Oxford: Oxford UP, 1999), p. 147.

'Irish-language audition': Ria Mooney, *Players and the painted stage, the autobiography of Ria Mooney, part two*, edited by Val Mulkerns. *George Spelvin's theatre book*, 1:3 (Fall 1978), 65–121, p. 119; Welch, pp 141–2.

'all actors' names were Gaelicized': Cast list, *King's son of reddened valour* [*The enemy within*], Abbey Theatre, NLI, BFP, MS 37,044/1.

'shunned Shakespeare': Patrick Lonergan, 'Queering Shakespeare at the Abbey: Wayne Jordan's *Twelfth Night*', *Scenes from the bigger picture* blog, 3 May 2014, accessed 11 September 2018.

'Sancho Panza, Don Cichote': *Gráinne na Long*, cast list 26 December 1959, Abbey Theatre Archives, https://www.abbeytheatre.ie/archives/production_detail/3731/

'Queen's Theatre in Pearse Street': Welch, T*he Abbey Theatre, 1899–1999*, pp 154–7; Cecil Allen, 'The Queen's Theatre', lecture at Pearse Street Library, recorded 24 August 2016, https://soundcloud.com/dublincitypubliclibrary/the-queens-theatre.

[**Page 76**] 'the script he received from Derry': 11 April 1961, '*King's son of reddened valour*, 3 act, submitted by Brian Friel', *Plays received, April 1955–April 1964*, ATC/LIT/SL/05, p. 86, Abbey Theatre archives.

'intrinsic merits': Ernest Blythe, letter to Brian Friel, 23 May 1961, NLI, BFP, MS 37,044/1.

'not likely to have a long run': Ernest Blythe, letter to Brian Friel, 23 May 1961, NLI, BFP, MS 37,044/1.

'he invited Blythe to visit him': Ernest Blythe, letter to Brian Friel, 25 May 1961, NLI, BFP, MS 37,044/1.

'Blythe sent a contract': Contract between Brian Friel and Abbey Theatre, 23 May 1961; Ernest Blythe, letter to Brian Friel, 25 May 1961, NLI, BFP, MS 37,044/1.

'commercial failure': BF to RA, 30 May 1961, *NY*.

'the saint's honorific': *The life of St Columba, founder of Hy, written by Adamnan, ninth abbot of that monastery*, ed. William Reeves (Dublin: Irish Archaeological and Celtic Society, 1857), p. 269.

'lame starters, or non-starters': Ernest Blythe, letter to Brian Friel, 2 August 1961, NLI, BFP, MS 37,044/1.

[**Page 77**] 'the private man': Brian Friel, Preface to *The enemy within*, NLI, BFP, MS 37,044/1.

'factual great-great-grandfather': *The life of St Columba, founder of Hy, written by Adamnán, ninth abbot of that monastery*, ed. William Reeves (Dublin: Irish Archaeological and Celtic Society, 1857), p. 269.

'modern prose' and 'violent and bloody': Brian Friel, Preface to *The enemy within*, NLI, BFP, MS 37,044/1.

'the grand error of his life': Reeves, p. 255.

'having fomented domestic feuds': Reeves, pp 247–53.

'all looking to him': Friel, notes for *King's son of reddened valour*, NLI, BFP, MS 37,044/1.

'Heroic sanctity is not a progression': Friel, notes for *King's son of reddened valour*, NLI, BFP, MS 37,044/1.

'I'm sorry for keeping you': Friel, *The enemy within*, in *Collected plays*, vol. 1 (Loughcrew: Gallery, 2016), I.i.113.
'a builder of churches': Friel, *The enemy within*, I.i.279.
'Do not think': Friel, *The enemy within*, I.i.231.
'the play's eventual title': Ernest Blythe (Earnán de Blaghd), letter to Brian Friel, 16 August 1961, NLI, BFP, MS 37,044/1. *The enemy within: the McClellan Committee's crusade against Jimmy Hoffa and corrupt labor unions* was also the title of Robert F. Kennedy's book about his work with the US Senate Committee on Improper Activities in Labor and Management, published in 1960. Blythe's letters to Friel about the Abbey's title selection make no reference to Kennedy.
[**Page 78**] 'the most beautiful play I have come across': Ray McAnally, letter to Brian Friel, 2 July 1962, NLI, BFP, MS 37,044/1.
'for a play I don't have to reconstruct': Ria Mooney, letter to Brian Friel, 21 July 1962, NLI, BFP, MS 37,044/1.
'More than three decades had passed': Ria Mooney, *Players and the painted stage, the autobiography of Ria Mooney*, edited by Val Mulkerns, in *George Spelvin's theatre book*, 1:2 (Summer 1978) and 1:3 (Fall 1978).
'her last great success': James McGlone, *Ria Mooney: the life and times of the artistic director of the Abbey Theatre, 1948–1963* (Jefferson, NC: McFarland, 2002), pp 195–8.
'the endings to Acts II & III': Ria Mooney, letter to Brian Friel, 21 July 1962, NLI, BFP, MS 37,044/1; Vincent Dowling played the novice, Oswald, in the original production of *The enemy within*. He later became a celebrated director of many plays, including the premiere of Friel's *The gentle island* at the Olympia Theatre in 1971.
[**Page 79**] 'to begin again': Friel, *The enemy within*, III.i.712.
'When we met': James MacGibbon, letters to Brian Friel, 30 August 1961 and 27 October 1961, NLI, BFP, MS 37,042/1.
'It was a hint he repeated half a dozen times': James MacGibbon, letters to Brian Friel, 30 August 1961, 27 October 1961, 15 March 1963, 13 June 1963, 9 July 1963, 19 November 1963, NLI, BFP, MS 37,042/1.
'this situation screams out': James MacGibbon, letter to Brian Friel, 15 March 1963, NLI, BFP, MS 37,042/1.
'If you break it all down': BBC – Plays – RM to BF, 2 February 1962.
'It has come back I am afraid with a rejection': BBC – Plays – RM to BF, 27 April 1962.
[**Page 80**] 'repeat the age-old pattern of argument': 'Radio and television', *Irish Press*, 7 January 1964.
'Yet Brian's script for a TV series': Hilton Edwards mentioned *Michael Mannion* in an essay for the *RTE guide* while he was head of drama for the new television service, quoted by Christopher Fitz-Simon in *The boys*, p. 242; and Brian Tobin, RTÉ script organiser, mentioned *Michael Mannion* in a letter to Friel dated 19 September 1963, NLI, BFP, MS 37,044/1.
'a weekly column for the *Irish Press*': See George O'Brien, '"Meet Brian Friel": the *Irish Press* columns', *Irish University Review*, 29:1 (1999), 30–41.
'the Intercontinental people know': Brian Friel, 'Haven for the harassed', *Irish Times*, 3 July 1959, and *Irish Press*, 29 December 1962. Other columns that appeared in both newspapers include 'Portrait of the artist', *Irish Times*, 11 December 1959, republished as 'Music hath charms, or Why my mother breeds greyhounds' in the *Irish Press*, 16 June 1962; 'The gamecock', *Irish Times*, 14 March 1962, republished as 'A bird in the bog' in the *Irish Press*, 18 August 1962; 'Friel and Boswell', *Irish Times*, 6 August 1958, republished as 'Lost: a good biographer' in the *Irish Press*, 15 September 1962; 'Quisling Rafteri', *Irish Times*, 30 January

1962, republished as 'After the catastrophe' in the *Irish Press*, 22 September 1962; and 'Behind the bars', *Irish Times*, 19 April 1960, republished as 'A warm afternoon in the cooler' in the *Irish Press*, 26 January 1963.

'Brian's Dublin editors': Brian Friel, 'When the bomb fell on Derry', *Irish Press*, 2 June 1962.

'not the first to see it in print': Brian Friel, 'Old memories', *Irish Press*, 12 May 1962.

'plenty of material': Brian Friel, 'The afternoon of a fawn pup', *Irish Press*, 7 July 1962; 'Brian Friel's seaside adventures: Donegal diary', *Irish Press*, 21 July 1962; 'A bird in the bog', *Irish Press*, 18 August 1962.

'I spend the greater part of my working day': Brian Friel, 'Now about these rats', *Irish Press*, 12 January 1963.

[**Page 81**] 'made the acquaintance': Brian Friel, 'Waiting in the rain', *Irish Press*, 30 June 1962.

'33 years of age': Brian Friel, 'Meet Brian Friel', *Irish Press*, 28 April 1962.

'Readers of the *Irish Press* look on me': BF to RA, 13 May 1963, *NY*.

'average in execution': BF to RA, 22 May 1963, *NY*.

'the very northern tip of Ireland': BF to RA, 6 April 1960, *NY*.

[**Page 82**] 'combined weekday circulation': Mark O'Brien, *De Valera, Fianna Fáil and the* Irish Press (Dublin: Irish Academic Press, 2001), p. 129.

'daily circulation of the *Irish Times*' and 'the *Press*' editor Douglas Gageby': Mark O'Brien, *The Irish Times: a history* (Dublin: Four Courts Press, 2008), pp 164–72.

'In the year after': Ernest Blythe, letters to Brian Friel, 24 October 1961; 2 February 1962, NLI, BFP, MS 37,044/1.

'publicity value': Ernest Blythe, letter to Brian Friel, 18 May 1962, NLI, BFP, MS 37,044/1.

'as often as you can': Ria Mooney, letter to Brian Friel, 21 July 1962, NLI, BFP, MS 37,044/1.

'find some way of rallying': Ray McAnally, letter to Brian Friel, 2 July 1962, NLI, BFP, MS 37,044/1.

'meanly intended to exploit as a baby-sitter' and 'day of indescribable wretchedness': Brian Friel, 'It's a long way to Dublin', *Irish Press*, 25 August 1962.

'rented house near Phoenix Park': Telegram from Limavady to 'MR AND MRS BRIAN FRIEL C/O CURRAN 73 SKREEN ROAD OFF NAVAN ROAD DUBLIN / BEST WISHES ON YOUR OPENING NIGHT', 6 August 1962, in NLI, BFP, MS 37,044/1.

'Once at the Abbey': Programmes for *This other Eden*, *Mac Uí Rudaí* and *Strange occurrence on Ireland's Eye*, NLI, BFP, MS 37,044/1.

[**Page 83**] 'performance as the brisk saint': *The enemy within* review, photocopy, 29 August 1962, NLI, BFP, MS 37,044/1.

'Over six weeks, Brian earned': Abbey Theatre returns for *The enemy within*, 11 August 1962, 18 August 1962, 25 August 1962, 8 September 1962, 15 September 1962, NLI, BFP, MS 37,044/1.

'He has contributed so much to this region': BBC – Plays – Ronald Mason, memo to head of Northern Ireland programmes, 20 August 1962.

'What is "The Enemy Within" about?': BBC – Plays – H.W. McMullan, memo to Ronald Mason, 21 August 1962.

'A former director and governor': 'Tyrone Guthrie', biographical statement, 15 April 1963, Guthrie Theater records, University of Minnesota, folder PA 3, Tyrone Guthrie general correspondence, 1963–69.

[**Page 84**] 'scores of young men': Friel, *The enemy within*, I.i.83.

'I love them, yes, I love them': Friel, *The enemy within*, I.i.524.

'goes on his knees', 'Home is a millstone': Friel, *The enemy within*, I.i.552, 556.

'Hoist your sails': Friel, *The enemy within*, I.i.631.

'I was tremendously impressed': BBC – Plays – RM to BF, 24 August 1962.

'shrewd, accurate, and vastly entertaining criticism': BBC – Plays – BF to RM, 6 September 1962.

[**Page 85**] 'This is the sort of play': BBC – Plays – RM to BF, 24 August 1962.

[**Page 86**] 'counter-balance' the 'often harsh realities': Edward Daly, *Mister, are you a priest?* (Dublin: Four Courts Press, 2000), pp 80, 93, 113.

'Press photos': Photographs, Brian Friel, Ernest Blythe and Father Edward Daly; Brian Friel with cast of *The enemy within*, NLI, BFP, MS 37,044/1.

'He and Anne invited Blythe': Ernest Blythe, letter to Brian Friel, 12 September 1962, NLI, BFP, MS 37,044/1.

'while the teetotalling Father Daly': Edward Daly, *Mister, are you a priest?*, p. 116.

'perfectly suited to the seminary situation': St Mary of the Lake Seminary, Archdiocese of Chicago, letter to Brian Friel, 14 September 1962, NLI, BFP, MS 37,044/2.

'Brian's name circulated': Father Edward L. Mason, Blessed Sacrament Rectory, Sioux City, Iowa, letter to Brian Friel, 30 January 1963, NLI, BFP, MS 37,044/2.

'In 1963, Ronnie Mason directed': Mary O'Malley, letter to Brian Friel, 28 January 1963, NLI, BFP, MS 37,044/1; programme for *The enemy within* at Lyric Theatre, Belfast, September 1963, NLI, BFP, MS 37,044/1.

'1963 is the millennium-and-a-half': BBC – Plays – Ronald Mason, memo to T.V. Centre, BBC, London, 1 October 1962.

'unenthusiastic': BBC – Plays – Ronald Mason, notes on telephone conversation with Brian Friel, 12 February 1963.

'commissioned Brian to adapt': BBC – Plays – Ronald Mason, memo to AHNIP, 14 February 1963.

'a producer asked to see Brian's script': Brian Tobin, Drama Department, Radio Éireann Irish Television, letter to Brian Friel, 19 September 1963, NLI, BFP, MS 37,048/1.

'Ray McAnally did his best': Ray McAnally, letter to Brian Friel, 11 January 1963, NLI, BFP, MS 37,048/1. McAnally loved *The enemy within* so much that he staged his own revival at the Olympia Theatre, Dublin, in 1968, but Columba and his fellow monks didn't generate the same buzz on their second outing ('RAY MCANALLY TO STAR IN BRIAN FRIEL PLAY,' press release, 20 June 1968, NLI, BFP, MS 37,044/4).

'likely at Guthrie's prompting': Guthrie was patron of the Ballymoney Drama Festival from 1961 until his death in 1971 (Friel became patron in 1988). S. Alexander Blair, *The golden years: the story of Ballymoney Drama Festival* (Ballymoney: Committee of Ballymoney Drama Festival, 1989).

'Hilton Edwards adjudicated': Ulster Drama Festival 1964, postcard, NLI, BFP, MS 37,048/1.

[**Page 88**] 'by going through the prayers': John Casey, 'Winter 1952–1953', *The Far East*, 38, March 1955, p. 8, quoted in Neil Collins, *The splendid cause: The Missionary Society of St Columban 1916–1954* (Dublin: Columba, 2009), p. 184.

'was allowed to buy grapes': John Casey, 'Winter 1952–1953', quoted in Collins, *The splendid cause*, pp 184–5.

'Bishop Patrick Cleary': Collins, *The splendid cause*, p. 175.

'The script opens': Brian Friel, *The blind mice*, typescript, NLI, BFP, MS 37,046/3.

'His movements are jerky': Brian Friel, *The blind mice*, typescript, NLI, BFP, MS 37,046/3, p. 25.

'You blighted my childhood': Brian Friel, *The blind mice*, typescript, NLI, BFP, MS 37,046/3, p. 61.

[**Page 89**] 'Brian's confirmation name': Brian Friel, 'Meet Brian Friel', *Irish Press*, 28 April 1962.

'"bought" his way': BF to RA, 29 November 1961, *NY*.

'an excellent subject for a story': RA to BF, 7 September 1961, *NY*.

'slender encouragement': BF to RA, 29 November 1961, *NY*.

'does not seem to us to be much of an improvement': RA to BF, 6 December 1961, *NY*.

'They were manna to me' and 'He was slipping from me': Brian Friel, *The blind mice*, typescript, p. 35, NLI, BFP, MS 37,046/1.

[**Page 90**] 'No torturing?': Brian Friel, *The blind mice*, typescript, p. 33, NLI, BFP, MS 37,046/1.

'Don't judge, don't judge': Brian Friel, *The blind mice*, typescript, p. 46, NLI, BFP, MS 37,046/1.

'A stone crashes through the family's front window': Brian Friel, *The blind mice*, typescript, pp 51–2, NLI, BFP, MS 37,046/1.

'There's going to be a riot!': Brian Friel, *The blind mice*, typescript, p. 49, NLI, BFP, MS 37,046/1.

'A great day for Ireland!': Brian Friel, *The blind mice*, typescript, p. 52, NLI, BFP, MS 37,046/1.

'I could hear some of Devlin's louts': Brian Friel, *The blind mice*, typescript, p. 49, NLI, BFP, MS 37,046/1.

'Protect us from what?': Brian Friel, *The blind mice*, typescript, p. 50, NLI, BFP, MS 37,046/1.

'merely triggers all the action': BBC – Plays – BF to RM, 17 October 1963.

'at 17 I presented myself at Maynooth': Brian Friel, handwritten draft of biographical statement for *The saucer of larks*, undated, NLI, BFP, MS 37,042/1.

'The Abbey wouldn't touch it': Abbey Theatre archives, ATC / LIT / SL / 05, p. 94.

'Brian's opinion that it was his best play yet': Brian Friel, handwritten draft of biographical statement for *The saucer of larks*, undated, NLI, BFP, MS 37,042/1.

'His Doubleday editor enjoyed it': Daniel R. Hayes, Catholic division editor, Doubleday & Company, letter to Brian Friel, 17 November 1961, NLI, MS 37,042/1.

[**Page 91**] 'débuted at the Abbey as a child actor': Phyllis Ryan, *The company I kept* (Dublin: Town House, 1996), pp 27–32.

'would need to become versed in Irish history and language': Ryan, pp 90–1.

'bullied': Ryan, p. 93.

'ruthless politician': Ryan, pp 84–5.

'The audience came in downstairs': Ryan, pp 141–6.

'News Cinema': Ryan, p. 141.

'John B. Keane, whose script for *The field* was unearthed by Ryan': Ryan, pp 195, 203–4.

'Barry Cassin, whom Ryan chose': *The blind mice* programme, Eblana Theatre, 19 February 1963, NLI, BFP, MS 37,046/2.

[**Page 92**] 'a moving play': BBC – Plays – Ronald Mason, memo to H.W. McMullan, 1 March 1963.

'to allow anyone else to adapt it': BBC – Plays – RM to BF, 4 June 1963.

'Once a play has been on the boards': BBC – Plays – BF to RM, 16 July 1963.

'Donal Donnelly would be cast': BBC WAC – *The blind mice*, Brian Friel, broadcast 28 November 1963, Northern Ireland Home Service.

'"Ulster Presbyterian" Derek Young': *The blind mice* programme, Eblana Theatre, 19 February 1963, NLI, BFP, MS 37,046/2; 'Ulster Presbyterian' quoted from Sean J. White, 'Sam Thompson returns to Dublin', *Irish Press*, 18 February 1963.

'actors recruited and recorded in London': BBC – Plays – Diana Hyde, memo to programme organiser, Chinese section, 15 October 1963; Ronald Mason, memo to A.H.D. (Sound), 18 October 1963.

'It is by Brian Friel' and 'My only concern': BBC – Plays – H.W. McMullan, memo to R.B.O., 1 October 1963.

'hotted up, sub-Billy Graham style': Sean J. While, 'Sam Thompson returns to Dublin', *Irish Press*, 18 February 1963.

'cleaning up of the motive' and 'As a hardened Protestant': BBC – Plays – H.W. McMullan, memo to Ronald Mason, 8 October 1963.

'one very easily forgets': BBC – Plays – BF to RM, 17 October 1963.

'And I think Papes & Proddydogs': BBC – Plays – BF to RM, 17 October 1963.
[**Page 93**] 'the torture of despair': Brian Friel, *The blind mice*, typescript, p. 45, NLI, BFP, MS 37,046/1.
'marching feet': BBC WAC – *The blind mice*, Brian Friel, broadcast 28 November 1963, Northern Ireland Home Service, p. 31.
'superimposed on the distant sound': BBC WAC – *The blind mice*, Brian Friel, broadcast 28 November 1963, Northern Ireland Home Service, p. 41. The script's final page: BBC WAC – *The blind mice*, Brian Friel, broadcast 28 November 1963, Northern Ireland Home Service, p. 65.
'"correlate" the "Communist technique"': BBC – Plays – BF to RM, 16 July 1963.
'Say a prayer for me, Father': Brian Friel, *The blind mice*, typescript, p. 75, NLI, BFP, MS 37,046/1.

CHAPTER 5: The giant of Minneapolis, 1962–3
[**Page 94**] 'My resolve to go to the US for a year' and 'US critics are much more open-handed': BF to RA, 12 July 1962, *NY*.
'a handful of which were published': Brian Friel, *The saucer of larks: stories of Ireland* (New York: Doubleday, 1962), p. 4.
'very uneven': BF to RA, 12 July 1962, *NY*.
'exhausted looking for a holiday house' and 'Friel's Folly': Brian Friel, 'The wild life: Brian Friel goes to the country', *Irish Press*, 14 July 1962.
[**Page 95**] 'oyster farming in Omagh's local river': Brian Friel, 'Pearls in the Strule', *Housewife*, 24:11 (November 1962), 44–7.
'agonizes over his first confession': Brian Friel, 'The first of my sins', *The Critic*, 21:4 (February–March 1963), 20–3.
'a failed fishing trip to Donegal': Brian Friel, 'The wee lake beyond', first published in *The Critic*, and in *The gold in the sea* (New York: Doubleday, 1966), pp 69–78.
'feared he would be cast out': EH to RA, 19 December 1962, *NY*.
'strange': EH to RA, 19 December 1962, *NY*.
'idea for this story is a really original one': RA to BF, 2 January 1963, *NY*.
'an alliance and a plan': Tyrone Guthrie, *A new theatre* (New York: McGraw-Hill, 1964), pp 10, 22.
[**Page 96**] 'audiences are composed of very rich, elderly people': Guthrie, *A new theatre*, p. 26.
'a shared experience': Guthrie, *A new theatre*, p. 69.
'Artists are ministers': Guthrie, *A life in the theatre*, p. 145.
'the abbot of a monastery': Guthrie, *A life in the theatre*, pp 152–3.
'bring healing and knowledge': Guthrie, *A life in the theatre*, p. 145.
'could not talk seriously nor think clearly in New York': Guthrie, *A new theatre*, p. 10.
'in the depths of very remote country': Guthrie, *A new theatre*, p. 11.
'Long talks over the ruins of breakfast': Guthrie, *A new theatre*, p. 35.
'missionary zeal': Guthrie, *A new theatre*, pp 35–6.
'permanent company that would perform classics': Guthrie, *A new theatre*, p. 45; Louis Calta, 'Stage unit slated outside of city', *New York Times*, 30 September 1959.
[**Page 97**] 'reached catastrophic proportions': Brian O'Doherty, 'Tyrone Guthrie producing jam to bolster Ireland home town', *New York Times*, 28 August 1962; Darac, 'The jam factory at Newbliss Railway Station, Co. Monaghan', https://www.darac.ie/History_of_Station/history_of_ station.html
'A local development committee' and 'jam jars as props': Brian O'Doherty, 'Tyrone Guthrie producing jam to bolster Ireland home town', *New York Times*, 28 August 1962.

'sold in Dayton's department stores': Will Jones, 'Sir Tyrone peddles jam', *Minneapolis Star Tribune*, 6 March 1964.
'When James Ellis and Sam Thompson visited Annaghmakerrig': James Ellis, *Troubles over the bridge*, p. 68.
'It was a felicitous piece of casting': Tyrone Guthrie, *A life in the theatre* (New York: McGraw-Hill, 1959), p. 16.
'watching the play take shape': Guthrie, *A life in the theatre*, p. 17.
'ugly, fascinating city': Guthrie, *A life in the theatre*, p. 39.
'militantly provincial': Guthrie, *A life in the theatre*, p. 44.
[**Page 98**] 'curfew pass in his pocket': James Forsyth, *Tyrone Guthrie: a biography* (London: Hamish Hamilton, 1976), p. 56.
'a theatrical Sahara': Guthrie, *A life in the theatre*, p. 90.
'vocation': Guthrie, *A life in the theatre*, p. 45.
'professional attitude': Guthrie, *A life in the theatre*, p. 44.
'as commercial travellers': Guthrie, *A life in the theatre*, p. 45.
'happy': Guthrie, *A life in the theatre*, p. 44.
'Ulster Literary Theatre invited him': Guthrie, *A life in the theatre*, p. 45.
'after marrying his childhood friend': Forsyth, *Tyrone Guthrie: a biography*, pp 107–9.
'rose to the attention of the Old Vic Shakespeare Company': Guthrie, *A life in the theatre*, pp 46–86.
'one or two little notions and wheezes': Guthrie, *A life in the theatre*, pp 187–93.
'it became clear to me': Tyrone Guthrie, 'A director views the stage', *Design Quarterly*, 58 (1963).
'mongrel Scot': Guthrie, *A life in the theatre*, p. 306.
'dimly lit rows of people similarly focused': Guthrie, *A life in the theatre*, p. 311.
[**Page 99**] the Canadian town of Stratford: Guthrie, *A life in the theatre*, p. 315.
'she designed a five-sided stage': David Jays, Obituary for Tanya Moiseiwitsch, *The Guardian*, 20 February 2003.
'The goal of theatre': Guthrie, 'A director views the stage', *Design Quarterly*, 58 (1963).
'spiritual life': Guthrie, *A life in the theatre*, p. 62.
'masterpieces', 'guarantee each season' and 'an extraordinary sense': Guthrie, 'Repertory theatre – ideal or deception?', *New York Times*, 26 April 1959.
[**Page 100**] 'penthouse with Chinese décor': Guthrie, *A new theatre*, pp 48–9.
'in brilliant starlight': Guthrie, *A new theatre*, p. 52.
'They flew from Minneapolis to Cleveland': Guthrie, *A new theatre*, pp 52–4.
'no more than a sleeping partner': Guthrie, *A new theatre*, p. 54; Forsyth, *Tyrone Guthrie: a biography*, p. 268.
'committed $500,000': H. Frederick Koeper, 'Introduction', *Design Quarterly* 58 (1963).
'artistic control over the interior design': Oliver Rea, letter to Harlan Hatcher, undated, General correspondence 1960–61, PA003 Guthrie Theater, series 6: Admin. files, box 197, Guthrie Theater records, University of Minnesota.
'insisted that the house capacity be restricted': Peter Zeisler, letter to Oliver Rea, undated, General correspondence 1960–61, PA003 Guthrie Theater, series 6: Admin. files, box 197, Guthrie Theater records, University of Minnesota.
'proceed very cautiously': Peter Zeisler, letter to Oliver Rea, undated, General correspondence 1960–61, PA003 Guthrie Theater, series 6: Admin. files, box 197, Guthrie Theater records, University of Minnesota.
'In the final design': 'Cost, dimensions and capacity', *Design Quarterly*, 58 (1963), Tyrone Guthrie papers, PRONI D3585/F/7/7/5. When the building was completed, total audience seating was 1,437. The original Tyrone Guthrie Theater was demolished in 2006 and a new

building, offering a thrust stage as well as proscenium and black box theatre spaces, opened on the opposite bank of the Mississippi River.

'an intimate actor-audience relationship': Ralph Rapson, 'The architect's design', *Design Quarterly*, 58 (1963).

'Walker Theater-in-the-round': Rapson A.I.A. Architects, cost list for 'Walker Theater-in-the-round', undated, General correspondence 1960–61, PA003 Guthrie Theater, series 6: Admin. files, box 197, Guthrie Theater records, University of Minnesota.

'steeply raked orchestra': Peter Zeisler, letter to Oliver Rea, undated, General correspondence 1960–61, PA003 Guthrie Theater, series 6: Admin. files, Box 197, Guthrie Theater records, University of Minnesota; 'Cost, dimensions and capacity', *Design Quarterly* 58, 1963, Tyrone Guthrie papers, PRONI D3585/F/7/7/5.

'eliminate the distinction': Ralph Rapson, 'The architect's design', *Design Quarterly* 58 (1963).

'The Alpine Climb': Alfred Rossi, 'The Hamlet log', *Minneapolis rehearsals: Tyrone Guthrie directs Hamlet* (Berkeley: University of California Press, 1970), p. 65. Rossi was a graduate student at the University of Minnesota who served as an assistant to Guthrie and acted the role of Rosencrantz in the Guthrie Theater's opening production of *Hamlet* in 1963.

'the desirability of making an audience feel': Tyrone Guthrie, *A new theatre*, p. 60.

'ranging from orange and violet': Ralph Rapson, 'The architect's design', *Design Quarterly* 58 (1963).

[Page 101] 'a Howard Johnson motel': Peter Zeisler, letter to John Cowles, Jr., March 13, 1961, General correspondence 1960–61, PA003 Guthrie Theater, series 6: Admin. files, box 197, Guthrie Theater records, University of Minnesota.

[Page 102] 'a model': Peter Zeisler, letter to John Cowles, Jr., March 13, 1961, General correspondence 1960–61, PA003 Guthrie Theater, series 6: Admin. files, box 197, Guthrie Theater records, University of Minnesota.

'revolutionary': Tyrone Guthrie, typescript of article for *Minneapolis Tribune*, 15 September 1963, PA003 Guthrie Theater series 1: Production, box 1, Guthrie Theater records, University of Minnesota.

'whose purpose is to serve the community': Tyrone Guthrie, typescript of article for *Minneapolis Tribune*, 15 September 1963, PA003 Guthrie Theater series 1: Production, box 1, Guthrie Theater records, University of Minnesota.

'Don't think I should take it': Forsyth, *Tyrone Guthrie: a biography*, p. 270.

'deeply impressed with the show': Tyrone Guthrie, in interview with Charlie Rice, 'Queen dubs knight', *This Week magazine*, 8 September 1963, PA3, Administrative files, GTF meeting minutes, 1960–72, box 407, Guthrie Theater records, University of Minnesota.

'Have you paid £150': Alec Guinness, letter to Tyrone Guthrie, 28 February 1964, Tyrone Guthrie papers, PRONI, folder D3585/F/5/1/10.

'writ on water': Tyrone Guthrie, *A life in the theatre*, p. 146.

'remembered by a few': Tyrone Guthrie, *A life in the theatre*, p. 147.

'addressed all letters home': Tyrone Guthrie papers, PRONI.

'airless + cheerless': Tyrone Guthrie, letter to Lady Guthrie, 9 September 1962, Tyrone Guthrie papers, PRONI, folder D3585/F/5/2/25.

'an indication, we hoped' and 'a clear, if implicit, statement of policy': Guthrie, *A new theatre*, p. 89.

[Page 103] 'Literally hundreds of actors': Guthrie, *A new theatre*, p. 82.

'so that we could form some opinion': Guthrie, *A new theatre*, p. 86.

'intelligence, wit, and humour': Guthrie, *A new theatre*, p. 87.

'uninvited': Guthrie, *A new theatre*, p. 88.

'stunned his associates': Robert Berkvist, 'George Grizzard, 79, dies; actor noted for Albee roles', *New York Times*, 3 October 2007.
'departure was expected': 'Corrections: For the Record', *New York Times*, 11 October 2007.
'He was small, lithe' and 'He could suggest a prince': Guthrie, *A new theatre*, p. 88.
'The building begins to look exciting': Tyrone Guthrie, letter to Lady Guthrie, 9 September 1962, Tyrone Guthrie papers, PRONI, folder D3585/F/7/7/5.
'*The saucer of larks* had sold': John R. O'Connor, Doubleday, letter to Brian Friel, 4 October 1962, NLI, BFP, MS37,042/1.
'slated for publication in the United Kingdom': James MacGibbon, Gollancz, letter to Brian Friel, 31 October 1962, NLI, BFP, MS37,042/1.
'deft, skillfully written': Edna O'Brien, letter to James MacGibbon, 26 November 1962, NLI, BFP, MS37,042/1.
'Doubleday sent statements': Doubleday & Company, statements, 23 October 1962; 31 October 1962; 30 April 1963; 31 October 1963; 30 April 1964; 30 April 1965; 1 August 1965, NLI, BFP, MS 37,042/3.
'his agent sold "Ginger Hero"': EH to RA, 19 December 1962, *NY*.
'He broadcast a Christmas Eve story': BBC – Plays – Contract signed by Brian Friel for 'Thoughts on Christmas', 18 December 1962, for broadcast on Northern Ireland Home Service, 24 December 1962.
'two inexorable dwarfs': Brian Friel, 'The letter writers: solemn and silent', *Irish Press* 15 December 1962, p. 8.
[**Page 104**] 'charmed my heart away' and 'six-foot-five-inch man': Brian Friel, 'The giant of Monaghan', *Holiday*, 35:5 (May 1964), 89–96, p. 92.
'Very briefly the idea is to go to Minneapolis': BF to RA, 5 January 1963, *NY*.
'We had no income': Anne Friel, in *Brian Friel: shy man, showman*, produced by Marie-Louise Muir, BBC Northern Ireland, 2022.
'Brian received a £100 advance': Victor Gollancz royalty statement, *The saucer of larks*, 25 July 1963, NLI, BFP, MS37,042/1.
'Months later': Victor Gollancz royalty statement, *The saucer of larks*, 25 July 1963, NLI, BFP, MS37,042/1; Bank of England inflation calculator, https://www.bankofengland.co.uk/monetary-policy/inflation/inflation-calculator.
'I am not going out to a job': BF to RA, 5 March 1963, *NY*.
'to get myself some sort of American correspondent job': BF to RA, 5 March 1963, *NY*.
'Angell assured him they would': RA to BF, 11 March 1963, *NY*.
'there are a million complications': BF to RA, 15 March 1963, *NY*.
'We are all madly excited': BF to RA, 15 March 1963, *NY*.
'Brian invited Angell to stay': BF to RA, 15 March 1963, *NY*.
[**Page 105**] 'Rehearsals at the Guthrie Theater were due to start': Alfred Rossi, 'The *Hamlet* log', *Minneapolis rehearsals: Tyrone Guthrie directs* Hamlet (Berkeley: University of California Press, 1970). p. xii.
'not-too-elegant apartments': BBC WAC – 'An observer in Minneapolis', Brian Friel, broadcast 16 August 1965, Northern Ireland Home Service; Minutes, Guthrie Theater Foundation meeting, 20 March 1963, PA3, Administrative files, GTF meeting minutes, 1960–72, box 407, Guthrie Theater Records, University of Minnesota.
'Sir Tyrone and Lady Guthrie rented a flat' and 'each scene, each speech, each sentence': Tyrone Guthrie, letter to George Grizzard, 16 January 1963, transcribed in Rossi, pp 9–11.
'Grizzard fenced': Rossi, p. 11.
'Campbell took the lead': BBC WAC – 'An observer in Minneapolis', Brian Friel, broadcast 16 August 1965, Northern Ireland Home Service; Rossi, p. 5.

'First Unitarian Society': Rossi, p. 4.
'Brian packed his typewriter': Brian Friel, 'American diary 1: arrival in New York', *Irish Press*, 20 April 1963.
'sightseeing at Rockefeller Center': Brian Friel, 'American diary 2: sight-seeing', *Irish Press*, 27 April 1963; 'American diary 5: at the United Nations', *Irish Press*, 18 May 1963.
'meet those people': BF to RA, 5 March 1963, *NY*.
'Top of the list': BF to RA, 31 March 1963, *NY*.
'lots and lots of thunderstorms': Brian Friel, 'American diary 9: wings on his heart', *Irish Press*, 15 June 1963; BBC WAC – 'An observer in Minneapolis', Brian Friel, broadcast 16 August 1965, Northern Ireland Home Service.
'The ballad of Ballybeg': 'Brian Friel's first book', *The Belfast Telegraph*, 25 February 1963, NLI, BFP, MS 37,042/2.
'Drinks on the house?': Brian Friel, 'Brian Friel's secret thoughts: at the annual P.P.U. meeting', *Irish Press*, 1 December 1962.
[**Page 106**] 'mentally marking time': BF to RA, 31 March 1963, *NY*.
'the Oak Grove apartment hotel': Forsyth, *Tyrone Guthrie: a biography*, p. 305.
'the feeling of creative joy': Rossi, pp 22, 32–3.
'hammers banging': Guthrie, letter to George Grizzard, 16 January 1963, transcribed in Rossi, pp 9–11.
'Guthrie started experimenting', 'seemed to enjoy this game' and 'So did the actors': Rossi, p. 37.
'New work must have something interesting': Guthrie, *A life in the theatre*, p. 69.
'He opposed the Method school of acting': Guthrie, *A life in the theatre*, p. 237.
'Because it says so in the script': Rossi, p. 55.
'to make absolutely clear what is going on': Rossi, p. 52.
'to participate in lavish and luxurious goings-on': Guthrie, *A life in the theatre*, p. 53. Friel quoted this phrase in 'The giant of Monaghan' and again in 'An observer in Minneapolis'.
[**Page 107**] 'how to manage great rhetorical speeches': Guthrie, *A life in the theatre*, p. 245.
'people who normally have to be frugal': Guthrie, *A life in the theatre*, p. 53.
'It occurred to me, too': Friel, letter to Roger Angell, 31 March 1963, *NY*.
'castle': Brian Friel, 'The giant of Monaghan', *Holiday*, 35:5 (May 1964), 89–96, p. 89.
'ad by the Irish Tourist Board': 'In Ireland, you'll forgive inconveniences that would cause you to boil anywhere else', advertisement by Irish Tourist Board, *Holiday*, 35:5 (May 1964), p. 88a.
'comes to rehearsal': Friel, 'The giant of Monaghan', p. 92.
'there is not one Guthrie': Friel, 'The giant of Monaghan', p. 92.
'What you wanted was right': Friel, letter to Roger Angell, 5 April 1963, *NY*.
'does not strike us as being much of an improvement', 'This version seems dogged and unimaginative', 'I hope you will put it aside again', 'there may be too many scenes now' and 'This must be your own story': RA to BF, 11 April 1963, *NY*.
[**Page 108**] 'The weather has me hopelessly confused': BF to RA, 5 April 1963, *NY*.
'It's always the same with a rewrite': BF to RA, 15 April 1963, *NY*.
'incident at Ballymanus': Marie O'Halloran, 'Doherty calls for war mine apology', *Irish Times*, 9 June 2011.
'I'll leave "Everything neat & tidy" aside': BF to RA, 15 April 1963, *NY*.
'After Easter, Brian returned to New York': BF to RA, 15 April 1963, *NY*.
'a very quiet life here': BF to RA, 22 May 1963, *NY*.
'opened each rehearsal with recitation of Psalm 118': Rossi, p. 32.
'in the gloom of the auditorium': BBC WAC – 'An observer in Minneapolis', Brian Friel, broadcast 16 August 1965, Northern Ireland Home Service.
'The company is enthused': Rossi, p. 22.

'Rehearsals continued six days a week': Rossi, p. 5.
'I attend dutifully': BF to RA, 22 May 1963, *NY*.
'a singularly inspiring event': Rossi, p. 68. Guthrie also describes the dedication service in *A new theatre*, p. 108.
'a couple of hundred photos' and 'The gown was made to look regal': Rossi, p. 67.
[**Page 109**] 'a great feeling of pride and *esprit de corps*': Rossi, p. 69.
'an emotional audience': Rossi, p. 70.
'when he and Stephen Rea launched the Field Day Theatre Company': see Richtarik, *Acting between the lines: the Field Day Theatre Company and Irish cultural politics 1980–1984* (Oxford, Oxford UP, 1994) for more detail on the founding of the Field Day Theatre Company in Derry in 1980.
'new one': BF to RA, 2 May 1963, *NY*.
'I do not share your glooms and despairs': RA to BF, 30 April 1963, *NY*.
'it's as stolid as dough' and 'I only hope that you are right': BF to RA, 2 May 1963, *NY*.
'Everyone who was Anyone in the Twin Cities': Guthrie, *A new theatre*, p. 108.
'Society Ladies began fidgeting' and 'At this point, I realised with painful clarity': Guthrie, *A new theatre*, p. 109.
[**Page 110**] 'It was miserable': Guthrie, *A new theatre*, pp 110–11.
'more for the entire venture': Rossi, p. 70.
'no comments from Guthrie': Rossi, p. 6.
'humour, which is never expressed in wisecracks or gags': Tyrone Guthrie, 'Guthrie takes stock of premiere season', *Minneapolis Star and Tribune*, 15 September 1963.
'must aim higher': Tyrone Guthrie and Tanya Moiseiwitsch, 'The production of *King Oedipus*', in *Thrice the brinded cat hath mew'd: a record of the Stratford Shakespearean Festival in Canada, 1955*, pp 137–8.
'ahead of his time': Guthrie, *A new theatre*, p. 139.
'the adventures and bafflements': BF to RA, 13 May 1963; RA to BF, 20 May 1963, *NY*.
'I am especially grieved at this rejection', 'first rate' and 'I'm afraid there's just no hope': RA to BF, 7 June 1963, *NY*.
[**Page 111**] 'the Macaulay Fellowship': Editorial, 'The Arts Council', *Irish Times*, 23 October 1964.
'young Irish writers, painters, sculptors and composers': 'Fellowship for Brian Friel', *Irish Press*, 6 June 1963.
'I am a little sorry that this wonderful fillip': James MacGibbon, letter to Brian Friel, 13 June 1963, BFP, National Library of Ireland, MS 37,042/1.
'Hell!': BBC – Plays – BF to RM, 8 June 1963.
'They departed': BBC – Plays – BF to RM, 8 June 1963.
'squirrels, escalators, sherbet': BF to RA, 22 May 1963, *NY*.
'Brian even considered staying': Anne Friel, in conversation, 26 August 2017.

CHAPTER 6: **Waiting in the wings, 1963–4**
[**Page 112**] 'cheer for one and pray for the other' and 'This has never been a rich or powerful country': 'Climax to historic visit', *Irish Press*, 29 June 1963.
'It is useless to protest': Brian Friel, 'The returned Yank', *Irish Press*, 10 August 1963.
'the most treacherous and unpredictable of emotions' and 'side-step': Brian Friel, 'American diary 4: the news from home', *Irish Press*, 11 May 1963.
[**Page 113**] 'Ronnie Mason had visited New York as well': BBC – Plays – RM to BF, 4 June 1963.

'While the BBC hesitated over': BBC – Plays – Ronald Mason, memo regarding projected costs of television production of *The enemy within*, 14 February 1963; Doris Johnston, memo to Record Library Clerk, 31 May 1963 regarding radio transmission of *The enemy within* on 6 June.
'Now Mason wanted to broadcast *The blind mice*': BBC – Plays – RM to BF, 4 June 1963.
'If you can make it down here': BBC – Plays – BF to RM, 16 July 1963.
'still on a Guthrie high': Brian Friel, letter to Joe Dowling, 14 June 1996, NLI archives, BFP, MS 37,048/1.
'the onionskin notes he had typed and handwritten': Brian Friel, notes for *Philadelphia, here I come!*, NLI archives, BFP, MS 37,047/1.
'1. There must be reactions of hearty (from the heart & belly) laughter': Friel, notes for *Philadelphia, here I come!*, NLI archives, BFP, MS 37,047/1.
'directing is aimed primarily at the heart and the belly': Brian Friel, 'The giant of Monaghan', p. 93.
'Little journalistic plays': Guthrie, *A life in the theatre*, p. 245.
[**Page 114**] 'marches': Brian Friel, *Philadelphia, here I come! in Collected plays*, vol. 1 (Loughcrew: Gallery, 2016), I.i.2.
'nosedives, engines screaming': Friel, *Philadelphia, here I come!*, I.i.61.
'goes through all sorts of contortions': Friel, notes for *Philadelphia, here I come!*, NLI archives, BFP, MS 37,047 / 1.
'Don't go for the easy tear and pathos': Rossi, 'The *Hamlet* log', *Minneapolis rehearsals*, p. 67.
'All this bloody yap': Friel, *Philadelphia, here I come!*, II.i.811.
'I have heightened the comic element': Brian Friel, synopsis of *Philadelphia, here I come!*, undated, NLI, BFP, MS 37,048/1.
'pupils called Master Friel "Scobie"': Tommy Doherty, in conversation, 27 August 2017.
'This is not another "American wake" story': Brian Friel, synopsis of *Philadelphia, here I come!*, undated, NLI, BFP, MS 37,048/1.
[**Page 115**] 'a surly, taciturn gruffness': Friel, *Philadelphia, here I come!*, I.i.148.
'make one unpredictable remark': Friel, *Philadelphia, here I come!*, I.i.570.
'Say it, and I'll stay!': Friel, draft of *Philadelphia, here I come!*, NLI, BFP, MS 37,047/2.
'moment of happiness caught in an album' and 'The fact is a fiction': Brian Friel, 'Self-portrait', *Aquarius* 5, 1972, 17–22, p. 18.
'between us at that moment there was this great happiness': Friel, *Philadelphia, here I come!*, III.i.63.
'I'm going into my Daddy's business': Friel, *Philadelphia, here I come!*, III.2.201.
'He never had a sailor suit': Friel, *Philadelphia, here I come!*, III.2.196.
'did both of you imagine them?': Brian Friel, draft of *Philadelphia, here I come!*, NLI, BFP, MS 37,047/2.
'He originally planned': Brian Friel, draft of *Philadelphia, here I come!*, NLI, BFP, MS 37,047/2.
[**Page 116**] 'that the ideal lake': Brian Friel, 'To the wee lake beyond', *Irish Press*, 4 August 1962, p. 8.
'The ideal Ireland that we would have': Éamon de Valera, radio address 17 March 1943, RTÉ archives, www.rte.ie/laweb/ll/ll_t09b.html.
'to illustrate the private world': BBC – Plays – BF to RM, 28 September 1960.
'the private man in each of us': BF to RA, 18 March 1961, *NY*.
'lengthy asides': Friel, synopsis of *Philadelphia, here I come!*, undated, NLI, BFP, MS 37,048/1.
'*The disagreeable oyster*': 'The BBC Drama Repertory Company in "THE DISAGREEABLE OYSTER", A new radio play by Giles Cooper with Hamilton Dyce and John Graham as Mervyn Bundy', *Radio Times*, Issue 1761, 15 August 1957, p. 43, BBC Genome Project, accessed 13 May 2020.

'tribute series to Cooper': 'THE DISAGREEABLE OYSTER, Third Programme, 22 October 1962,' *Radio Times*, Issue 2032, 18 October 1962, p. 27, BBC Genome Project, accessed 13 May 2020.

'I've got thirty-four pounds!': Giles Cooper, *The disagreeable oyster*, BBC broadcast audio file, https://clyp.it/l1awe5u2, accessed 13 May 2020.

'Passionate Bundy!': Giles Cooper, *The disagreeable oyster*, BBC broadcast audio file, https://clyp.it/l1awe5u2 , accessed 13 May 2020.

[**Page 117**] 'Alter Ego': Friel, notes for *Philadelphia, here I come!*, NLI archives, BFP, MS 37,047 / 1.

'1. Gar is an individual of two people': Friel, notes for *Philadelphia, here I come!*, NLI archives, BFP, MS 37,047 / 1.

'never sees him': Friel, 'Set' for *Philadelphia, here I come!* (Loughcrew, 2016), p. 89.

[**Page 118**] 'And now for our nightly lesson': Friel, *Philadelphia, here I come!*, I.i.526.

'the new Irish': Friel, notes for *Philadelphia, here I come!*, NLI archives, BFP, MS 37,047 / 1.

'Kate … sweet Katie Doogan': Friel, *Philadelphia, here I come!*, I.i.322.

'Keep the humour high': Friel, notes for *Philadelphia, here I come!*, NLI archives, BFP, MS 37,047 / 1.

a 'late' child: Friel, notes for *Philadelphia, here I come!*, NLI archives, BFP, MS 37,047 / 1.

[**Page 119**] 'EVERYBODY WANTS SOMETHING': Friel, notes for *Philadelphia, here I come!*, NLI archives, BFP, MS 37,047 / 1.

'Madge wants to marry Gar's father': Friel changed the father character's name twice in his early notes, from Dan to F.X. to S.B. for Sean Bernard, nicknamed Screwballs. His earliest notes state that Madge 'thinks she'll marry Dan; has thought so for 20 years', and in his list of characters' desires, Madge's is 'F.X.' Friel, notes for *Philadelphia, here I come!*, NLI, BFP, MS 37,047 / 1.

'what? peace? escape?': Friel, notes for *Philadelphia, here I come!*, NLI archives, BFP, MS 37,047 / 1.

'a comedy besieged': Friel, synopsis of *Philadelphia, here I come!*, undated, NLI, BFP, MS 37,048/1.

'Could the young Gar be identified by a cobeen': Friel, notes for *Philadelphia, here I come!*, NLI archives, BFP, MS 37,047/1.

'I have no physical identity of my own': Friel, draft of *Philadelphia, here I come!*, NLI archives, BFP, MS 37,047/2.

'a time is reached': Friel, notes for *Philadelphia, here I come!*, NLI archives, BFP, MS 37,047/1.

[**Page 120**] 'I'm in great form': Friel, draft of *Philadelphia, here I come!*, NLI archives, BFP, MS 37,047/2.

'his Alter Ego keeps up an endless stream': Friel, notes for *Philadelphia, here I come!*, NLI archives, BFP, MS 37,047/1.

'should some dramatist': Brian Friel, 'The giant of Monaghan', p. 96.

'A bed is ready and aired for you': BBC – Plays – RM to BF, 3 September 1963.

'nervous at being left alone': BBC – Plays – BF to RM, 4 September 1963.

'Postage to America, plus insurance': Certificates of posting, 11:00 a.m., 9 September 1963, to Miss D. Daly, Curtis Brown, Covent Garden, London and Mr Warren Baylis, Curtis Brown, 575 Madison Ave., New York. NLI Manuscripts collection, BFP, MS 37,047/2.

'That night': BBC – Plays – Internal memo covering sheet for 'The enemy within' transmission on Light Programme at 75 minutes, edited down from 80 minutes, 9th September 1963, 8.45–10.00 p.m.

'one of the most successful': BBC – Plays – Ronald Mason, programme note for *Radio Times*, 9 September 1963; Ronald Mason, director's note for *The enemy within* programme, Lyric Theatre, September, 1963. NLI, BFP, MS 37,044/3.

'The broadcast seems to have gone down very well': BBC – Plays – Internal memo from drama producer to HNIP, CNI, I.O., Registry, 11 September 1963.
'the price I pay': BBC – Plays – Doris Johnston, letter to Brian Friel, 12 September 1963; Brian Friel, letter to Doris Johnston, 13 September 1963.
[**Page 121**] 'royalty cheque from the Lyric': Undated note from Lyric Players Theatre, 23 Grosvenor Road, Belfast 12, to Brian Friel, to accompany payment of £12 2s. to Friel as 10% of box office takings of £120 18s. 6d. NLI, BFP, MS 37,044/3.
'alternating all four repertory plays': *Hamlet* performance schedule, PA 3, Ser. 1, Productions, Guthrie Theater records, University of Minnesota.
'Hope the baby has arrived': Tyrone Guthrie, letter to Brian Friel, 3 October 1963, NLI, BFP, MS 37,048/1.
'one single, solitary feature', 'just ripped apart', 'heartfelt and humble congratulations', 'Now for it', 'some leger de voix', 'a mistake', 'I somehow think', 'Honestly I wasn't that much impressed' and 'you're doing the right thing': Tyrone Guthrie, letter to Brian Friel, 7 October 1963, NLI , BFP, MS 37,048/1.
[**Page 122**] 'christened Judith, after Lady Guthrie': Anne Friel, in conversation, 9 December 2022.
'10 harrowing days overdue': BF to RA, 30 October 1963, *NY*.
'all through-other': BBC – Plays – BF to RM, 10 October 1963.
'I carried out all his suggestions': BBC – Plays – BF to RM, 16 October 1963; Friel, handwritten note on Guthrie letter of October 7, 1963, NLI, BFP, MS 37,048/1.
'I like it still': BF to RA, 30 October 1963, *NY*.
'I'm very excited about this play': BBC – Plays – Friel, letter to Ronald Mason, 16 October 1963.
'extraordinarily well written', 'static' and 'Most commercial managements': John Barber, letter to Brian Friel, 8 October 1963, NLI, BFP, MS 37,048/1.
[**Page 123**] 'the great man' and 'Would he ever be free to direct it himself': John Barber, letter to Brian Friel, 10 October 1963, NLI, BFP, MS 37,048/1.
'settle': John Barber, letter to Brian Friel, 8 October 1963, NLI, BFP, MS 37,048/1.
'I don't want to let myself in for an expense': BBC – Plays – Brian Friel, letter to Doris Johnston, 31 October 1963.
'He mailed the new version to his agents': Postage receipts from Marlborough Terrace P.O. to Warren Bayliss, John Barber and Ray McAnally in Artane, Dublin, 28 October 1963, NLI, BFP, MS 37,048/1; John Barber, letter to Brian Friel, 30 October 1963, NLI, BFP, MS 37,048/1.
'I have attempted the rewrite so often': BF to RA, 30 October 1963, *NY*.
'Remember the play I told you about': BBC – Plays – Friel, letter to Ronald Mason, 31 October 1963.
'Three cheers!' and 'I am really delighted': RA to BF, 19 November 1963, *NY*.
'that Carol and I were married three weeks ago' and 'Carol has given up her job here': RA to BF, addendum, 19 November 1963, NLI, BFP, MS 37,041/4.
[**Page 124**] 'I am really pleased': Roger Angell, letter to Emmy Jacobson, 11 December 1963, *NY*.
'Maybe I'm unduly nervy and depressive': BF to RA, 17 December 1963, *NY*.
'directorial problems' and 'I firmly believe': Warren Bayless, letter to Brian Friel, 4 November 1963, NLI, BFP, MS 37,048/1.
'the most revealing and alive': Tyrone Guthrie, letter to Brian Friel, 7 October 1963, NLI, BFP, MS 37,048/1.
'Vulgar. Negro haters, Jew haters': Friel, notes for *Philadelphia, here I come!*, NLI, BFP, MS 37,047/1.
'You got your own problems': Friel, draft of *Philadelphia, here I come!*, NLI, BFP, MS 37,047/2.

'You got your own problems to look after': Friel, *Philadelphia, here I come!*, II.i.241.
'I have little doubt': Warren Bayless, letter to Brian Friel, 26 November 1963, NLI, BFP, MS 37,048/1.
'a (scruffy) copy': BBC – Plays – BF to RM, 26 November 1963.
[**Page 125**] 'The play has now been written for about two months': BBC – Plays – Friel, letter to Ronald Mason, 26 November 1963.
'I began reading at one o'clock this morning', 'sophisticated' … 'It must be staged' and 'You must continue to have implicit faith in this play': BBC – Plays – RM to BF, 3 December 1963.
'gave me great, great pleasure, and assurance': BBC – Plays – BF to RM, 5 December 1963.
'As you know, I have no experience of theatre outside Ireland' and 'God, you've no idea': BBC – Plays – Friel, letter to Ronald Mason, 5 December 1963.
'he contacted his superiors in BBC London': BBC – Plays – Ronald Mason, memo to assistant head of drama (Sound), BBC, 30 December 1963.
'Well it's not that good': BBC – Plays – John Tydeman, memo to Michael Bakewell, 6 January 1964.
[**Page 126**] 'vulgarity keeps sadness at bay': Friel, notes for *Philadelphia, here I come!*, NLI, BFP, MS 37,047 / 1.
'by God I lashed so much salt': Friel, *Philadelphia, here I come!*, I.i.42.
'skirmishes over the sandwiches': Guthrie's description of 'Baddish press' in his letter to Brian about the Nottingham Playhouse opening was an uncharacteristic understatement. According to a retrospective article marking 75 years of the theatre's history, the earl of Snowdon, Princess Margaret's husband, gave keynote remarks for the opening on 11 December 1963, and afterward 'A civic reception had been laid on in the Council House, with buffet and drinks … but by the time Sir Tyrone and his company arrived, most of the food had gone and, having enjoyed the city's hospitality, few even noticed the actors among them. Sir Tyrone exploded with rage and threatened to walk out in search of sandwiches. According to the following day's *Post*, blows were exchanged between a corporation official and a member of the company.' Andy Smart, 'Skirmishes over the sandwiches at Nottingham Playhouse's opening night', *Nottingham Post*, 17 October 2018, https://www.nottinghampost.com/news/history/skirmishes-over-sandwiches-nottingham-playhouses–2118387
'N.I. is changing fast & radically': Tyrone Guthrie, letter to Hilton Edwards and Micheál MacLiammóir, 4 December 1963, Dublin Gate Theatre archive, Northwestern University, Correspondence box 17, folder 1.
'Off to Belfast tomorrow': Tyrone Guthrie, letter to Brian Friel, 15 December 1963, NLI, BFP, MS 37,048/1.
'the drive back home in the dark': Tyrone Guthrie, letter to Brian Friel, 2 January 1964 [misdated 1963], NLI, BFP, MS 37,048/1.
'would dearly love to make a short film of it': Alec Guinness, letter to Tyrone Guthrie, 28 February 1964, Tyrone Guthrie Papers, PRONI, folder D3585/F/5/1/10.
'Guinness drafted a screenplay': Correspondence between Brian Friel and Sir Alec Guinness, NLI, BFP, MS 37,042/6.
[**Page 127**] 'would give it an interesting send-off': John Barber, letter to Brian Friel, 6 January 1964, NLI, BFP, MS 37,048/1.
'Splendid! Warmest congratulations!': Tyrone Guthrie, postcard to Brian Friel, 10 January 1964, NLI, BFP, MS 37,048/1.
'Mr Shawn likes this story very much': RA to BF, 6 January 1964, *NY*.
'25% bonus': Brian Friel, First Reading Agreement, 1 January 1964 to 1 January 1965, *NY*.
'wonderfully alive': RA to BF, 12 December 1963, *NY*.

'I've been so long out of the pages of the *New Yorker*': BF to RA, 10 January 1964, *NY*.
'did not give me much trouble': BF to RA, 3 January 1964, *NY*.
'Naturally I would like it to be a success': BF to RA, 17 December 1963, *NY*.
'You're very lucky not to be involved in the theatre business': BF to RA, 3 January 1964, *NY*.

CHAPTER 7: **Broadway, here I come!, 1964–6**
[**Page 128**] 'wildly optimistic' and 'If the play does well': BF to RA, 10 January 1964, *NY*.
'premiered John Osborne's *Look back in anger*': Oscar Lewenstein, *Kicking against the pricks: a theatre producer looks back* (London: Nick Hern, 1994), pp 28–30.
'a Playwright's theatre': Lewenstein, p. 10.
'foreign writers we considered neglected': Lewenstein, pp 14–15. Lewenstein owned the London rights to Miller's *The crucible*, and he was later the first producer to stage Brecht's *Threepenny opera* in England (p. 12).
'Their first production was *Billy Liar*': Lewenstein, pp 99–101.
'Billy escapes his dreary job': Keith Waterhouse and Willis Hall, *Billy Liar: a comedy in three acts* (London: Samuel French, 1960).
'*Billy Liar* ran to packed houses': Lewenstein, p. 100.
'a steady policy': Lewenstein, p. 180.
'Russian Jew born in England': Lewenstein, p. 16.
[**Page 129**] 'taboo': Lewenstein, p. 50.
'affairs with other women': Lewenstein, pp 47–51.
'a distant, even mysterious figure': Lewenstein, p. 47.
'another language we didn't understand': Lewenstein, p. 47.
'Central School in Hackney': Lewenstein, pp 42–9.
'He and his siblings moved with their mother': Lewenstein, p. 50.
'joined the Young Communist League': Lewenstein, p. 51.
'to work for the betterment of society': Lewenstein, pp 65–6.
'a lasting friendship with Seán O'Casey': Lewenstein eventually acquired the rights to six O'Casey plays and staged two in London, *Juno and the Paycock* and *The shadow of a gunman*, for the centenary of the playwright's birth in 1980. Lewenstein, pp 76, 178.
'stars': John Barber, letter to Oscar Lewenstein, 13 February 1964, NLI, BFP, MS 37,048/1.
'Woodfall's blockbuster *Tom Jones*': Tony Richardson, producer; Oscar Lewenstein, associate producer, *Tom Jones*. London: Woodfall, 1963.
'by no means my brightest virtue': Brian Friel, letter to John Barber, 16 January 1964, NLI, BFP, MS 37,048/1.
'So far our winter has been as gentle': BF to RA, 5 February 1964, *NY*.
[**Page 130**] 'quite firm': Brian Friel, note to John Barber, undated [15 January 1964], NLI, BFP, MS 37,048/1.
'I think he could do a wonderful job': Brian Friel, letter to John Barber, 16 January 1964, NLI, BFP, MS 37,048/1.
'Lewenstein agreed': Brian Friel, notes, 12 March and 16 March 1964; Oscar Lewenstein, letter to Brian Friel, 16 March 1964, NLI, BFP, MS 37,048/1.
'arrived a week late': Tyrone Guthrie, letter to Brian Friel, 27 March 1964, NLI, BFP, MS 37,048/1. The previous year, during the theatre company's inaugural rehearsals, Guthrie distributed Irish shamrock to his actors for St Patrick's Day, 1963, a week before Brian arrived to observe (Rossi, 'The *Hamlet* log', p. 19).
'there isn't quite the thrill': Tyrone Guthrie, letter to Brian Friel, 27 March 1964, NLI, BFP, MS 37,048/1.

'His theatre needed $50,000 in upgrades and repairs': Tyrone Guthrie Theater Foundation, minutes of annual meeting of board of directors, 20 November 1963, Box PA3, series 6, Administration, Guthrie Theater records, University of Minnesota.

'His friend Frank Whiting': Frank M. Whiting, letter to Tyrone Guthrie, 26 February 1964, Box PA3, Series administrative, 1964, Guthrie Theater records, University of Minnesota.

'a stoodent cast': Tyrone Guthrie, letter to Brian Friel, 16 October 1964, NLI, BFP, MS 37,048/1.

'careful casting' ... 'I wish this letter could have said YES': Tyrone Guthrie, letter to Brian Friel, 27 March 1964, NLI, BFP, MS 37,048/1.

'going on outside': RA to BF, 17 March 1964, NY.

'all absolutely love THE DEATH OF A SCIENTIFIC HUMANIST': RA to BF, 17 March 1964, NY.

'For some reason I don't understand': BF to RA, 21 February 1964, NY.

[**Page 131**] 'far too obvious': RA to BF, 1 April 1964, NY.

'contract for *Philadelphia*': Brian Friel and Oscar Lewenstein, memorandum of agreement, 17 March 1964, NLI, BFP, MS 37,048/1.

'semiannual statements': Doubleday & Company, Inc., royalty statement issued to Brian Friel, 31 October 1963, NLI, BFP, MS 37,042/3.

'fighting flu': Tyrone Guthrie, letter to Oscar Lewenstein, 20 April 1964, NLI, BFP, MS 37,048/1.

'the Abbey's rejection': Abbey Theatre archives, ATC / LIT / SL / 05, p. 94.

'From then on': Brian Friel, letter to Suzanne Finlay, 23 May 1964, NLI, BFP, MS 37,489/1.

'extravagantly different and difficult': Phyllis Ryan, undated letter to Brian Friel, NLI, BFP, MS 37,048/1.

'Looking forward to almighty argument': Phyllis Ryan, undated letter to Brian Friel, NLI, BFP, MS 37,048/1.

'The Private and Public Gars work well': Phyllis Ryan, letter to Brian Friel, 28 April 1964, NLI, BFP, MS 37,048/1.

'Brian still wanted Ray McAnally': Phyllis Ryan, letter to Brian Friel, 14 May 1964, NLI, BFP, MS 37,048/1.

'I thought we agreed on most points': Brian Friel, letter to Curtis Brown agent Suzanne Finlay, 21 May 1964, NLI, BFP, MS 37,489/1.

[**Page 132**] 'idiosyncrasies', 'misleading and harmful' and 'We too have a reputation to consider': Phyllis Ryan, letter to Brian Friel, 14 May 1964, NLI, BFP, MS 37,048/1.

'Apparently your letter of the 14th May': Oscar Lewenstein, letter to Brian Friel, 1 June 1964, NLI, BFP, MS 37,048/1.

'reeling': Suzanne Finlay, letter to Brian Friel, 27 May 1964, NLI, BFP, MS 37,489/1.

'Phyllis & I did have our differences of opinion': Brian Friel, draft of letter to Oscar Lewenstein, 5 June 1964, handwritten on letter from Lewenstein dated 1 June 1964, NLI, BFP, MS 37,048/1.

'first prize in the Ulster Drama Festival': postcard for Ulster Drama Festival at the Grand Opera House, including Ballymoney Literary & Debating Society production of THE ENEMY WITHIN and 'Final Adjudication by Hilton Edwards', 18–23 May 1964, NLI, BFP, MS 37,044/1; Blair, S. Alexander, *The golden years: the story of Ballymoney Drama Festival* (Ballymoney: Committee of Ballymoney Drama Festival, 1989), p. 15.

'This whole business has distressed me deeply': Brian Friel, letter to Suzanne Finlay, 21 May 1964, NLI, BFP, MS 37,489/1.

'*The New Yorker* rejected': 'The highwayman and the saint' appeared in *Critic* and in Friel's second short story anthology, *The gold in the sea*, where 'The Barney game' was also published.

'The writing is good': Roger Angell, letter to Curtis Brown agent Emilie Jacobson, 20 May 1964, NY.
'double the BBC's usual rate': BBC – Plays – Elsie Wakeham, Copyright Department, memo to Peggy Wells, 25 May 1964.
'all the more important': BBC – Plays – RM to BF, 29 May 1964.
'I have long ceased': Brian Friel, letter to Suzanne Finlay, 1 June 1964, NLI, BFP, MS 37,489/1.
'I have no idea what Miss Ryan has told Oscar': Brian Friel, letter to Suzanne Finlay, 23 May 1964, NLI, BFP, MS 37,489/1.
[**Page 133**] 'What about a cheap flight' and 'At the moment I'm not actually writing a story': BF to RA, 5 June 1964, NY.
'I'm about tired of it': Brian Friel, letter to Suzanne Finlay, 19 June 1964, NLI, BFP, MS 37,489/1.
'an unpleasant, even repellant, play': Jim Mooney, report on script for KING OF THE CASTLE, 30 March 1964, Northwestern University Libraries, Gate Theatre archive, Correspondence box 19, folder 6.
'a very strong, if grim and unpalatable, work': Hilton Edwards, notes on KING OF THE CASTLE, 7 April 1964, Northwestern University Libraries, Gate Theatre archive, Correspondence box 19, folder 6.
'poetry and sheer genius': Jim Mooney, report on script for KING OF THE CASTLE, 30 March 1964, Northwestern University Libraries, Gate Theatre archive, Correspondence box 19, folder 6.
'Your play seems': Hilton Edwards, letter to Eugene McCabe, 7 April 1964, Northwestern University Libraries, Gate Theatre archive, Correspondence box 19, folder 6.
[**Page 134**] 'Dublin's senior producer': Brian Friel, letter to Suzanne Finlay, 13 June 1964, NLI, BFP, MS 37,489/1.
'He grew up in London': Christopher Fitz-Simon, *The boys: a biography of Micheál MacLiammóir and Hilton Edwards* (Dublin: New Island, 2005), pp 31–7.
'joined the Old Vic': Fitz-Simon, pp 47–8.
'He then joined another touring group': Fitz-Simon, pp 16–17.
'a dream they realized in 1928': Fitz-Simon, pp 50–2.
'inaugural head of drama': Fitz-Simons, 238–68.
'reverted with relief to the theatre': Hilton Edwards, letter to Edward J., 4 December 1964, Northwestern University Libraries, Gate Theatre archive, Correspondence box 17, folder 1.
'the best and most exciting': Harold Hobson, *Sunday Times*, quoted by Wolfe Kaufman in 'Even taxi drivers are playwrights during Theatre Festival in Dublin', *Variety*, 26 October 1966, p. 59.
'nuts': Kaufman, p. 59.
'The brainchild of actor and director Brendan Smith': Fitz-Simon, *The boys*, p. 184.
'That's the gimmick': Kaufman, p. 59.
'while we wasted our energies on An Tóstal': Editorial, 'Theatre Festival', *Irish Times*, 15 September 1964. For the history of An Tóstal, see Joan FitzPatrick Dean, *All dressed up: modern Irish historical pageantry* (New York: Syracuse UP), 2014.
[**Page 135**] 'killing Irish drama': 'Festival killing Irish drama?', *Irish Times*, 5 October 1964.
'lifeless': Peter Lennon, 'Irish drama, last act', *The Guardian*, 14 October 1965.
'three-year Bord Fáilte grant': 'Anonymous businessmen back Theatre Festival', *Irish Times*, 3 October 1964.
'the tundish through which State patronage flows to the arts': 'The Arts Council', *Irish Times*, 23 October 1964.

NOTES

'Edwards pitched it to the Festival board': Hilton Edwards, letter to Eugene McCabe, 29 May 1964, Dublin Gate Theatre archive, Northwestern University, Correspondence box 19, folder 6.
'in 1955, Edwards designed the lighting': Lewenstein, p. 17.
'Phyllis Ryan offered a higher bid': Patricia MacNaughton, letter on behalf of agent Christopher Mann to Hilton Edwards, 29 May 1964, Dublin Gate Theatre archive, Northwestern University, Correspondence box 19, folder 6.
'embroiled in a sort of Dutch auction': Hilton Edwards, letter to Cyril Cusack, 20 July 1964, Dublin Gate Theatre archive, Northwestern University, Correspondence box 19, folder 6. Cusack did not end up acting in *King of the castle*. Edwards later directed him as Fox Melarkey in Friel's *Crystal and Fox* in 1968.
'If you like it': Oscar Lewenstein, letter to Hilton Edwards, 10 June 1964, Dublin Gate Theatre archive, Northwestern University, Production box 87, folder 2.
'very enthusiastic': Brian Friel, letter to Suzanne Finlay, 13 June 1964, NLI, BFP, MS 37,489/1.
'Enterprising Brendan Smith': Brendan Smith, letter to Hilton Edwards, 25 August 1964, Dublin Gate Theatre archive, Northwestern University, Production box 87, folder 2.
'a beautiful elegant theatre': Brian Friel, letter to Suzanne Finlay, 13 June 1964, NLI, BFP, MS 37,489/1; Hilton Edwards, letter to Brendan Smith, 13 June 1964, NLI, BFP, MS 37,048/1.
'As ever, I'm opposed to the Festival': Brian Friel, letter to Suzanne Finlay, 13 June 1964, NLI, BFP, MS 37,048/1.
[**Page 136**] 'Edwards was about to depart': Hilton Edwards, letter to Donal O'Donovan, assistant editor, *Irish Times*, 16 May 1964, Dublin Gate Theatre archive, Northwestern University, Correspondence box 17, folder 2.
'in no mood for work': Hilton Edwards, letter to Louis Elliman, 1 June 1964, Dublin Gate Theatre archive, Northwestern University, Correspondence box 19, folder 6.
'He promised Brian': Hilton Edwards, letter to Brian Friel, 6 July 1964, NLI Archives, BFP, MS 37,048/1.
'At the moment the weather here is VILE' and 'Mails here are erratic and uncertain': BBC – Plays – BF to RM, 7 July 1964.
'It would mean a camp bed': BBC – Plays – BF to RM, 29 June 1964.
'This is nothing more' and 'On the other hand, perhaps this is my greatest fault': Brian Friel, journal entry, 2 August 1964, NLI, BFP, MS 37,048/1.
[**Page 137**] 'Absolutely no news': Brian Friel, letter to Suzanne Finlay, 22 July 1964, NLI, BFP, MS 37,489/1.
'If you wait for sunshine': Suzanne Finlay, letter to Brian Friel, 28 July 1964, NLI, BFP, MS 37,489/1.
'cook, chauffeur, nurse and *confidant*': Patrick Bedford, quoted in Fitz-Simon, p. 288.
'plump, balding, middle-aged man': Brian Friel, *The gentle island*, in *Collected plays*, vol. 1 (Loughcrew: Gallery), I.i.405.
'Patrick Bedford had played many roles': Hilton Edwards, letter to Brian Friel, 28 July 1964, NLI, BFP, MS 37,048/1.
'For Private Gar, Edwards wanted Donal Donnelly': Programme, *Philadelphia, here I come!*, Walnut Street Theatre, Philadelphia, January 1966, NLI, BFP, MS 37,048/4; *The blind mice*, radio script as broadcast, BBC Written Archives Centre.
'all sorts of plans & drawings': Brian Friel, letter to Suzanne Finlay, 1 August 1964, NLI, BFP, MS 37,489/1; Fitz-Simon, pp 275–6.
'He also requested' and 'The weather is still vile': Brian Friel, letter to Suzanne Finlay, 1 August 1964, NLI, BFP, MS 37,489/1.
'when a 60 m.p.h. gale' and 'Now to get back to work': BBC – Plays – BF to RM, 20 August 1964.

'Brian dug up one of his newspaper columns': Brian Friel, 'Down to the sea', *Irish Times*, 16 September 1960; 'Brian Friel's seaside adventures: Donegal diary', *Irish Press*, 21 July 1962; 'The demon fisherman', *Irish Press*, 20 October 1962.
[**Page 138**] 'charmed and interested': RA to BF, 17 September 1964, *NY*.
'delighted to have another solid piece of work from you': RA to BF, 3 November 1964, *NY*.
'money is not all that plentiful': BF to RA, 10 August 1964, *NY*.
'Brian sent his last copy of that script': BBC – Plays – BF to RM, 21 August 1964.
'Good luck with it': BBC – Plays – BF to RM, 20 August 1964.
'getting up steam' and 'By this stage in a production': Hilton Edwards, letter to Brian Friel, 21 July 1964, NLI, BFP, MS 37,048/1.
Brian's first revision for Edwards: Hilton Edwards, letter to Brian Friel, 7 July 1964, NLI, BFP, MS 37,048/1.
'I agree that the light note must be stressed': Hilton Edwards, letter to Brian Friel, 6 July 1964, NLI, BFP, MS 37,048/1.
'It is far better' and 'could dispense with': Hilton Edwards, letter to Brian Friel, 4 August 1964, NLI, BFP, MS 37,048/1.
'Edwards worked with Brian on introducing Gar's dual personae': BBC – Plays – BF to RM, 11 August 1964.
[**Page 139**] 'I don't want to be rushed': Hilton Edwards, letter to Brian Friel, 4 August 1964, NLI, BFP, MS 37,048/1.
'I have, with the utmost difficulty': Hilton Edwards, letter to Brian Friel, 31 August 1964, NLI, BFP, MS 37,048/1.
'a nosey neighbour': Eileen Crowe played Mrs Playfair in John Ford's 1952 film *The quiet man*.
'One would think': Hilton Edwards, letter to Brian Friel, 31 August 1964, NLI, BFP, MS 37,048/1.
'changed her mind': Hilton Edwards, letter to Brian Friel, 3 September 1964, NLI, BFP, MS 37,048/1.
'member of the Radio Éireann players': Programme, *Philadelphia, here I come!*, Walnut Street Theatre, Philadelphia, January 1966, NLI, BFP, MS 37,048/4.
'This completes the cast': Hilton Edwards, letter to Brian Friel, 3 September 1964, NLI, BFP, MS 37,048/1.
'On a Sunday afternoon': BBC – Plays – BF to RM, 7 September 1964.
'a few days to get things roughed out': Hilton Edwards, letter to Brian Friel, 3 September 1964, NLI, BFP, MS 37,048/1.
'At Lewenstein's expense': Elizabeth Lomas, letter to Brian Friel to accompany cheque from Oscar Lewenstein Plays Ltd for £57 10s. for expenses incurred during rehearsal and run of PHILADELPHIA in Dublin Theatre Festival, NLI, BFP, MS 37,048/1.
'Anne and the children': BF to RM, 7 September 1964, BBC Written Archives Centre; letter to Roger Angell, 7 October 1964, *NY*.
'Ronnie Mason brought Richard Imison': BBC – Plays – Richard Imison, letter to Margaret McLaren of Curtis Brown, 13 November 1964.
'a bit more of a "dying fall"': Tyrone Guthrie, letter to Brian Friel, 7 October 1963, NLI, BFP, MS 37,048/1.
'That'll get him a cup of tea on the plane': Friel, *Philadelphia, here I come!*, III.ii.236; BBC – Plays – BF to RM, 2 November 1964.
'God, boy, why do you have to leave?': Friel, *Philadelphia, here I come!*, III.ii.282.
'My original objection': Friel, letter to Oscar Lewenstein, 21 October 1964, NLI, BFP, MS 37,048/1.

[**Page 140**] 'I want to thank everyone very much': Fergus Linehan, 'All right on the night', *Irish Times*, 20 November 1964.

'touching impersonation of an opossum': 'Lavish praise for play by Brian Friel', *Irish Independent*, 30 September 1964.

'Derry wans': Unsigned note to Brian Friel, 28 September 1964, NLI, BFP, MS 37,048/1.

'you must be walking on air': Nanette Molloy, letter to Brian Friel, 29 September 1964, NLI, BFP, MS 37,048/1.

'headlines proclaimed': Desmond Rushe, 'At last – it's the best new Irish play of year', *Irish Independent*, 29 September 1964; M.M., 'Friel gives new twist to an "American wake"', *Irish Press*, 29 September 1964.

'the SURGE at the box office': Tyrone Guthrie, letter to Brian Friel, 11 October 1964, NLI, BFP, MS 37,048/1.

'wasn't nearly so queeny': Tyrone Guthrie, letter to Brian Friel, 11 October 1964, NLI, BFP, MS 37,048/1. Guthrie's biographer James Forsyth, writing in 1976, noted the director's own tendency toward effeminate gestures, and he strenuously defined Guthrie as 'non-sexual' despite his close relationship with college friend Christopher Scaife and his eventual marriage to Lady Guthrie: 'He often displayed the mannerisms – and mocked them in himself, too – of an over-energetic aunt; and in his hazy young days he was surrounded by giant female figures from whom he acquired the world's presumably proper gestures. He was not, however, a homosexual.' (Forsyth, p. 41)

'peevish instead of powerful': Tyrone Guthrie, letter to Brian Friel, 11 October 1964, NLI, BFP, MS 37,048/1.

'I guess it ought to be tried': Tyrone Guthrie, letter to Brian Friel, 7 October 1963, NLI, BFP, MS 37,048/1.

'the master has fucked up the arrangements': Tyrone Guthrie, letter to Brian Friel, 11 October 1964, NLI, BFP, MS 37,048/1.

[**Page 141**] 'gentle play', 'Having read most of what Mr Friel has written' and 'Taciturn and Talkative': Frank O'Connor, 'Edwards the magician turns gentle play into rip-roaring revue', *Sunday Independent*, 4 October 1964.

'as rich a piece of theatrical flamboyance': Hilton Edwards, 'Hilton Edwards replies to Frank O'Connor', *Sunday Independent*, 11 October 1964.

'the real-life Michael O'Donovan': O'Connor wasn't the only Irishman using a pen name. It was common in the mid-twentieth century for writers to hide their true identities, as, for example, in the pseudonyms Flann O'Brien and Myles na gCopaleen, both used by Brian O'Nolan to preserve his early anonymity and his employment in the Irish civil service. In the same era, Conor Cruise O'Brien published essays and a book as Donat O'Donnell, while Seán O'Faoláin used his Gaelicised name rather than his birth name, John Whelan. Arguably the most extravagant act of self-invention was Micheál MacLiammóir's adoption of not only a Gaelicized version of his birth name, Alfred Willmore, but a fictional Irish origin story that upheld his birthplace as Cork rather than Kensal Green, London and presented MacLiammóir as a native Irish speaker. The truth was hidden even from close friends until well after his death in 1978.

'Sir – it is beyond question': Brian Friel, 'Brian Friel, O'Connor and Edwards', *Sunday Independent*, 11 October 1964.

'still endeavouring to extract': Hilton Edwards, 'Hilton Edwards replies to Frank O'Connor', *Sunday Independent*, 11 October 1964.

'So I plead with Mr O'Connor': Brian Friel, 'Brian Friel, O'Connor and Edwards', *Sunday Independent*, 11 October 1964.

'attended by American reporters': Brian Friel, letter to Oscar Lewenstein, 21 October 1964, NLI, BFP, MS 37,048/1.
'a strong local b.o. click': Kauf. [Wolfe Kaufman], 'Shows abroad: *Philadelphia, here I come!*', *Variety*, 21 October 1964, p. 72.
'Brian received £290 in royalties': Brendan Smith, letter to Oscar Lewenstein, 16 October 1964; Suzanne Finlay, letter to Oscar Lewenstein, 14 October 1964; Suzanne Finlay, letter to Brian Friel, 9 November 1964, NLI, BFP, MS 37,048/1.
'a comedy of the absurd': Suzanne Finlay, letter to Brian Friel, 12 November 1964, NLI, BFP, MS 37,048/1.
[**Page 142**] 'still in such a fluid state': Oscar Lewenstein, letter to Brian Friel, 2 December 1964, NLI, BFP, MS 37,048/1.
'sent it to *Psycho* film star': Kermit Bloomgarden, letter to Anthony Perkins, 14 December 1964, Wisconsin Center for Film and Theater Research, KB papers, box 48, folder 23.
'no basis in reality': Kermit Bloomgarden, letters to John McMichael, 25 November 1964, and to Oscar Lewenstein, 31 December 1964, Wisconsin Center for Film and Theater Research, KB papers, box 48, folder 23.
'I hope your nerves will keep steady!': Oscar Lewenstein, letter to Brian Friel, 2 December 1964, NLI, BFP, MS 37,048/1.
'Throughout November and December': Brian Friel, letter to Spencer Curtis Brown, 10 December 1964, NLI, BFP, MS 37,489/2.
'His agent sold publication rights': Richard Simon of Curtis Brown, letter to Brian Friel, 16 October 1964, NLI, BFP, MS 37,046/5; Suzanne Finlay, letter to Brian Friel, 19 October 1964, NLI, BFP, MS 37,048/1.
'translated into German': Ruth Binde of Diogenes Verlag Zürich, letter to Suzanne Finlay of Curtis Brown, 4 December 1964, NLI, BFP, MS 37,489/2.
'Finnish': Suzanne Finlay, letter to Kai Savola, 11 November 1964, NLI, BFP, MS 37,489/2.
'Greek': Andrew Ganly, letter to Brian Friel, 12 October 1965, NLI, BFP, MS 37,048/1.
'amateur drama societies': Letters to Brian Friel from Tommy O'Doherty, Lifford Players, 12 October 1964; Bobby Byrne, Meath Drama Club, October 1964; Johnie J. Friel, Catholic Young Men's Society, Sligo, 13 October 1964; William C. Malone, Waterford Dramatic Society, 16 October 1964; and Tommy McArdle, Castleblaney, 13 October 1964, NLI, BFP, MS 37,048/1.
'pre-printed reply slips': Undated reply slip explaining Lewenstein's licence to *Philadelphia, here I come!*, NLI, BFP, MS 37,048/1.
'short run in the Gaiety': Ernest Blythe, letter to Brian Friel, 31 December 1964, NLI, BFP, MS 37,048/1.
'Lewenstein broke his silence': Elizabeth Lomas of Oscar Lewenstein Ltd, letter to Brian Friel, 4 January 1965, NLI, BFP, MS 37,048/1.
'flew to London for one day': Brian Friel, letter to Spencer Curtis Brown, 5 January 1965, NLI, BFP, MS 37,489/2.
[**Page 143**] 'keen interest', 'Gower would be an absolutely wonderful idea' and 'rather nervous of the idea of pitchforking you alone and unattended': Oscar Lewenstein, letter to Brian Friel, 18 January 1965, NLI, BFP, MS 37,048/1.
'Hartley had over a decade of experience': Obituary for Neil Hartley, *Variety*, 22 January 1995.
'one or two other possible directors': Oscar Lewenstein, letter to Brian Friel, 18 January 1965, NLI, BFP, MS 37,048/1.
'the US trip and all the negotiations so far' and 'as soon as he heard Broadway mentioned': Brian Friel, letter to Spencer Curtis Brown, 2 February 1965, NLI, BFP, MS 37,489/2.

'business was good', 'declared with some heat' and 'Undignified scenes in hotel rooms': Guthrie, *A life in the theatre*, p. 235.
'Speaking to *Time* magazine': 'The presentation and examination of the be(a)st of Broadway', *Time*, 87:12 (25 March 1966), 52–9.
'the Abominable Showman' and 'Between 1954 and 1965': 'The presentation and examination of the be(a)st of Broadway', p. 52.
[**Page 144**] 'promotional stunts': 'The presentation and examination of the be(a)st of Broadway', pp 52–9.
'cynically, successfully, and vulgarly sensational': Guthrie, *A new theatre*, p. 26.
'The Abbey Theatre had just named him': '25 agree to be "Abbey" shareholders', *Irish Press*, 17 February 1965.
'a lovely pile of money': Emilie Jacobson, letter to Brian Friel, 21 December 1964, NLI, BFP, MS 37,041/4; January 1, 1965, *The New Yorker* first reading agreement, NY.
'Brian opened a savings account': Brian Friel, calculations dated 29 January 1965, NLI, BFP, MS 37,041/4.
'a competent person at my elbow': Brian Friel, letter to Spencer Curtis Brown, 2 February 1965, NLI, BFP, MS 37,489/2.
'a small woman': Audrey Wood and Max Wilk, *Represented by Audrey Wood: a memoir* (New York: Doubleday, 1981), p. 54.
'endearingly tough': Studs Terkel, in Wood and Wilk, p. 300.
'a birthing process': Wood and Wilk, p. 12.
'As a young woman': Wood and Wilk, pp 129–203.
'His career entirely turned over': Roger Angell, interview, 18 November 2018.
'Brian met Yip Harburg': Brian Friel, letter to Kermit Bloomgarden, 28 February 1965, KB papers.
[**Page 145**] 'balletic approach' … 'former informer': Burton Lane, letter to Kermit Bloomgarden, 9 November 1965, KB papers.
'stage-Irish': Brian Friel, letter to Kermit Bloomgarden, 28 February 1965, KB papers.
'I know I could do the book to a T': Brian Friel, letter to Kermit Bloomgarden, 13 June 1965, KB papers.
'a $500 advance': Kermit Bloomgarden, letter to Brian Friel, 17 May 1965, KB papers.
'even if it meant': Kermit Bloomgarden, letter to Brian Friel, 31 March 1966, KB papers.
'dealing with the events and characters with absolute simplicity': Brian Friel, letter to Kermit Bloomgarden, 9 November 1966, KB papers.
'Bloomgarden sought Stephen Sondheim's advice': Kermit Bloomgarden, letter to Stephen Sondheim, 18 November 1966, KB papers.
'Richard Harris volunteered': Richard Harris, letter to Kermit Bloomgarden, 22 December 1965, KB papers.
'animal, bullish quality': Brian Friel, letter to Kermit Bloomgarden, 9 November 1966, KB papers.
'Guthrie signalled interest in directing': Paul A. Rosen, letter to Michael Burke, 6 January 1965, KB papers.
'the other "hot" directors in N.Y.': BF to RA, 27 February 1965.
'Wood shopped the play': Oscar Lewenstein, letter to Brian Friel quoting telegram from Audrey Wood, 26 February 1965, NLI, BFP, MS 37,048/1.
'Elia Kazan': Oscar Lewenstein, letter to Brian Friel, 12 April 1965, NLI, BFP, MS 37,489/2.
'Ronnie Mason directed the radio broadcast': BBC – Plays – Martin Esslin, memo to John Tydeman, 15 July 1964.
[**Page 146**] 'No one else from the original cast': BBC WAC – *Philadelphia, here I come!*, Brian Friel, broadcast 25 February 1965, Third Programme, p. 1.

'Take note, America!': BBC WAC – *Philadelphia, here I come!*, Brian Friel, broadcast 25 February 1965, Third Programme, cast list.
'the play scored 71': BBC – Plays – Audience research report, 18 March 1965.
'quite sure that a repeat on the Northern Ireland Home Service is not feasible': BBC – Plays – Memo from head of Northern Ireland Programmes to chief assistant, Home Service, 22 March 1965.
'television version of *The enemy within*': 'Fifty dramatic minutes in March', *Belfast Telegraph*, 5 February 1965; 'A first-rate production', *News Letter*, 31 March 1965.
'He had co-produced Brendan Behan's *The Hostage*': Oscar Lewenstein, p. 90; letter to Brian Friel, 22 April 1965, NLI, BFP, MS 37,048/1.
'I don't think this play is a sure thing': Oscar Lewenstein, letter to Brian Friel, 22 April 1965, NLI, BFP, MS 37,048/1.
'invite certain Americans': Oscar Lewenstein, letter to Brian Friel, 12 April 1965, NLI, BFP, MS 37,489/2.
'a huge loss': Brian Friel, letter to Oscar Lewenstein, 14 April 1965, NLI, BFP, MS 37,048/1.
[**Page 147**] 'because we know one another': Brian Friel, letter to Oscar Lewenstein, 14 April 1965, NLI, BFP, MS 37,048/1.
'I have got to earn money from this play': Brian Friel, letter to Oscar Lewenstein, 14 April 1965, NLI, BFP, MS 37,048/1.
'Donal Donnelly's calendar': Spencer Curtis Brown, letter to Brian Friel, 5 May 1965, NLI, BFP, MS 37,489/2.
'The news cheered Brian enough', 'took a mad notion' and 'The theatre is absorbing me more and more': BF to RA, 14 June 1965, *NY*.
'you complain to me': RA to BF, 21 June 1965, *NY*.
'The queen of Troy Close': RA to BF, 6 April 1965, *NY*.
'You are at least twice the writer': RA to BF, 21 June 1965, *NY*.
'British pop culture reigned': *Festival de Cannes, 1965, les médias*, Association Française du Festival International du Film, https://www.festival-cannes.com/fr/72-editions/retrospective/1965/medias#; Getty Images, https://www.gettyimages.com/photos/cannes-film-festival-1965?mediatype=photography&page=2&phrase=cannes%20film%20festival%201965&sort=mostpopular.
'so busy with film affairs': Spencer Curtis Brown, letter to Brian Friel, 5 July 1965, NLI, BFP, MS 37,489/2.
'esoteric literary plays': Michael White, *Empty seats* (London: Hamish Hamilton, 1984), p. 44; Lewenstein, p. 107.
[**Page 148**] '*The Connection*': White, pp 37–42.
'White would later produce': Bruce Weber, 'Michael White, impresario of the outrageous, dies at 80', *New York Times*, 13 March 2016.
'Brian instructed': Brian Friel, draft of letter to Michael White, 13 August 1965, NLI, BFP, MS 37,048/3.
'difficulty in mustering a cast': Brian Friel, letter to Spencer Curtis Brown, 6 July 1965, NLI, BFP, MS 37,489/2.
'Impact of a newspaper strike': Brian Friel, letter to Spencer Curtis Brown, dated 'Friday' [23 July 1965], NLI, BFP, MS 37,489/2.
'Lewenstein was on location in France': Spencer Curtis Brown, letter to Brian Friel, 27 July 1965, NLI, BFP, MS 37,489/2.
'Michael White arranged travel': Brian Friel, letter to Spencer Curtis Brown, dated 'Friday' [23 July 1965], NLI, BFP, MS 37,489/2; Spencer Curtis Brown, letter to Brian Friel, 27 July 1965, NLI, BFP, MS 37,489/2.

'reprised their roles': Programme, *Philadelphia, here I come!*, 10 August 1965, NLI, BFP, MS 37,489/2.

'flawless in Casting, Direction, and Acting': Ria Mooney, postcard to Brian Friel, 15 August 1965, NLI, BFP, MS 37,048/3.

'more than slightly perplexed' and 'We all agree': Brian Friel, draft of letter to Michael White, 13 August 1965, NLI, BFP, MS 37,048/3.

[**Page 149**] 'To keep the Irish cast together': Spencer Curtis Brown, letter to Brian Friel, 24 August 1965; Brian Friel, letter to Spencer Curtis Brown, 1 September 1965, NLI, BFP, MS 37,489/2.

'madness': Michael White, letter to Hilton Edwards, 6 September 1965, NLI, BFP, MS 37,048/1.

'all were fully booked': Michael White, letter to Hilton Edwards, 6 September 1965, NLI, BFP, MS 37,048/1.

'More bad news': Lord Chamberlain's office, letter to Michael White, 26 August 1965, NLI, BFP, MS 37,048/3.

'grips his loins, doubles up' and 'With regard to this section': Assistant comptroller, letter to Michael White, 10 September 1965, NLI, BFP, MS 37,048/3.

'anti-war trilogy *America hurrah*': White, *Empty seats*, pp 90–4.

'"stunned" and "disturbed"': Brian Friel, letter to Spencer Curtis Brown, 1 September 1965, NLI, BFP, MS 37,489/2.

'I have had so many disappointments over this play': Brian Friel, letter to Spencer Curtis Brown, 1 September 1965, NLI, BFP, MS 37,489/2.

'SEND TRUSTWORTHY SPY': Tyrone Guthrie, draft of telegram to Harry Saltzman, 3 September 1965, NLI, BFP, MS 37,048/1.

'extremely intelligent': Spencer Curtis Brown, letter to Brian Friel, 25 August 1965, NLI, BFP, MS 37,489/2.

'bankrolled *A streetcar named Desire*': Wood and Wilk, pp 150–1.

'enormously moved and impressed': Spencer Curtis Brown, letter to Brian Friel, 7 September 1965, NLI, BFP, MS 37,489/2.

'we can still work out a deal': Audrey Wood, letter to Spencer Curtis Brown, 22 September 1965, NLI, BFP, MS 37,489/2.

[**Page 150**] 'AGREEABLE USING EDWARDS AS DIRECTOR': Audrey Wood, telegram to Brian Friel, 24 September 1965, NLI, BFP, MS 37,489/2.

'Brian consented': Brian Friel, letter to Michael White, 28 September 1965, NLI, BFP, MS 37,048/3.

'I could do with the money': Brian Friel, letter to John Fernald, 19 October 1965, NLI, BFP, MS 37,489/2.

'he collected his royalties': Mary Cannon, letter to John Fernald, 27 October 1965; John Fernald, letter to Brian Friel, 2 November 1965, NLI, BFP, MS 37,489/2.

'He found Mavis Villiers': *Playbill* program for *Philadelphia, here I come!*, Walnut St. Theatre, Philadelphia, NLI archives, BFP, MS 37,048/4.

'Experienced television actors': *Playbill* program for *Philadelphia, here I come!*, Helen Hayes Theatre, New York, 16 February 1966, NLI archives, BFP, MS 37,048/4.

'Gar's friends Ned, Tom and Joe': Before the New York opening, Merrick summoned Eamon Morrissey from Dublin to play Joe because the American actor that Edwards cast could not perfect his Irish accent. Morrissey had played Ned in the original Dublin Festival production (Colin Murphy, 'Eamon Morrissey and *Philadelphia, here I come!*', *Irish Independent Review*, 6 March 2010).

'Kelly was a veteran of the Radio Éireann Player's: *Playbill* program for *Philadelphia, here I come!*, Walnut St. Theatre, Philadelphia, NLI, BFP, MS 37,048/4.
'The one piece of casting': Tyrone Guthrie, letter to Brian Friel, 11 October 1964, NLI, BFP, MS 37,048/1.
'Two days after Christmas 1965': 'On the way to Broadway', photo of Friel, Edwards and *Philadelphia* Irish cast members, undated, NLI, BFP, MS 37,048/4.
'Irish culture was in vogue': See Mary Burke, 'The cottage, the castle, and the couture cloak: "traditional" Irish fabrics and "modern"' Irish fashions in America, c.1952–1969', *Journal of Design History*, 31:3 (September 2018).
'We were invited to luncheon parties': BBC WAC – 'Philadelphia, here the author comes: a talk by Brian Friel', Brian Friel, broadcast 21 July 1966. Bobby Kennedy attended: Anne Friel, video introduction to the American Conference for Irish Studies, 2 June 2021, https://www.youtube.com/watch?v=hbZ2ukPv3Dw.
[Page 151] 'Brian, Edwards and the cast': Undated photograph, NLI, BFP, MS 37,048/4.
[Page 152] 'In Boston': George Ryan, letter to Brian Friel, 1 February 1966, NLI, BFP, MS 37,048/4.
'Brian spent his thirty-seventh birthday in New York': BBC WAC – 'Philadelphia, here the author comes: a talk by Brian Friel', Brian Friel, broadcast 21 July 1966.
'for the statue not the store': White, p. 86.
'do something to liven this play up': White, p. 86.
'a sort of Irish "Death of a salesman"': Gagh., 'Legit tryout: *Philadelphia, here I come*', *Variety*, 19 January 1966, p. 3.
'It grossed $27,428': 'Road sizzles', *Variety*, 26 January 1966, p. 63.
'and $35,557 in its second': 'Road healthy', *Variety*, 2 February 1966, p. 59.
'hackneyed': Kevin Kelly, 'Inner self, outer self; just another comedy', *Boston Globe*, 1 February 1966.
[Page 153] 'the Wilbur Theatre reaped $25,650': 'Road perky', *Variety*, 9 February 1966, p. 58.
'and $30,161 in its second': 'Road iffy', *Variety*, 16 February 1966, p. 57.
'a tightening of the nerves': BBC WAC – 'Philadelphia, here the author comes: a talk by Brian Friel', Brian Friel, broadcast 21 July 1966. Merrick and other producers: Bert Cardullo, 'Interview with Stanley Kauffmann', *The Missouri Review*, 25:3 (Winter 2002), https://www.missourireview.com/article/interview-with-stanley-kauffmann/
'either bonanza time or sudden death': Hobe Morrison, 'Biz like New Year's Eve on B'way, but disaster time for 3 preems', *Variety*, 2 March 1966, p. 57.
'At your peril', 'technical difficulties': 'the sell-out crowd' and '*New York Times* carried the story on its front page': 'The dark preview, or "At your peril"', *New York Times*, 16 February 1966.
'*The New Yorker* and *Time* were agog': 'The talk of the town: notes and comment', *The New Yorker*, 26 February 1966, p. 26; 'Smelling a rat', *Time*, 87:8 (25 February 1966), p. 64.
'Merrick appeared on the *Merv Griffin* TV show': 'The dark preview, or "At your peril"', *New York Times*, 16 February 1966.
'a million dollars worth of publicity': Fitz-Simon, p. 279.
'Billy-Liar youths': Stanley Kauffmann, 'Theatre: an Irish play', *New York Times*, 17 February 1966.
'a promising box office start': Hobe Morrison, 'B'way spotty; may ditto this week', *Variety*, 23 February 1966, p. 65.
'One corpulent, silver-haired lady': BBC WAC – 'Philadelphia, here the author comes: a talk by Brian Friel', Brian Friel, broadcast 21 July 1966.
[Page 154] 'The play's second week brought in $34,427': Hobe Morrison, 'Biz like New Year's Eve on B'way, but disaster time for 3 preems', *Variety*, 2 March 1966, p. 57.
'steady climb': Hobe Morrison, 'B'way spotty, but slightly better', *Variety*, 23 March 1966, p. 66.

'Brian's contracts with Lewenstein and Merrick': Brian Friel and Oscar Lewenstein, memorandum of agreement, 17 March 1964, NLI, BFP, MS 37,048/1.
'Ex-teacher Friel hits cash mark as "Phila." hits', and 'struck gold': 'Ex-teacher Friel hits cash mark as "Phila." hits', *Variety*, 2 March 1966, p. 1.
'it ran for 41 weeks on Broadway': *Variety* weekly ticket sales reports, 2 March 1966 through 30 November 1966.
'took a mighty leap': 'Road perky, even for so-so draws', *Variety*, 18 January 1967, p. 69.
'Brendan Smith's royalty agreement': Brendan Smith, letter to Hilton Edwards, 25 August 1964, Dublin Gate Theatre archive, Northwestern University, Production box 87, folder 2.
'Patrick Bedford negotiated a salary raise': Peter Witt, agent, letter to Jack Schlissel, c/o David Merrick, 13 October 1966, NLI, BFP, MS 37,048/1.
'smiling for press photos': Becky Blum, 'Irish actor learned to cook in self-defense', *Chicago Sun-Times*, 17 February 1967, p. 22, NLI, BFP, MS 37,048/1.
'longest-running Irish play in Broadway history': 'Friel record', *Irish Press*, 1 December 1966.
'had to pester Gaiety management': Suzanne Finlay, letter to Brian Friel, 12 November 1964, NLI, BFP, MS 37,048/1.

EPILOGUE: **Curtain call**
[**Page 155**] 'the role of my life': Patrick Bedford, letter to Brian Friel, 6 April 1996, NLI, BFP, MS 37,048/2.
'a year and a half': 'Roadshow slump', *Variety*, 24 May 1967, p. 61.
'The play transferred from the US to London': Hawk, 'Shows abroad', *Variety*, 27 September 1967, p. 62.
'but its West End box office returns were disappointing': Lewenstein, p. 122.
'When Hilton Edwards died in 1982': Fitz-Simon, pp 308–9.
'in 1988 he became a Gate trustee': Christine Newman, 'Actor Patrick Bedford (67) dies in New York', *Irish Times*, 22 November 1999.
'it was in Chicago when they told me': Patrick Bedford, letter to Brian Friel, 6 April 1996, NLI, BFP, MS 37,048/2.
'the Royalty Arms': RA to BF, 6 April 1967, *NY*.
[**Page 156**] 'with a squad of builders': BF to RA, 20 April 1967, *NY*.
'in a wild effort': BF to RA, 12 August 1968, *NY*; 'Brian Friel unable to attend Olympia', press release, 1 July 1966, NLI, BFP, MS 37,044/4.
'Ray McAnally's revival': *The enemy within* ran for two weeks at the Olympia Theatre, Dublin in July 1968. See NLI, BFP, MS 37,044/4.
'Teach Annie': 'Building of the month – May 2017 – Teach Annie', https://www.equitone.com/en-ie/blog/64365/teach-annie/ 'Teach' translates as 'house' in English.
'just too good for your old friends': RA to BF, 15 April 1966, NLI, BFP, MS 37,041/4.
'I did make several attempts at stories recently': BF to RA, 19 December 1967, *NY*.
'severe doubts that Brian Friel will ever write another short story': Roger Angell, letter to Emilie Jacobson to accompany First Reading Agreement, 13 December 1967, *NY*. Friel had repeatedly corrected Angell's naming of 'North Ireland' as early as 1961, to no avail: 'Our severed portion of the country is usually referred to as Northern Ireland, not North Ireland. A simple error like that could bring a terrible Irish wrath down on our heads!' (Friel, letter to Roger Angell, 30 June 1961, *NY*),
'glorious performance': Hobe Morrison, review of *The loves of Cass McGuire*, *Variety*, 12 October 1966, p. 70.

'The play ran for only twenty nights': 'B'way zooms again', *Variety*, 19 October 1966, p. 57; 'Broadway slightly off', *Variety*, 26 October 1966, p. 61.

'"blame" for what happened in America': Brian Friel, letter to Hilton Edwards, 13 December 1966, NLI, BFP, MS 37,062/2.

'He quickly submitted the play to the Abbey': 5 December 1966, '*The loves of Cass McGuire*, 3 act, submitted by Brian Friel', *Plays received, April 1964–*, ATC/LIT/SL/06, p. 34, Abbey Theatre archives.

[**Page 157**] 'It opened in Dublin': Roche, pp 48–50.

'I don't like America at all': Brian Friel, 'Interview with Desmond Rushe, 1970' in *Brian Friel, essays, diaries, interviews: 1964–1999*, edited by Christopher Murray (London: Faber, 1999), pp 25–34, p. 34.

'efforts to transfer *Philadelphia*'s success to film': 'International soundtrack', *Variety*, 13 January 1971, p. 33; Roy Loynd, '"Runaway" Robert Altman operates "images" free style in Ireland', *Variety*, 15 December 1971, pp 4, 20; 'Brian Friel rights clearance is clouded', *Variety*, 2 April 1975, p. 38.

'Lewenstein produced Brian's 1973 play *The freedom of the city*': Lewenstein, p. 150; Stephen Rea, in *Brian Friel: shy man, showman*, 2022.

'hostile reviews': Lewenstein, p. 150.

'a bit of a dog's tail': BF to RA, 15 December 1964, *NY*.

'expect writers to approach them with awe': Brian Friel, 'Self-portrait', *Aquarius* 5 (1972), 17–22, p. 21.

[**Page 158**] 'took their seats after being frisked': Anne Friel, in *Brian Friel: shy man, showman*, 2022.

'Field Day launched annual plays': Seamus Deane, Seamus Heaney, Richard Kearney, Declan Kiberd and Tom Paulin, *Ireland's Field Day* (London: Hutchinson, 1985), pp vii–viii.

'market towns north and south of the border': from September through December, 1980, Field Day performed *Translations* in Belfast, Dublin, Magherafelt, Dungannon, Newry, Carrickmore, Armagh, Enniskillen, Ballyshannon, Coleraine, Galway, Tralee and Cork. NLI, BFP, MS 37,086/1 – 3.

'An Grianán Theatre, Letterkenny': Katy Hayes, 'Seán McGinley: "We're all asking why this play hasn't been done more often', *Irish Independent*, 20 November 2021.

'Housebound audiences in seventy-one countries': https://www.oldvictheatre.com/whats-on/2020/old-vic-in-camera/faith-healer

[**Page 159**] 'so poor that I still have bad dreams about it': Brian Friel, letter to Elizabeth Stevens of Curtis Brown, 15 April 1965, NLI, BFP, MS 37,489/2.

'ruthless use of a blue pencil': BBC – Plays – RM to BF, 25 March 1958.

'memorial fidelity': Roger Angell, 'This old man', *The New Yorker*, 17 February 2014, 60–5, p. 65.

'Brian had a wonderful voice': Roger Angell, interview, 18 November 2018.

'a hiding place': *Sir Tyrone Guthrie: a voluntary exile*, RTÉ archives, 1962, https://www.rte.ie/archives/2017/0517/875878-tyrone-guthrie-theatre-man/

Bibliography

Archival sources

Abbey Theatre archives
BBC Written Archives Centre (WAC)
Brian Friel papers, National Library of Ireland (NLI)
Dublin Gate Theatre archives, Northwestern University
Guthrie, Sir Tyrone, and Lady Guthrie papers, Public Records Office of Northern Ireland (PRONI)
Guthrie Theater records, University of Minnesota
Kermit Bloomgarden papers, Wisconsin Center for Film and Theater Research
The New Yorker archives, New York Public Library

Interviews and conversations

Roger Angell, interview, 18 November 2018, New York
Tommy Doherty, conversation, 27 August 2017, Derry
Anne Friel, conversations, 26 August 2017, Derry and 9 December 2022, Belfast
Michael Longley, conversation, 18 March 2019, Cambridge, Massachusetts
Paul Muldoon, conversation, 3 March 2018, Boston
John Tydeman, interview, 21 June 2016, via telephone

Periodicals

Boston Globe
The Critic
Derry Journal
Donegal Democrat
Evening Herald
The Guardian
Housewife
The Independent
Irish Independent
The Irish Press
Irish Times
Minneapolis Star Tribune
New York Times
The New Yorker
News Letter
Nottingham Post
Radio Times
The Sign
St Jude
The Telegraph
Time
The Times
Ulster Herald
Variety

Published works consulted

Abbotson, Susan C.W., 'Production history of *Death of a Salesman*', https://www.ibiblio.org/miller/Production%20History%20of%20SalesmanearlyFinal.

Alexander, James D., 'Frank O'Connor in the *New Yorker*, 1945–1967', *Éire-Ireland* 30:1 (Spring 1995), 130–44.

Andrews, Elmer, *The art of Brian Friel: neither reality nor dreams* (London: Macmillan, 1995).

Bank of England Inflation Calculator, https://www.bankofengland.co.uk/monetary-policy/inflation/inflation-calculator.

Bardon, Jonathan, *Beyond the studio: a history of BBC Northern Ireland* (Belfast: Blackstaff, 2000).

Barton, Brian, *Northern Ireland in the Second World War* (Belfast: Ulster Historical Society, 1995).

Blair, S. Alexander, *The golden years: the story of Ballymoney Drama Festival* (Ballymoney: Committee of Ballymoney Drama Festival, 1989).

Boltwood, Scott, '"An emperor or something": Brian Friel's Columba, migrancy and postcolonial theory', *Irish Studies Review*, 10:1 (2002), 51–61.

— *Brian Friel, Ireland, and the North* (Cambridge: Cambridge University Press, 2007).

— *Brian Friel: Readers' guide to essential criticism* (London: Palgrave Macmillan, 2018).

— '"Mildly eccentric": Brian Friel's writings for the *Irish Times* and the *New Yorker*', *Irish University Review*, 44:2 (Autumn–Winter 2014), 305–22.

— '"More real for Northern Catholics than anybody else": Brian Friel's earliest plays', *Irish Theatre International*, 2:1 (2009), 4–15.

— '"Swapping stories about Apollo and Cuchulainn": Brian Friel and the de-gaelicizing of Ireland', *Modern Drama*, 41 (1998), 573–83.

Briggs, Asa, *The BBC: the first fifty years* (Oxford: Oxford University Press, 1985).

'Building of the month – May 2017 – Teach Annie', https://www.equitone.com/en-ie/blog/64365/teach-annie/

Burke, Mary, 'The cottage, the castle, and the couture cloak: "traditional" Irish fabrics and "modern" Irish fashions in America, c.1952–1969', *Journal of Design History*, 31:3 (September 2018), 364–82.

Cardullo, Bert, 'Interview with Stanley Kauffmann', *The Missouri Review*, 25:3 (Winter 2002), https://www.missourireview.com/article/interview-with-stanley-kauffmann/

Collins, Neil, *The splendid cause: the Missionary Society of St Columban 1916–1954* (Dublin: Columba Press, 2009).

Cooper, Giles, *The disagreeable oyster*, BBC broadcast audio file, https://clyp.it/l1awe5u2, accessed 13 May 2020.

Cronin, John, '"Donging the tower" – the past did have meaning: the short stories of Brian Friel' in A. Peacock (ed.), *The achievement of Brian Friel* (Gerrards Cross: Colin Smythe, 1993), pp 1–13.

Daly, Edward, *Mister, are you a priest?* (Dublin: Four Courts Press, 2000).

Dantanus, Ulf, *Brian Friel: a study* (London: Faber and Faber, 1988).
Darac, 'The jam factory at Newbliss railway station, Co. Monaghan', https://www.darac.ie/History_of_Station/history_of_station.html
Davies, Robertson, *Thrice the brinded cat hath mew'd: a record of the Stratford Shakespearean Festival in Canada, 1955* (Toronto: Clarke, Irwin, 1955).
de Valera, Éamon, Radio address 17 March 1943, RTÉ Archives, www.rte.ie/laweb/ll/ll_to9b.html.
Deane, Seamus, and Seamus Heaney, Richard Kearney, Declan Kiberd, and Tom Paulin, *Ireland's Field Day* (London: Hutchinson, 1985).
Delaney, Paul (ed.), *Brian Friel in conversation* (Ann Arbor: University of Michigan Press, 2000).
Drakakis, John (ed.), *British radio drama* (Cambridge: Cambridge University Press, 1981).
Ellis, James, *Troubles over the bridge: a first hand account of the* Over the bridge *controversy and its aftermath* (Belfast: Lagan, 2015).
Esslin, Martin, 'Drama and the media in Britain', *Modern Drama* 28:1 (Spring 1985), 99–109.
Festival de Cannes, 1965, Les médias. Association Française du Festival International du Film, https://www.festival-cannes.com/fr/72-editions/retrospective/1965/medias#.
Fitz-Simon, Christopher, *The boys: a biography of Micheál MacLiammóir and Hilton Edwards* (Dublin: New Island, 2005).
Fitzpatrick, David, *Ernest Blythe in Ulster: the making of a double agent?* (Cork: Cork University Press, 2018).
Foley, Dermot, 'The young librarian' in M. Sheehy (ed.), *Michael/Frank: studies on Frank O'Connor* (New York: Knopf, 1969), pp 50–63.
Forsyth, James, *Tyrone Guthrie: a biography* (London: Hamish Hamilton, 1976).
Franklin, Nancy, 'Lady with a pencil', *The New Yorker*, 26 February 1996.
Franzen, Jonathan, 'The birth of "*The New Yorker* story"', *The New Yorker*, 27 October 2015, www.newyorker.com
Friel, Brian, *Aristocrats* in *Collected plays*, vol. 2 (Loughcrew: Gallery, 2016), pp 266–358.
— 'The Child', *The Bell*, 18:4 (July 1952), 232–3.
— *The enemy within*, in *Collected plays*, vol. 1 (Loughcrew: Gallery, 2016), pp 9–84.
— *Essays, diaries, interviews: 1964–1999*, ed. Christopher Murray (London: Faber and Faber, 1999).
— 'The first of my sins', *The Critic*, 21:4, February–March 1963, 20–3.
— 'For export only', *The Commonweal*, 15 February 1957, 509–10.
— 'The giant of Monaghan', *Holiday*, 35:5, May 1964, 89–96.
— *The gold in the sea* (New York: Doubleday, 1966).
— 'The green years', broadcast 30 April 1964, Northern Ireland Home Service.
— 'Pearls in the Strule', *Housewife*, 24:11, November 1962, 44–7.
— *Philadelphia, here I come!* in *Collected plays*, vol. 1 (Loughcrew: Gallery, 2016), pp 87–175.

— 'Philadelphia, here the author comes!', broadcast 21 July 1966, Northern Ireland Home Service.
— *The saucer of larks: stories of Ireland* (New York: Doubleday, 1962).
— 'Self-portrait', *Aquarius*, 5 (1972), 17–22.
— 'Some people and places', broadcast 7 November 1962, Northern Ireland Home Service.
Froggatt, Richard, 'Harold Goldblatt (1899–1982)', *New Ulster biography*, www.newulsterbiography.co.uk.
Getty Images, Cannes Film Festival 1965, https://www.gettyimages.com/photos/cannes-film-festival-1965?mediatype=photography&page= 2&phrase=cannes%20film%20festival%201965&sort=mostpopular.
Gill, Brendan, *Here at the New Yorker* (New York: Random House, 1975).
'Glencree German war cemetery', *Atlas Obscura*, https://www.atlasobscura.com/places/glencree-german-war-cemetery
Gussow, Mel, 'From Ballybeg to Broadway', *New York Times magazine*, 29 September 1991, 30, 56–61.
Guthrie, Tyrone, 'A director views the stage', *Design Quarterly*, 58 (1963). Tyrone Guthrie papers, PRONI D3585/F/7/7/5.
— *A life in the theatre* (New York: McGraw-Hill, 1959).
— *A new theatre* (New York: McGraw-Hill, 1964).
— *Sir Tyrone Guthrie: a voluntary exile*, RTÉ archives, 1962, https://www.rte.ie/archives/2017/0517/875878-tyrone-guthrie-theatre-man/
Guthrie, Tyrone, and Tanya Moiseiwitsch, 'The production of *King Oedipus*', in *Thrice the brinded cat hath mew'd: A record of the Stratford Shakespearean Festival in Canada, 1955* (Toronto: Clarke, Irwin & Company, 1955), pp 111–78.
Hewitt, John, 'Writing in Ulster', *The Bell*, 18:4 (July 1952), 197–202.
Koeper, H. Frederick, 'Introduction', *Design Quarterly*, 58 (1963). Tyrone Guthrie papers, PRONI D3585/F/7/7/5.
Lewenstein, Oscar, *Kicking against the pricks: a theatre producer looks back* (London: Nick Hern, 1994).
The Life of St Columba, founder of Hy, written by Adamnan, ninth abbot of that monastery, ed. William Reeves (Dublin: Irish Archaeological and Celtic Society, 1857).
Lojek, Helen, 'Stage Irish-Americans in the plays of Brian Friel', *Canadian Journal of Irish Studies*, 17:2 (December 1991), 78–85.
Lonergan, Patrick, 'Queering Shakespeare at the Abbey: Wayne Jordan's *Twelfth Night*', *Scenes from the bigger picture* blog, 3 May 2014, accessed 11 September 2018.
Loughran, Gráinne, and Marian McCavana (eds), *The radio catalogue: BBC Northern Ireland radio archives at the Ulster Folk and Transport Museum* (Belfast: Ulster Folk and Transport Museum, 1993).
Matthews, James, *Voices: a life of Frank O'Connor* (New York: Atheneum, 1987).
Matthews, Kelly, *The Bell magazine and the representation of Irish identity* (Dublin: Four Courts Press, 2012).

Maxwell, D.E.S., *Brian Friel* (Lewisburg: Bucknell University Press, 1973).

Maxwell, William, 'Frank O'Connor and the *New Yorker*', in M. Sheehy (ed.), *Michael/Frank: studies on Frank O'Connor* (New York: Knopf, 1969), pp 140–7.

McGlone, James, *Ria Mooney: the life and times of the artistic director of the Abbey Theatre, 1948–1963* (Jefferson, North Carolina: McFarland, 2002).

McMullan, Anna, 'Performativity, unruly bodies and gender in Brian Friel's drama' in A. Roche, *The Cambridge companion to Brian Friel* (Cambridge, 2006), pp 142–53.

Mooney, Ria, *Players and the painted stage, the autobiography of Ria Mooney*, edited by Val Mulkerns, in *George Spelvin's Theatre Book*, 1:2 (Summer 1978) and 1:3 (Fall 1978).

Morash, Christopher, *A history of Irish theatre, 1601–2000* (Cambridge: Cambridge University Press, 2004).

— *A history of the media in Ireland* (Cambridge: Cambridge UP, 2010).

Muir, Marie-Louise, *Brian Friel: shy man, showman* (BBC Northern Ireland, 2022).

Murray, Christopher, *The theatre of Brian Friel: tradition and modernity* (London: Bloomsbury, 2014).

Newtownabbey: 50 years of progress, 1958–2008 (Newtownabbey: *Newtownabbey Times* and *East Antrim Times*).

Northern Ireland Statistics and Research Agency, 1937 census, http:// www.histpop.org/ohpr/servlet/PageBrowser?path=Browse/Census%20(by%20date)/1937&active=yes&mno=341&tocstate=expandnew&tocseq=4100&display=sections&display=tables&display=pagetitles&pageseq=first-nonblank and https://www.nisra.gov.uk/statistics/2001-and-earlier-censuses/1937-census

O'Brien, George, *Brian Friel: a reference guide, 1962–1992* (New York: Simon & Schuster Macmillan, 1995).

— '"Meet Brian Friel": the *Irish Press* columns', *Irish University Review*, 29:1 (1999), 30–9.

O'Brien, Mark, *De Valera, Fianna Fáil and the* Irish Press (Dublin: Irish Academic Press, 2001).

— *The* Irish Times*: a history* (Dublin: Four Courts Press, 2008).

O'Connor, Frank, *My father's son* (London: Macmillan, 1968).

O'Faoláin, Seán, 'F.R. Higgins, died, January 7th, 1941', *The Bell*, 3:4 (January 1942), 251–3.

— 'Frederick Robert Higgins (1897–1941)', *The Bell*, 1:5 (February 1941), 53–5.

Old Vic *In Camera*, https://www.oldvictheatre.com/whats-on/2020/old-vic-in-camera/faith-healer

Pelletier, Martine, 'Telling stories and making history: Brian Friel and Field Day', *Irish University Review*, 24:2 (Autumn–Winter 1994), 186–97.

— *Le théâtre de Brian Friel: histoire et histoires* (Villeneuve d'Ascq: Septentrion, 1997).

Pilkington, Lionel, 'Theatre and cultural politics in Northern Ireland: the *Over the bridge* Controversy, 1959', *Éire-Ireland*, 30:4 (1996), 76–93.

Pine, Richard, *Brian Friel and Ireland's drama* (London: Routledge, 1990).

— *The diviner: the art of Brian Friel* (Dublin: UCD Press, 1999).

Radharc Programme 2, broadcast 1962, available via Irish Film Institute courtesy of *Donegal Today*, https://www.youtube.com/watch?v=hQqek PeNPWY

Rapson, Ralph, 'The architect's design', *Design Quarterly*, 58 (1963). Tyrone Guthrie papers, PRONI D3585/F/7/7/5.

Richardson, Tony (producer), *Tom Jones*. London: Woodfall, 1963.

Richtarik, Marilynn J., *Acting between the lines: The Field Day Theatre Company and Irish cultural politics 1980–1984* (Oxford: Clarendon, 1994).

Roche, Anthony, *Brian Friel: theatre and politics* (Basingstoke: Palgrave Macmillan, 2011).

— (ed.), *The Cambridge companion to Brian Friel* (Cambridge: Cambridge University Press, 2006).

Rossi, Alfred, 'The *Hamlet* log', *Minneapolis rehearsals: Tyrone Guthrie directs* Hamlet (Berkeley: U of California Press, 1970).

Russell, Richard Rankin, 'Brian Friel's short fiction: place, community, and modernity', *Irish University Review*, 42:2 (Autumn–Winter 2012), 298–326.

— 'Brian Friel's transformation from short fiction writer to dramatist', *Comparative Drama*, 46:4 (Winter 2012), 451–74.

— *Modernity, community, and place in Brian Friel's drama* (Syracuse: Syracuse University Press, 2014).

Ryan, Phyllis, *The company I kept* (Dublin: Town House, 1996).

Stingone, William, *The New Yorker: Records*, New York Public Library humanities and social sciences library manuscripts and archives division (New York, 1996).

Stulberg, Jacob, 'How (not) to write broadcast plays: Pinter and the BBC', *Modern Drama* 58:4 (Winter 2015), 502–23.

Verma, Neil, *Theater of the mind: imagination, aesthetics, and American radio drama* (Chicago: University of Chicago Press, 2012).

Waterhouse, Keith, and Willis Hall, *Billy Liar: a comedy in three acts* (London: Samuel French, 1960).

Welch, Robert, *The Abbey Theatre, 1899–1999: form and pressure* (Oxford University Press, 1999).

White, Michael, *Empty seats* (London: Hamish Hamilton, 1984).

Wood, Audrey, and Max Wilk, *Represented by Audrey Wood: a memoir* (New York: Doubleday, 1981).

Index

A Jew called Sammy by John McCann, 83
A satire of the three estates by Sir David Lyndsay, 98
Abbey Theatre, 8, 42, 66, 75–9, 85–7, 120, 122, 131, 134, 142, 144, 148, 156–7, 158
Academy Awards, 129
Actors' Equity Association, 96, 148
Adamnán, St, 76–7, 84
After the fall by Arthur Miller, 145
Albee, Edward, 103, 156
Alexandra College, 91
Algonquin Hotel, 144
America hurrah by Jean-Claude van Itallie, 149
An Grianán Theatre, Letterkenny, 158
An Tóstal, 134
Angell, Carol Rogge, 14, 105, 123–4, 159
Angell, Roger, 8, 9, 10, 14–5, 23, 35–40, 42–54, 57, 59–74, 76, 80–1, 88–9, 94–5, 103–11, 116, 122–4, 127–33, 138, 141, 144–5, 147, 155–7, 159
Annaghmakerrig House, 55, 95–8, 100, 103, 121, 126, 140
Archer, William, 31
Ardmore Studios, 82, 157
Argosy magazine, 93
Arts Council, Ireland, 111, 135
Arts Over Borders Festival, 158
Atkinson, Brooks, 96
Ave Maria magazine, 61, 94

Bakewell, Michael, 58
Ball, William, 145
Ballymoney Literary and Debating Society, 86, 132
Beatles, 147

Bedford, Patrick, 136–8, 140, 148, 150–2, 154, 155
Behan, Brendan, 76, 146
Belfast News Letter, 55
Belfast Telegraph, 105
Berlin Wall, 51, 112
Billy Budd film, 76
Billy Liar by Keith Waterhouse, 128, 153
Bleakley, David, 27
Bloody Sunday, Derry, 85, 157
Bloomgarden, Kermit, 142, 144–5, 147, 149
Blythe, Ernest, 8, 75–9, 82–3, 85–6, 90–1, 134, 142, 157
Bord Fáilte, 49, 53, 62, 134–5
Boston *Globe*, 152
Boucicault, Dion, 76
Bowen, Evelyn, 48
Boyd, John, 22, 24, 27, 28, 136
Brandeis University, 99–100
Brecht, Bertolt, 128
Bretherton, Judith, 98; *see also* Guthrie, Lady Judith
Bristol Old Vic, 41
British Broadcasting Corporation (BBC), 8, 9, 10, 14, 15, 22, 23–35, 41, 53, 54, 58, 60, 74, 83, 86, 92, 97–8, 103, 113, 115, 116, 120, 123, 125–7, 132, 136, 137, 139, 145–7
  Northern Ireland Home Service, 22, 29, 52, 103, 146, 153
  payment rates, 22, 29–30, 52, 62, 103, 132
Britten, Benjamin, 99
Brown, Graham, 103, 114
Burke, Edmund, 138, 141
Bye bye Birdie by Michael Stewart, 13, 143

Campbell, Douglas, 99, 102, 105
Campbell, Patrick, 63
Camus, Albert, 103
Cannes Film Festival, 147
Carlisle and Blake Premium, 17, 34
Cassin, Barry, 91, 132
Champion, Gower, 13, 14, 142, 143, 145
Cheever, John, 23, 37
Chekhov, Anton, 55, 97, 102, 103, 107, 110–11
Chiang Kai-shek, 88
Chicago Sun-Times, 154
Christie, Julie, 128
civil war, 17, 144
Clancy Brothers, 13, 150
Cleary, Bishop Patrick, 88
Cleopatra film, 129
Colmcille, 83; *see also* Columba, St
Columba, St, 8, 15, 66, 69, 74, 76–9, 84–7, 88, 93, 95, 96, 116, 120, 146, 159
Comgall, St, 77, 84
Connery, Sean, 147
Cooper, Giles, 116–17
Courtenay, Tom, 128
Cronin, Anthony, 19
Cronyn, Hume, 102
Crowe, Eileen, 139
Culmore Primary School, 17, 70
Curtis Brown literary agency, 22, 69, 79, 120, 122, 124, 127
Curtis Brown, Spencer, 142, 148–9
Cusack, Cyril, 57, 135

D'Alton, Louis, 82
Da by Hugh Leonard, 91
Dáil Éireann, 112
Daly, Fr Edward, 8, 85, 86
de Valera, Éamon, 17, 75, 82, 116
de Valera, Vivion, 82
Death of a salesman by Arthur Miller, 35, 102, 121, 142, 152
Deevy, Teresa, 78
Devlin, J.G. (James Gerard), 62, 90
Donnelly, Donal, 92, 123, 137–8, 142, 146–8, 150

Doubleday & Co., publishers, 69, 74, 90, 103, 131
Dowling, Vincent, 75, 181
Dr Who film, 147
Dublin Grand Opera Company, 135
Dublin Theatre Festival, 14, 127, 130–1, 133–41, 142, 145–50, 154
Duddy, Jackie (John), 85

Eblana Theatre, 90–2, 104, 131
Edinburgh International Festival, 98, 134
Edwards, Hilton, 8, 11, 80, 86, 132, 133–9, 141, 146–8, 150–2, 155–8
Éire Society, Boston, 152
electrification, Ireland, 17, 81
Ellis, James, 41, 54, 55, 97
Empire Theatre, Belfast, 55
English Stage Company (ESC), 26, 123, 127–8
Enniscorthy Athenaeum, 134
Envoy magazine, 126
Ervine, St John, 31, 41
Esslin, Martin, 125

Faber and Faber, publishers, 142
Fagan, James B., 97–8
Festival Theatre, Cambridge, 98–9
Field Day Theatre Company, 95, 109, 157–8
film rights, 127, 129, 157
Finian's rainbow by Yip Harburg and Fred Saidy, 145
Finlay, Suzanne, 137, 141
Finney, Albert, 128–9, 157
Finnian, St, 77
First World War, 136
FitzGerald, Jim (James), 132
Flanagan, Sinéad, 75
Fleming, Tom, 8, 25, 146
Flynn, Philip, 75
Ford, John, 13, 144
Forristal, Fr Desmond, 63
Friel, Anne, 8, 10, 14, 20–2, 27–9, 32–3, 41, 44, 59, 60–1, 68, 70, 82, 86, 94, 103–6, 108, 111, 113, 120–2, 136, 139–40, 143, 147–8, 155–6

FRIEL, BRIAN, written works, published and unpublished
  'CASUALS' submitted to *New Yorker*
    'Downstairs no upstairs', 70, 80–1, 109
    'Hams versus harmony', 60
    'NATO at night', 59–61
    'The night the bomb fell', 60
    'The rest of the four million', 63
  JOURNALISM
    'American diary', 110
    'Brian Friel's secret thoughts', 105
    'De mortuis', 50, 54
    'Down to the sea', 62, 138
    'For export only', 23
    'Friel and Boswell', 45
    'Glenties Abu!', 62
    'Gunning for Sheriff', 29
    'Haven for the harassed', 80
    'Lunchtime interlude', 54
    'Money for putty', 32–3
    'Old memories', 80–1; see also 'Downstairs no upstairs'
    'Roundabouts and swings', 33
    'Taking one's oil', 63
    'The demon fisherman', 138
    'The game bookseller', 63
    'The giant of Monaghan', 107
    'When the bomb fell on Derry', 80
  PLAYS
    A cottage in Devon, 22
    A sort of freedom, 23–9, 32, 40, 113
    Crystal and Fox, 65, 157
    Dancing at Lughnasa, 15, 19, 46–7, 69, 89, 158–9
    Faith healer, 65, 158
    King's son of reddened valour, 66, 76; see also *The enemy within*
    Lovers, 15, 132, 157
    Make vile things precious, 30–3; see also *To this hard house*
    Michael Mannion, proprietor, 80
    Philadelphia, here I come!, 8, 13–14, 18, 24, 47, 69, 71, 113–57
    Post mortem, 79
    The ballad of Ballybeg, 105, 107, 115; see also *Philadelphia, here I come!*
    The blind mice, 19, 24, 54, 88–93, 104, 113, 116, 123, 131–2, 137, 138, 159
    The communication cord, 158
    The doubtful paradise, 55
    The enemy within, 8, 25, 66, 74, 76–9, 82–7, 88, 93, 95, 113, 116, 120, 122, 132, 147, 156–8
    The Francophile, 15, 40–2, 54–6, 62, 145, 159; see also *The doubtful paradise*
    The freedom of the city, 18, 145, 157, 159
    The gentle island, 52, 137
    The hero of Thian–Hee, 87, 88; see also *The blind mice*
    The loves of Cass McGuire, 137, 142, 147, 156–7
    The making of Mark, 44
    The world of Johnny del Pinto, 58–60, 116
    Three fathers, three sons, 79
    Three sisters (adapted from Chekhov), 158
    To this hard house, 30, 35, 42, 70, 113
    Translations, 30, 62, 157–9
  SHORT STORIES
    'A late child', 35, 42
    'A man's world', 15, 30, 46
    'Among the ruins', 61–2, 66–70, 115
    'Aunt Maggie, the strong one', 61
    'Bark mats for the Toners', 88; see also 'The perfect gentleman'
    'Barry', 52; see also 'Stories on the verandah'
    'Everything neat and tidy', 73, 95, 107–8, 123
    'Foundry House', 15, 30, 66–7
    'Ginger Hero', 72, 80, 103
    'Jimmy Gleeson's cats', 42
    'Mr Sing my heart's delight', 58
    'My famous grandfather' (later titled 'Kelly's Hall'), 45

FRIEL, BRIAN, written works, published and unpublished (*continued*)
  SHORT STORIES (*continued*)
    'My father and the sergeant', 52, 70–1
    'My fine white boy', 42
    'My little girl Joan', 42
    'My true kinsman', 29, 52–3, 115
    'Obscene, indecent and unhealthy in character', 61
    'Pearls in the Strule', 95
    'Segova, the savage Turk', 65
    Selected stories, Gallery Press, 158
    'Stories on the verandah', 63
    'Straight from his colonial success', 66
    'The Barney game', 131
    'The Child', 19, 43
    'The death of a scientific humanist', 130
    'The Diviner', 71
    'The fawn pup', 42–5, 68, 94
    'The first of my sins', 95
    'The flower of Kiltymore', 108–11
    'The Giant', 44
    The gold in the sea (anthology), 61, 62, 147, 158
    'The gold in the sea' (short story), 62, 136–8, 144, 156
    'The highwayman and the saint', 15, 30, 132
    'The king of Knock Island', 45, 48
    'The perfect gentleman', 89
    'The potato gatherers', 51
    'The queen of Troy Close', 147
    'The Return', 42
    The saucer of larks (anthology), 8, 61, 69, 79, 94, 103, 104, 113, 131, 147, 158
    'The saucer of larks' (short story), 47–8, 50–1, 68, 126
    'The Skelper', 14, 36, 37, 39–40, 42, 44, 48, 52, 68
    'The wee lake beyond', 73, 95
    'The widowhood system', 127
  TALKS (radio)
    'Self-portrait', 115, 157
    'Thoughts on Christmas', 103
Friel, Judith (Judy), 122
Friel, Mary, sister of Brian Friel, 18
Friel, Mary, daughter of Brian Friel, 27, 94, 105, 108, 122
Friel, Nanette, 18, 140
Friel, Patricia (Paddy), 22, 27, 81, 108, 122
Friel, Patrick, 17–18, 34, 47, 70, 114

Gaelic League, 75
Gageby, Douglas, 82
Gaiety Theatre, 91, 134, 135, 137, 140–2, 154
Gallant, Mavis, 37
Gallery Press, 158
Gate Theatre, 9, 11, 86, 91, 133–4, 136–7, 139, 147–50, 155
Geer, Ellen, 103
Gemini Productions, 91
Gielgud, Sir John, 31
Gielgud, Val, 31
Gill, Brendan, 49
Globe Theatre, 99
Goldblatt, Harold, 40–1, 54–5, 145–6
Goodman, Jonathan, 55, 56
Gordimer, Nadine, 23
Gordon, Ruth, 156
Grace, princess of Monaco, 59, 150
Graham, Billy, 92
Grand Opera House, Belfast, 44, 86, 132
Granville-Barker, Harley, 31
Greenhalgh, Mollie, 22
Gregory, Lady Augusta, 76
Grizzard, George, 103, 105
Grosbard, Ulu, 145
Guildhall, Derry, 109, 145, 157–8
Guinness, Sir Alec, 98, 99, 102, 126
Guthrie Theater, 8, 11, 100–10, 130
Guthrie, Lady Judith, 98–9, 102–3, 105, 122, 126, 140
Guthrie, Sir Tyrone, 8, 11, 14, 22, 41, 55, 74, 83–6, 93, 95–110, 113–15, 120–7, 130–2, 138–40, 143–5, 149–50, 156–9

Haggard, Edith Sewell, 15, 22–3, 35–6, 42–7, 59–61, 63, 65, 68, 73, 103
Hanna Bell, Sam, 54
Harburg, Yip, 144, 145
Harris, Richard, 145
Hartley, Neil, 143
Harvard University, 159
Harvard Club, Boston, 152
Helen Hayes Theatre, New York, 153
Hello, Dolly! by Michael Stewart, 13, 143–4
Help! film, 147
Henry IV parts I and II by William Shakespeare, 99
Henry V by William Shakespeare, 98, 99, 130
Henry VIII by William Shakespeare, 99
Hewitt, John, 20
Higgins, F.R. (Frederick Robert), 75
Hobson, Harold, 134
Holiday magazine, 37, 39, 107, 111, 113, 120, 136
homosexuality, 24, 52, 63, 71, 134, 140
How the West was won film, 129

Ibsen, Henrik, 78, 125
Idlewild Airport, New York, 13, 113, 144
Imison, Richard, 139
Intimate Theatre Company, 134
IRA, 29, 83, 109
Irish language, 75–6, 78, 91, 157
Irish Press, 9, 14, 18, 58, 80–2, 94, 103, 105, 110, 112–13, 116, 138
Irish Times, 9, 14, 18, 29, 32, 41–2, 45, 48, 50, 53, 59, 60, 62–3, 80–2, 113, 136, 138

Jam, Irish Farmhouse Preserves co-operative factory, 96–7, 121, 126
James Bond 007 film series, 147, 149
Jellicoe, Ann, 142
Jewish Institute Dramatic Society, 40
Johnston, Denis, 78, 82, 83, 91
Joyce, James, 20, 23, 125, 146
Juno and the Paycock by Seán O'Casey, 129

Kabosh Theatre Company, 158
Kauffmann, Stanley, 153
Kazan, Elia, 145
Keane, John B., 78, 91
Kelly, Eamon, 148, 150, 151, 152, 157
Kelly, Grace; *see* Grace, princess of Monaco
Kennedy, John F., 63, 112, 124
Kennedy, Robert, 151
Kennelly, Brendan, 91
Kiely, Benedict, 48, 73
King of the castle by Eugene McCabe, 133, 135

Lane, Burton, 145
Lavin, Mary, 48
Lennon, John, 147
Leonard, Hugh, 78, 91, 132, 146
Lewenstein, Oscar, 127–32, 135, 138–49, 154, 155, 157
Liebling, William, 144, 153
Lincoln Center, 145
Liverpool Playhouse, 55
Look back in anger by John Osborne, 26, 123, 128
Lorca, Federico, 82–3
Lord Chamberlain, 149, 155
Lurie, Louis, 100
Lyric Players Theatre, 86, 120–1, 138, 158

Mac Anna, Tomás, 75, 78, 83, 157
Mac Uí Rudaí by Mairéad Ní Ghrada, 82
Macaulay Fellowship, 111, 113
MacGibbon, James, 79, 111
MacLiammóir, Micheál, 11, 129, 134, 137, 155
MacLoone, Fr Bernard Joseph, 19, 47, 87
MacLoone, Kathleen, 19
Mademoiselle film, 148
Mao Tse-tung, 88
Marx, Groucho, 143
Mason, James, 98
Mason, Ronald, 8, 9, 14, 23–35, 40–2, 44, 52, 56, 57–60, 62, 74, 79, 83–5, 86, 90, 92–3, 113, 120, 122, 123, 124–5, 127, 132–3, 136–9, 145–6, 157, 159

Maxwell, William, 48–9
Mayer, Louis B., 149
Maynooth College, 19, 87, 90
Maynooth Mission to China, 87–8
McAlinney, Patrick, 55
McAnally, Ray, 76, 78–83, 85–6, 91, 120, 123, 131, 145, 156
McCabe, Eugene, 133–6
McCann, John, 87
McCarthy, Senator Joseph, 145
McKee, Ritchie, 54–5
McKellen, Ian, 126
McKelway, St Clair, 65
McKenna, Siobhán, 157
McMaster, Anew, 134
McMullan, H.W. (Harry), 24, 26, 32, 54–5, 58, 83, 92, 146
Melville, Herman, 76
Merrick, David, 13, 14, 143–5, 148–54, 156
Merv Griffin television show, 253
Mhac an tSaoi, Máire, 91
Miller, Arthur, 35, 102, 128, 145
Minneapolis Star and Tribune, 8, 100, 104
Moby Dick by Herman Melville, adapted by Orson Welles, 135
Moiseiwitsch, Tanya, 99, 106
Molière, 97, 102, 107
Monty Python and the Holy Grail film, 148
Mooney, Ria, 76, 78, 82–3, 91, 148
Moore, Marianne, 23
Moorman, Peggy, 159
Moreau, Jeanne, 148
Mulkerns, Val, 19
Murphy, John, 42

na gCopaleen, Myles, 32, 53
National Theatre, London, 158
Neeson, Liam, 62
New Republic magazine, 141
New York Times, 96, 97, 99, 103, 153
New Yorker magazine, 8, 9, 14–5, 19, 22–3, 29, 35–40, 42–54, 57–60, 63–74, 79–80, 88–9, 94–5, 105, 107, 113, 123–4, 127, 130, 132–3, 138, 140, 144, 153, 156, 159

first reading agreement, 53, 54, 57, 59, 65, 66, 68, 70, 95, 104, 124, 127, 144, 156
Ní Ghrada, Mairéad, 82
Niall of the Nine Hostages, 77
Northern Ireland Education Act of 1947, 17
Northern Ireland Players, 40
Nottingham Playhouse, 126

Ó hAongusa, Micheál, 157
O'Casey, Seán, 23, 75, 129
O'Brien, Edna, 103
O'Brien, Kate, 19
O'Connor, Frank, 46, 47–50, 52, 53, 69, 140–1, 153, 156
O'Donovan, Michael; *see* O'Connor, Frank
O'Faoláin, Seán, 19
O'Flaherty, Liam, 144
O'Malley, Mary, 86, 120, 138
O'Neill, Eugene, 116
O'Prey, George, 55
O'Reilly, Alpho, 137
O'Sullivan, Máirín, 139, 148, 150, 155
Oak Grove Apartment Hotel, 105–6
Oh! Calcutta! by Kenneth Tynan, 148, 149
Old Vic Theatre, 83, 98, 99, 134, 158
Olivier, Sir Laurence, 98
Olympia Theatre, 91, 134, 156
Orion Productions, 91
Osborne, John, 26, 123, 128, 129
Over the bridge by Sam Thompson, 27, 54–5, 91, 97
'Over the rainbow' song by Yip Harburg, 144
Oxford Playhouse, 99
Oxford University, 97

Paisley, Ian, 24
Perkins, Anthony, 142
Pinter, Harold, 25
Plunkett, James, 19, 78
Priestley, J.B., 31
Project Arts Centre, 132
Psycho film, 142

INDEX

Queen Elizabeth II, 102
Queen's Theatre, 75, 76, 83, 134
Queen's University Belfast, 10, 24, 41, 126

Radio Éireann, 58, 86, 139, 150
Radio Times, 24, 120
Rapson, Ralph, 100–2
Rea, Oliver, 95–6, 99–102
Rea, Stephen, 67, 109, 157
Reagan, Ronald, 64
Reeves, William, 77
Reilly, Fr Patrick, 88
Richard II by William Shakespeare, 99
Richard III by William Shakespeare, 99
Richardson, Tony, 128, 129, 143, 148
Robbins, Jerome, 145
Ross, Harold, 23
Rossi, Alfred, 106, 108–10
Royal Court Theatre, 127, 142, 157; see also English Stage Company (ESC)
Royal Opera House, Covent Garden, 99
RTÉ, 80, 137; see also Radio Éireann, Telefís Éireann
Ryan, John, 126
Ryan, Phyllis, 90–1, 131–3, 135

Saint Joan by George Bernard Shaw, 187
Saltzman, Harry, 129, 149
Saturday Evening Post, 103
Scottish National Players, 98
Second World War, 18, 48, 108
Selznick, Irene, 149
Shakespeare, William, 75, 97, 99, 102, 107, 134
Shannon Airport, 49
Shawn, William, 22, 39, 51, 69, 72, 127
Shepard, Alan, 68
Six characters in search of an author by Luigi Pirandello, 130
Smith, Brendan, 134, 135
Sondheim, Stephen, 145
St Columb's Hall, 85–6, 116
St Columb's College, 19
St Columba's, Long Tower, Derry, 17, 18, 47
St Jude magazine, 61, 94

Stephen D by Hugh Leonard, 132, 146
Stoppard, Tom, 25
Stormont, 97
Strange interlude by Eugene O'Neill, 116
Strange occurrence on Ireland's Eye by Denis Johnston, 82
Stratford Shakespearean Festival, Ontario, 83, 99, 102
Sun Yat-sen, 88
Synge, John Millington, 69

Taibhdhearc Theatre, Galway, 134
Tandy, Jessica, 102, 108, 110
Tartuffe, 145
Tate, James, 8, 152
Teach Annie, 156
Telefís Éireann, 79, 134
The Bell magazine, 14, 19–20, 22, 53
The Connection by Jack Gelber, 148
The Critic magazine, 61, 110
The disagreeable oyster by Giles Cooper, 116–7
The Guardian, 104
The Far East magazine, 87–9
The Field by John B. Keane, 91
The Hill film, 147
The Hostage by Brendan Behan, 146
The house of Bernarda Alba by Federico Lorca, 82
The Informer by Liam O'Flaherty, 144–5, 147
The knack ... and how to get it film, 142, 147
The lark's nest screenplay by Sir Alec Guinness, 126
The Laurels, 19
The Matchmaker by Thornton Wilder, 143–4, 156
The McCooeys, 62
The moon in the Yellow River by Denis Johnston, 91
The Observer, 104
The quiet man film, 13, 139, 150
The Rocky Horror show by Richard O'Brien, 148, 149

The Sign magazine, 45, 61, 94
The subject was roses by Frank D. Gilroy, 145
This other Eden by Louis D'Alton, 82
Thompson, Sam, 27, 54–5, 91, 92, 97
Threepenny opera by Bertolt Brecht, 128
Thurber, James, 37, 60, 80
Tidy Towns competition, 53–4, 62–3
Time magazine, 141, 143, 153
Tom Jones film, 129, 143
Tommy Baxter, shop steward by Sam Thompson, 27, 54
Tony Awards, 13, 19, 46, 91, 144, 154, 156
Trevor, William, 39
Trinity College Dublin, 112
Troubles, Northern Ireland, 158
tuberculosis, 26, 52, 63
Tydeman, John, 24, 125

Ulster Drama Festival, 86, 132
Ulster Group Theatre, 40–2, 54–6, 145
Ulster Literary Theatre, 98
Ulster Theatre, 40
Unity Theatre Society, 129
University College Dublin, 112
University of Minnesota, 100, 130
Updike, John, 23, 37, 39, 63
US–Soviet space race, 68, 94

Van Druten, John, 31
Variety magazine, 55, 134, 141, 152, 154
Victor Gollancz Ltd, publishers, 79
Villiers, Mavis, 150, 157
Vivante, Arturo, 65

Walker Foundation, Minneapolis, 100, 105
Walnut Street Theatre, Philadelphia, 152, 153
Washington Post, 141
Waterhouse, Keith, 128
Welles, Orson, 135
West Side story by Arthur Laurents, 145
White, E.B., 23, 37, 159
White, Katharine, 22–3, 37–9, 48–9
White, Michael, 147–9, 152
Whiting, Frank, 100, 130
Wilbur Theatre, Boston, 150, 153
Wilder, Thornton, 143
Williams, Tennessee, 14, 144
Wood, Audrey, 14, 144–5, 149, 153
Woodfall Films, 129, 143

Yeats, William Butler, 76
Young, Derek, 92

Zeisler, Peter, 95–6, 100–1